CHRIS PETERSON
DEPARTMENT OF PSYCHOLOGY
UNIVERSITY OF MICHIGAN
580 UNION DRIVE
ANN ARBOR, MI 48109

A SOCIAL HISTORY OF
MADNESS

A SOCIAL HISTORY OF
MADNESS

The World
Through the Eyes
of the Insane

ROY PORTER

WEIDENFELD & NICOLSON • NEW YORK

Published by Weidenfeld & Nicolson, New York
A Division of Wheatland Corporation
10 East 53rd Street
New York, NY 10022

Published in Canada by General Publishing Company, Ltd.

First published in Great Britain in 1987 by George Weidenfeld and Nicolson Limited.

Library of Congress Cataloging-in-Publication Data

Porter, Roy, 1946–
  A social history of madness: the world through the eyes of the insane / Roy Porter.
  —1st American ed.
      p.   cm.
  Bibliography: p.
  Includes index.
  ISBN 1-555-84185-6
    1. Mentally ill—Biography. 2. Mental illness—Case studies.
I. Title.
RC464.A1P67 1988   87-33979
362.2′092′2—dc19   CIP

Manufactured in the United States of America

First American Edition, 1988

10 9 8 7 6 5 4 3 2 1

To My Parents

Contents

Acknowledgements

Over the years, I have benefited vastly from conversations – indeed often arguments – on the theme of this book with far too many people to list here. Likewise I have found stimulus from far more works than I can list in the brief reading suggestions which appear at the end of the book. Some particular friends and colleagues have been kind enough to read through earlier drafts of this book and to debate the issues with me. I am particularly grateful to William F. Bynum, Tony Delamothe, John Forrester, Godelieve van Haeteren, Margaret Kinnell, Sue Limb, Charlotte Mackenzie, Michael Neve, Christine Stevenson, Sylvana Tomaselli, Jane Walsh, Dorothy Watkins and Andrew Wear. They are emphatically not responsible for the opinions and interpretations expressed below. The Wellcome Institute has proved a wonderful environment for writing this book. And I would like to say a thank you to everyone I have dealt with at Weidenfeld and Nicolson. They have been exemplary publishers; Juliet Gardiner in particular has been the best of editors.

ROY PORTER
The Wellcome Institute for the History of Medicine
London

1 · Introduction

What is it like to be mad? This book explores the lives of a couple of dozen 'mad people' as they themselves recorded them.

It is not a medical history of insanity viewed as a disease. Much less is it a history of psychiatry. Above all, it is not an exercise in psycho-history, nor an attempt to set the civilizations of the past on the couch and analyse their collective psyches. My aims are far more modest. I shall explore the thoughts and feelings of a number of mad people from earlier centuries, primarily making use of their own autobiographical writings.

There is of course nothing new in focusing attention upon the lives of the neurotic and the insane. Quite a few psychiatrists and like-minded scholars have undertaken extensive retrospective diagnoses of the dead, analysing the 'madness' of factual personages such as George III, Goethe, Daniel Schreber and Virginia Woolf, and of fictional ones besides, such as Hamlet, King Lear and Oedipus himself. Usually the aim has been to plumb the hidden depths of their mental illness; sometimes it has been to acquit them of madness altogether.

But my aims in this book are rather different. They are not psychiatric or psychoanalytic. I am not attempting to decode what mad people said, wrote and did in the light of some or other psychiatric theory, to reveal what disease or syndrome they really had or even to discover the 'real' (that is, unconscious) meaning of their actions. Sensitively attempted, that can be a fruitful and illuminating enterprise. As a mere historian, I don't feel qualified, however, to undertake it. Neither is it my principal interest.

Rather I wish to examine not the unconscious of the mad but their consciousness. Instead of principally reading between the lines, searching out hidden meanings, reconstructing lost childhoods, baring unspoken desires, I wish to explore what mad people meant to say, what was on their minds. Their testimonies are eloquent of their hopes and fears, the injustices they suffered, above all of what it was like to be mad or to be thought to be mad. I wish simply and quite literally to see what they had to say. It is curious how little this has been done; we have been preoccupied with explaining away what they said.

My readings of mad people's writings will not therefore be grounded in theories of psychic development, will not demonstrate how universal facts of psychic life – such as the Oedipus Complex – find expression in them. Rather I am concerned with how the mad tried to explain their own behaviour to themselves and others in the language available to them. My points of reference, therefore, are language, history and culture. The writings of the mad can be read not just as symptoms of diseases or syndromes, but as coherent communications in their own right. Psychiatric doctors have commonly denied intelligibility to madness: for Kraepelin that was one of the typical features of *dementia praecox*. They often portrayed insanity as irrational, as nonsense – what the mad said was no better than meaningless babble. Perhaps that is often true. But mad people's autobiographies are hardly likely to fall into that category. Madness may be typically incomprehensible or just badly comprehended; but a glance at those writings by mad people which have come down to us from previous centuries confirms that even if we diagnose their condition as madness, yet there is method in it.

I seek to tease out the inner logic of the texts by exploring them as products of their situation and their times. Although the mad often seemed so alien, so alien of mind as (it was believed) to require exclusion from society, their testaments plainly echo, albeit often in an unconventional or distorted idiom, the ideas, values, aspirations, hopes and fears of their contemporaries. They use the language of their age, though often in ways which are highly unorthodox. When we read the writings of the mad, we gain an enhanced insight into the sheer range of what could be thought and felt, at the margins. We might compare the way historians of popular culture have told us to listen sympathetically to the popular idiom of graffiti, to riddles, to the lore and language of schoolchildren, or to the cosmologies of heretics arraigned before the Inquisition.

Posterity has treated the writings of mad people with enormous condescension. Either they have been ignored altogether, or they have been treated just as cases. But it would be foolish to fly to the other extreme and try to turn the mad *en bloc* into folk heroes, into radicals and rebels. It would be mistaken and terribly sentimental to rush headlong into concluding that the voice of the mad is the authentic voice of the excluded, that somehow madness leads the chorus of protest against dominant elite consciousness, indeed sings the song of the repressed. Sometimes it may, as for example with John Clare, the peasant poet, who certainly did see the world from below. And some mad people such as Artaud have identified madness with insurrection. But often enough the mad have no grudge against their society as such, though once mad they often utter the fiercest protests against their treatment.

Rather, what the mad say is illuminating because it presents a world through the looking-glass, or indeed holds up the mirror to the logic (and psycho-logic) of sane society. It focuses and puts to the test the nature and limits of the rationality, humanity and 'understanding' of the normal. In that sense, the late French philosopher Michel Foucault was quite right to insist that the history of unreason must be coterminous with the history of reason. They are doubles.

Furthermore, examined in this light, the consciousness of the mad confronts that of the sane to constitute a kind of hall of mirrors. When we juxtapose the mind of the insane with that of reason, society and culture, we see two facets, two expressions, two faces, and each puts the question to the other. If normality condemns madness as irrational, subhuman, perverse, madness typically replies in kind, has its own *tu quoque*. Rather like children playing at being adults, the mad highlight the hypocrisies, double standards and sheer callous obliviousness of sane society. The writings of the mad challenge the discourse of the normal, challenge its right to be the objective mouthpiece of the times. The assumption that there exist definitive and unitary standards of truth and falsehood, reality and delusion, is put to the test.

And we are left essentially with stories about reality told by the public authorities on the one hand and different tales told by the mad on the other. To adjudicate between these rival myths – or, often, rival tellings of the same myths – there stands no contemporary court of appeal, but merely the voice of the majority. Emily Dickinson put this point in verse:

> Much Madness is divinest Sense –
> To a discerning Eye –
> Much Sense – the starkest Madness –
> 'Tis the Majority
> In this, as All, prevail –
> Assent – and you are sane –
> Demur – you're straightway dangerous –
> And handled with a Chain.

The seventeenth-century mad playwright Nathaniel Lee, protesting against his consignment to Bethlem, made the same point more graphically: 'They called me mad, and I called them mad, and damn them, they outvoted me.'

But isn't psychiatry precisely that sought-after court of appeal? On the contrary; for a key feature of the chapters that follow is the suggestion that from the viewpoint of the writings analysed, psychiatry is itself part of the problem not the solution – it is just another rival, plausible mythology. As I have just stated, I shall try to show that the beliefs of mad people make sense when read as part of a dialectic of consciousness between them and their times. Why shouldn't the same apply to the theories of psychiatry? It is much debated today whether psychiatry and psychoanalysis are properly sciences, and anti-psychiatrists such as Thomas Szasz would contend that psychiatry has served as a mode of repressive ideology, that mental illness is the invention, the delusion, of psychiatry. My aim, however, is not to victimize the pioneers of psychiatry. Particularly in the past, psychiatrists themselves were often highly marginal men, misunderstood and vilified by society at large for advancing beliefs commonly called just as crazy as those of the mad themselves. The mad psychiatrist is of course a stock figure of fun.

Yet I see, on the other hand, no reason for according the myths advanced by earlier mad-doctors and psychiatrists any privileged truth status. The eternal joke in the history of lunacy involves a series of variations on the theme that madmen and mad-doctors switch identities and are impossible to tell apart. And it seems to me that in many of the encounters between 'mad people' and their doctors which I shall examine below – Alexander Cruden and Dr Monro, John Perceval and Dr Fox, Daniel Schreber, Dr Weber, Freud, and so forth – common humanity and often common sense perhaps lie squarely on the side of the mad.

But my intention in this is not to add the guns of history to the anti-psychiatry broadside. Rather it is to show how psychiatry has itself formed part of a common consciousness. The mad and the mad-doctors are often saying intriguingly comparable things about agency and action, rights and responsibility, reason and nonsense, though applying them in fundamentally reversed ways. Indeed, in this century, as psychiatry has become part of the common cultural coinage, it is often hard to tell when the psychiatrist is speaking and when the patient.

One of Freud's monumental insights is that man makes myths. Ceaselessly. He is always telling stories. This book examines consciousness – mainly that of mad people, partly that of psychiatrists, and (more by implication than explicitly) that of society at large. The delusions of the mad, the myths of psychiatry and the ideologies of society at large all form part of a common ideological fabric. Liliane Feder has phrased this well:

> The madman, like other people, does not exist alone. He both reflects and influences those involved with him. He embodies and symbolically transforms the values and aspirations of his family, his tribe, and his society, even if he renounces them, as well as their delusions, cruelty

and violence, even in his inner flight.

To say this is of course to say something which, left as a generality, is utterly banal: no man is an island, consciousness is a linguistic continuum. The age of the Reformation produced lots of religious maniacs and expert religious exorcists to heal them. *Fin de siècle* Vienna threw up plenty of sexually disturbed patients for the sex-obsessed Freudians to treat. Yet contemporary psychiatry in highminded Boston found both patients and their doctors silent about sex but preoccupied with problems of the will and spirit.

When put into practice, however, by setting the main expressions of madness in their historico-cultural context, the point takes on greater significance. For it suggests that there is indeed a history, not just of psychiatry, but of madness itself. Insanity is not just an individual atom, a biological accident, but forms an element in the history of sub-cultures in their own right. The cultures of madness differ radically between advanced and tribal societies, male and female communities. As I shall outline, religious madness has given way to secular, outwardly controlled to inner-directed. We see the emergence of the family as a nexus for explaining insanity amongst both mad people and psychiatrists at the very time when the ideology of bourgeois happy families becomes dominant in society at large. Highly individualistic perceptions amongst the mad mirror ego-psychiatry in self-help modern times. There are shared cultural assumptions. Even the mad are men of their times. It is possible to be odd, to be strange, in ways that still make sense.

There may be a practical moral in this. The history of psychiatry shows generations of doctors and other experts doubting that there was any reason in madness. Minds were being possessed and limbs manipulated by Powers from Beyond or by a poison in the blood or through a twisted mentality. In so far as the behaviour of the disturbed made sense, it was not in terms of their intentions, of the here-and-now, of social relations and the loom of language, but in extraneous terms – diabolical possession or an infantile neurosis. This has led, as Peter Barham, a critic of orthodox psychiatry, has argued, to an extraordinary deafness towards the communications of the disturbed, and in particular a discounting of their reactions to, and complaints against, the psychiatric treatment meted out to them. The protests of the mad have been interpreted as symptoms of their madness.

But with hindsight – or perhaps with distance, but certainly with sympathy – we can see how much sense the voices of the mad commonly made, in the desperate attempts of isolated, troubled and confused people to grasp their actual situations, their own urges, impulses, memories. They form the struggles of the despairing and powerless to exercise some control over those – devils, spooks, mad-doctors, priests – who had them in their power. The logic is there for those who look. We don't yet have hindsight to explain what baffles us about the behaviour of crazy people today. But history shows we would be foolish to dismiss it as 'meaningless'.

A few further remarks may be helpful by way of explanation, apology and acknowledgement. First, as will be quite clear, this book is highly selective and episodic. I have focused upon a small number of relatively famous cases, for which the documentation is particularly rich or the issues sharply drawn. Clearly the mad people who wrote their autobiographies are a highly unrepresentative sample of all mad people. I am not advocating the 'great madman' approach to history. My selection has resulted in an over-representation of English and English-language cases.

My sheet anchor has been authentic autobiographical records, used alongside other well-authenticated utterances. Here and there, however, I have drawn upon literary and other similar evidence to make a point. There are obviously profound dangers in the uncritical use of such texts; I hope I have avoided the worst of these. I have in some sense let my figures speak for themselves. Obviously this is literally impossible, and I have had to make sense of them making sense of themselves. In a book of this size and nature, it has, regretfully, proved impracticable to discuss alternative interpretations at any length, or even to begin to raise and explore the enormous problems which the very acts of 'reading' or 'interpretation' raise. Neither have I been able to acknowledge the range, variety and subtlety of the present scholarship on many topics upon which I have obviously drawn deeply. I have told a simple story. I hope it doesn't betray simplistic thinking.

Throughout this book I have referred to the 'mad' as a generic name for the whole range of people thought to be in some way, more or less, abnormal in ideas or behaviour. The label is obviously unsatisfactory. I hope that its very unsatisfactoriness will help to draw attention to its shortcomings, and show that it is merely being used as a collective shorthand. Similarly, I have used the term 'psychiatry' as a generic word to include all attempts to treat mad people, and 'psychoanalysis' to refer to the therapies developed by Freud and ones broadly consonant. Whether those called 'mad' really were insane or whatever, or were merely stigmatized as such, has aroused animated scholarly debate. The issue is not, however, central to this book, and I pass no judgements on it. Suffice to say here that all the autobiographical accounts used in this book were by people thought to be, or to have been, mad. Some of them accepted that they were, at some time or another, truly mad. Others fiercely contested the name.

My debts to other scholars are obviously enormous. A special mention of gratitude is due to Dale Peterson. His book, *A Mad People's History of*

Madness, constitutes the first proper scholarly account and anthology of mad people's writings over a long historical span. Peterson was the first to show that a history of the consciousness of the mad was feasible. I hope that this book proves a worthy complement to his.

2 · Madness and Psychiatry Talking: A Historical Dialogue

The core of this book in the chapters to follow will be an investigation into the minds of mad people through their own autobiographical writings. By way of preliminary, this discussion will first attempt to set these in context. What conditions led mad people to write and publish their stories? Or, in other words, what special features of our culture down the centuries have led some people – the 'mad' – to feel that they are a very special group, set apart from the rest of society, who particularly need to vindicate themselves by telling the stories of their lives?

To grapple with the issues raised by these questions it is first important to remember that even today we possess no rational consensus upon the nature of mental illness – what it is, what causes it, what will cure it. That is true even amongst psychiatrists. This admission of ignorance must colour our attitudes towards the mass of competing explanations of insanity held in the past by psychiatrists, society and mad people alike. Madness has been and remains an elusive thing. Of course most people, and practically all psychiatrists, would affirm what seems like a common-sense proposition, the reality of mental illness, as the title of a recent defence of psychiatry by the psychiatrists Martin Roth and Jerome Kroll invites us to do. But it is equally possible to think in terms of the manufacture of madness, that is, the idea that labelling insanity is primarily a social act, a cultural construct (or, in its weaker form, the adage that every society gets the mad people it deserves). And it is noteworthy that the book called *The Manufacture of Madness* was not written, as one might imagine, by a revolutionary relativist but by a practising psychiatrist and indeed a university professor of psychiatry, Dr Thomas S. Szasz.

In other words, debate is still raging, not least amongst psychiatrists themselves, about the basic object of their study. Is insanity truly a 'disease', rather in the way that we all accept that measles is? Or might it not be better regarded essentially as a badge we pin on people displaying a rather subjectively defined bundle of symptoms and traits, but who at bottom are just mildly or severely 'different' or 'odd'? In which case, is the bottom line simply that we call people mentally 'confused' because we find them 'confusing', 'disturbed' essentially because we find them 'disturbing'? – itself a highly disturbing possibility. The mad are 'strange'. But does that mean anything more than to say that they are strange to us? And then what about the fact that we are strange to them?

The question of what insanity really amounts to remains open. Short of the discovery tomorrow of the schizophrenia gene, these controversial issues will not be quickly settled. The point now is that we should keep in mind – lest we are tempted to feel superior to the inquirers of former times – that madness retains its enigma. And we must see that *strangeness* has typically been the key feature in the fractured dialogues that go on, or the silences that intrude, between the 'mad' and the 'sane'. Madness is a foreign country.

All societies make arrangements for coping with peculiar people whose behaviour is weird, disruptive or dangerous: to that degree madness forms a universal fact of life. But the ways such peculiarities are described, judged and handled differ quite profoundly from society to society, from era to era, and from symptom to symptom. Here we encounter an element of irreducible relativism.

To take an instance, in the West today, relatively mild mental and emotional incapacity is commonly called 'neurosis'. It is often regarded not as organic but as merely 'functional' (for example, a product of worry or 'tension'), and may well be treated – at least for those who can afford it – by essentially psychiatric means such as psychotherapy. The exact opposite is true in China. There, by the concurrence of doctors and sufferers alike, broadly comparable disabilities are described as being due to 'neurasthenia', a diagnosis once common but now extinct in the West. This is regarded essentially as a disease of the body itself. The contrasting diagnoses (and often treatments) follow from divergent socio-cultural priorities. In the individualistic West, mental disorder, if mild, is relatively 'legitimate'. Because we believe we have a right to happiness, we also believe we have a right to complain when we are miserable, a right to redress. In the much more rigid and communal society of the Communist East, on the other hand, to confess to such weakness would be regarded as shameful and self-indulgent, and would forfeit claims to sympathy and attention. There 'somatization' – the presentation of symptoms in physical form linked to an organic diagnosis – by contrast, gives dignity and credibility to the sufferer. Samuel Butler's Victorian fantasy novel, *Erewhon*, makes these alternatives and reversals particularly clear. In Erewhonian society, crime was universally seen as a disease, but being ill was criminal.

These instances point to something frequently visible in the discussions

9

which follow: the fact that the language, ideas and associations surrounding mental illness do not have scientific meanings fixed for all time, but are better viewed as 'resources' which can be variously used by various parties for various purposes. What is mental and what is physical, what is mad and what is bad, are not fixed points but culture-relative.

In this book, I am not interested in playing doctor to the dead and performing a series of psychiatric autopsies, trying to work out precisely what form of mental illness various people had. Rather I am concerned to use their writings to see how they 'made sense of self', how they tried to show there was (to use John Perceval's phrase) 'reasonableness in lunacy'. And by doing so I aim to look, from an uncommon angle, at the traditions of culture and knowledge which have given rise to particular ways of thinking, talking and acting about mental disorder in the West – from the viewpoint of the sufferers rather than the psychiatrists. These meanings of madness have been many and they have been deeply contested. Here I shall offer a thumbnail sketch of mad people, their social place and displacement into institutions, and their treatment (what Andrew Scull in a felicitous phrase has called 'madhouses, mad doctors, and madmen'). This will serve as a backdrop to those attempts of the mad to make sense of their plight – their experience of madness and of psychiatry – which will be explored in individual detail in the heart of the book.

Reasoning about Madness

For the Western intellectual tradition, it is with the Greeks that making sense of madness first became a problem, raising alternatives and requiring explanations. In Greek mythology and in the Homeric epics we probably encounter the remnants at least of archaic attitudes towards the mad and their deeds. The Greek heroes go mad; some are driven wild with frenzy; others become beside themselves with fury, revenge or grief. But the myths do not present insanity in the terms later pioneered by Classical medicine and philosophy, and their heroes do not possess psyches comparable to that of Oedipus in Sophocles' play, still less to that of Hamlet or Sigmund Freud. The ancient epic, and we might say the mentality it represents, gives its characters no sensitive, reflective inner self, no mind of their own grappling with what Dr Johnson was to call 'the choice of life'. It is not 'psychological' like the novel.

Homer's heroes are instead more like puppets, players at the mercy of forces essentially from Beyond and beyond their control: gods, demons, the fates, the furies. They each have their own destiny as warrior, king, son, daughter, father; they possess powerful physical bodies for doing deeds (legs that run, arms that strike blows). We are told far more about their deeds than about their deliberations, and their fates are decided largely by instructions from above, often revealed to them through auguries or in dreams. They are often cursed and pursued by terrible powers, which punish, avenge and destroy, sometimes by driving the demented mad. The process of pollution and purification drives many to distraction. But the inner life, with its dilemmas of reason and conscience and the torments of mental strife, is not yet the centre of attention.

But that more modern mental landscape and its symbols were already emerging by the apogee of Greek civilization in the fifth and fourth centuries BC. Indeed the psychiatrist and historian Bennett Simon has argued, in a way which is illuminating if consciously anachronistic, that Athenian thinking on the psyche as developed during those centuries has set the mould for reasoning about minds and madness in the Western mind ever since. Freud in effect made the same point by calling infantile sexual conflicts the 'Oedipus Complex'.

Greek philosophers energetically set about subjecting nature, society and consciousness to reason. They wished to tame anarchy, establish order, impose self-discipline. Rationality became definitive of the noblest faculty in man. Through logic and theory, cosmic order could be perceived, and so man's unique place in nature understood. But reason could also, through self-knowledge ('know thyself'), understand human nature itself and thereby control the lower 'animal' urges, the baser appetites within. Thus philosophy enthroned reason.

But in doing so the Greeks did not deny the reality of all that was not rational. Indeed, the very adulation they accorded to reason surely attests to the strength which they attributed to the mysterious forces of passion, of destiny, of fate which reason opposed. But schools of Greek philosophers – the Stoics in particular – clearly exposed the irrational as a problem, a menace, a scandal, which reason should combat. The Greeks never lost their terror at the titanic and primordial forces possessing the mind and often toying with human destiny, or their admiration for the 'fire' which seized geniuses and artists, lighting up visions of the divine. But from Plato onwards, philosophy defined how the madness of the irrational was the antipodes of human dignity; and the dichotomy between the rational and the irrational, and the rightful sovereignty of the rational, became fundamental to both their moral and their scientific vocabulary, and, through them, to ours.

If the invention of philosophy enabled the Greeks to reflect upon madness, how did they then explain it? How did they expect to prevent or cure it?

11

Simon has suggested a useful schematic approach. There were two main traditions, he argues, through which they principally made sense of madness, and which have proved templates for future formulations. One lay in speech and drama, art and theatre, in tragedy in particular. The Greek tragedians made the stuff of their drama the great unbearable elemental conflicts of life – the trauma of the individual will crushed under ineluctable destiny, the rival demands of love and hate, pity and revenge, duty and desire, individual, family and state battling in the breast.

Moreover, they showed these terrifying conflicts becoming – as they never could have been in so many terms for Homer's heroes – the *conscious* objects of reflection, responsibility and guilt, of inner conflict, of minds divided against themselves. Witness the functions of the chorus in tragedy. The destructive powers were no longer essentially those of external fate, of mischievous gods and furies, but were now self-inflicted; heroes were now eaten up with shame, guilt, grief; they tore themselves apart. The new heroes brought their own madness upon themselves and civil war within became integral to the human condition.

But the drama also suggested paths of resolution, or (as Simon puts it) theatre as 'therapy'. Madness might of course simply be punished in death. But, as with Oedipus, suffering could eventuate in a higher wisdom, blindness could lead to insight, and the public enactment of drama itself could be a collective catharsis. Playing madness out, forcing the unthinkable to be spoken, bringing the monsters of the human deep into the open, formed a ritual reclamation of the terrain for reason, spelling order restored.

Thus madness could be the sickness of the soul as expressed by art. Yet the Greeks also developed a quite different way of coping with madness, a tradition not of moral but of medical theory. Faced with what had always been seen as the sacred disease – epilepsy – the scientific doctors of the Hippocratic tradition now daringly denied that it was supernatural, a miraculous visitation from above. On the contrary, they argued, it was but a physical sickness, a product of the regular powers of nature. By implication, all abnormalities, all madness too, could be claimed for naturalistic medicine. Explanations would draw upon physical causes and effects, centring on organs such as the heart or brain, blood, spirits and humours, and cures would rely upon regimen and medicines. In other words, to the scientific temper, mania and melancholy were essentially diseases, intelligible in terms of anatomy and pathology.

Classical thinkers thus defined – but did not solve! – the problem of madness for future ages by elevating *mind*, by valuing reason, order and cosmic intelligibility so highly. Through making man the measure of all things, they made madness human. They also specified alternative and rival schemes for explaining madness, the negation of their ideal. On the one hand, insanity might be the extremes of experience: mind at the end of its tether. As such, madness certainly had its meanings, even if they largely showed man being tortured as part of the terrible workings of a pitiless universe. On the other hand, mental derangement might be essentially a somatic condition, a delirious disease symptom much like fever. In that case, less responsibility was attached to the sufferer, but the explanation also offered less meaning, less reason in madness. Both formulations – madness as badness, madness as sickness – had a fearful potential for regarding the insane person as less than fully human.

The inheritors of the Greek legacy – and in the end that means us – never resolved the Sphinx's riddle of the divide between the psychological and the somatic theories of madness. Both theories have had their attractions and their drawbacks. The culture of medieval Latin Christendom absorbed and made use of both of the Greek alternatives (madness as moral trauma, madness as disease). But it also fitted them within a cosmic Christian scheme – madness as divine Providence – which could impart a higher significance to either. Christian theology could also, of course, treat madness in quite distinctive ways, ones essentially alien to Greek man-centred philosophy; this lay in seeing mental disorder as a mark of the war for the possession of the soul (the 'psychomachy') waged between God and Satan. Medieval and Renaissance minds could regard madness as religious, as moral or as medical, as divine or diabolical, as good or bad.

The modern world dawned with the coming of the Renaissance, the Scientific Revolution and the Enlightenment. But in the short term none of the old multitude of meanings of madness was refuted or became obsolete: the mystery of madness was not cracked. The reader of Robert Burton's compendious *Anatomy of Melancholy* (1621) comes away with the melancholy impression that there are as many theories of madness as there are mad people. And in the event the major change in reasoning about insanity did not come from a great scientific or medical breakthrough. There was no Newton of insanity, no Copernican revolution in psychiatry discovering the secrets within the skull.

The real watershed in attitudes towards, and the treatment of, the mad came rather from a long-term shift in policy towards those displaying delinquent and dangerous traits: the rise of exclusion. Through the Middle Ages and well beyond, crazy people had rarely had any special, formal provision made for them. Refuges specifically for lunatics were almost unknown. A very small number of homes for the insane were set up – a few asylums appeared in fifteenth-century Spain, and around the same time Bethlem Hospital in London began to specialize in caring for mad people. Some monasteries accepted the odd lunatic. Mostly, however, lunatics were looked after (or neglected) within the family, kept under the watch of the village community, or were simply allowed to wander (the English 'Tom o' Bedlam').

It would be inappropriate to deplore this indifference as especially cruel or to praise it as especially enlightened. It was simply that the traditional state undertook limited welfare functions. Yet the old intermingling of lunatics with people at large possibly preserved some residual sense of common humanity; at least it did not foster a 'them and us' estrangement of the mad as essentially alien beings, as a race apart. This was in line with Christian teachings, which perhaps helped to maintain some sense of the mad person or idiot as a fellow human being, a creature made in God's image, the same as all other believers. If all men were sinners, then the distinctions of the world – the outward appurtenances of rank, wealth, education, success – might in the end count for little in God's eye.

Moreover, under very special circumstances, Christian belief could set a positive value upon madness. Insanity might of course be God's punishment for crime, as the favourite case of Herod's madness exemplified. But madness could also be holy. A faith founded upon the madness of the Cross, which crusaded against worldliness, which lauded the innocence of the infant, which valued the spiritual mysteries of contemplation, asceticism and the mortification of the flesh, and prized faith over intellect, could not help but see gleams of godliness in the simplicity of the fool or in ecstasies and transports (witness the life of Margery Kempe in chapter 6 below).

At least in theory, if perhaps less so in practice, medieval and Renaissance Christianity thought that the voice of folly might be a medium for the voice of God and bade it have its hearing. In the more secular sphere, Court jesters were granted folly's privilege to turn normality topsy-turvy and utter truths denied to politic courtiers; and literary vehicles, from Erasmus' *Praise of Folly* onwards, pointed paradoxically to a simpleton wisdom higher than that of the pompous professors, thus wittily making a nonsense of the very categories securing reason's sovereignty over madness.

Michel Foucault has argued that back in those good old days madness really did utter its own truths and engage in a full dialogue with reason. We need not go all the way with this romantic primitivism. But we can accept his further contention that from the seventeenth century onwards movements were activated which led for the next three centuries to mad people increasingly being segregated from sane society, both categorically and physically. In particular, the institutionalization of the insane inexorably gathered momentum.

The Enlightenment endorsed the Greek faith in reason ('I *think*, therefore I am,' Descartes had claimed). And the enterprise of the age of reason, gaining

14

authority from the mid-seventeenth century onwards, was to criticize, condemn and crush whatever its protagonists considered to be foolish or unreasonable. All beliefs and practices which appeared ignorant, primitive, childish or useless came to be readily dismissed as idiotic or insane, evidently the products of stupid thought-processes, or delusion and daydream. And all that was so labelled could be deemed inimical to society or the state – indeed could be regarded as a menace to the proper workings of an orderly, efficient, progressive, rational society.

In the long run, the distinction which the Greeks had drawn between 'reason' and 'unreason', between fully rational members of society and the sub-rational, came to weigh increasingly heavily. The growing importance of science and technology, the development of bureaucracy, the formalization of the law, the flourishing of the market economy, the spread of literacy and education – all made their contribution to this amorphous but inexorable process of prizing 'rationality', as understood by those 'right-thinking' members of society who had the power to impose social norms. Abnormality provoked anxiety. The men of the Enlightenment doubtless felt benevolent sympathy towards the insane, as likewise towards savages and slaves, but only through first seeing them as quite alien from themselves.

From around the mid-seventeenth century, a similar process of redefinition was afoot within Christianity itself, tending to deny the validity of traditional forms of religious madness. The Reformation and Counter-Reformation ages had of course made great play of the reality of religious madness: some of it 'good', derived directly from God and manifested in ecstasies or in prophetic powers; much of it evil, originating from the Devil and all too obvious in witches, demoniacs and heretics. The lives of George Trosse and Christoph Haitzmann, discussed below, show the ramifications of such views.

But, from the second half of the seventeenth century, Church leaders had become thoroughly sickened by the carnage and chaos these endless conflicts of good and evil spirits had caused. The reality (or at least the validity) of religious madness came into question. Even the pious admitted that claims to speak with divine tongues had to be treated with extreme suspicion. Most such 'ranters' were probably mere enthusiasts, blind zealots, suffering from credulity and superstition. 'Pretended inspiration' was most probably just delusion or even disease. At the end of the seventeenth century John Locke argued in favour of *The Reasonableness of Christianity*. Even religion now had, it seemed, to be rational.

The same reversal also applies to 'witches'. In the great Europe-wide witch-craze of the sixteenth and seventeenth centuries, the authorities, civil and ecclesiastical, had treated witches as authentically possessed or obsessed by the Devil. Increasingly, from the seventeenth century, the manifestations

15

of witchcraft came to be reinterpreted, at least by the social elite controlling the printing presses and the law courts, essentially as delusions, as products of individual and collective hysteria, the work of ignorant, self-deluding minds. Witches themselves were, after all, no more than crazy civil nuisances, hysterical teenagers or old women.

These intellectual and cultural *voltes-faces* of course served to widen the divide between 'normal' people – those subscribing to the norms of politeness and propriety demanded by a progressive and increasingly secular civil society – and the strange. It would be too glib to see this newly crucial gulf between the rational and the irrational simply in terms of naked class power: reason as a tool for putting down the poor. After all, within elite culture itself, eccentricity had its vogue, later leading to Romantic ideas of the mad genius and dandyish degeneracy. All the same, public opinion from the age of the Enlightenment onwards readily identified the attitudes and behaviour of marginal social elements – criminals, vagrants, the religious 'lunatic fringe' – with false consciousness and madness. It was easy to slide from finding such outsiders disturbing to calling them disturbed, from seeing them as 'alien' to polite society to assuming that they were 'alien' or 'alienated' in mind. The higher the expectations imposed by the central state or the market economy, the greater the apparent divide between those who set and met the norms, and those who did not.

Increasingly, institutions were provided for locking away the worst offenders, both to prevent society itself from being swamped and sabotaged, and as engines to reform delinquents. All over Europe the eighteenth and nineteenth centuries witnessed a proliferation of schools, prisons, houses of industry, houses of correction, workhouses and, not least, madhouses to deal with the menace of unreason.

Foucault called this move to shut difficult, dangerous and just different people away 'the Great Confinement'. He saw it as deliberate policy. In many ways his analysis requires qualification and refinement. But there is no gainsaying that the confinement of weird and worrisome people, of the perverse and the peculiar, gathered momentum from the latter part of the seventeenth century onwards. This movement particularly accelerated in the nineteenth century, continuing its numerical expansion till little more than a generation ago. Since then the policies of confining the insane have been reversed. Closed institutions are now being shut down, and community care ('decarceration') is today's answer for the mentally disturbed. The totals of those confined as insane have steadily diminished within the last generation. The asylum movement marks the great watershed in the way the mad have been seen and treated.

In the early public madhouses, lunatics were commonly handled with great harshness – though there always existed a small number of posh private mad-houses offering *de luxe* conditions for patients paying hefty fees. Critics complained that madhouse inmates were often treated no better than wild animals. This however seemed quite defensible to influential currents of opinion. After all, were not those who lost their minds by that very fact reduced to the condition of a brute, and capable of responding only to force and fear? Indeed brutalization might be seen as their just deserts, for it was widely believed that the mad were the victims of their own vanity, pride, sloth and sin.

It is an open question whether the lunatic confined to a madhouse in 1650, 1750 or 1850 got a rougher deal than his non-Bedlamite brother still permitted to haunt the hedgerows, or chained up in a barn, or kept, like Mrs Rochester in *Jane Eyre*, locked away in the attic. And it would, in any case, be a mistake to depict the movement to institutionalize the mad as essentially repressive and punitive. What it principally was, was segregative. Its rationale first and foremost expressed the notion that locking up the mad was best for everyone, essential both for the wellbeing of the lunatic and for the safety of society.

Increasingly, from perhaps the mid-eighteenth century, the case for segregating the insane was reinforced by a new faith in therapy and the dream of curing. Lunatics, the argument went, ought to be confined, because new management techniques would make them well. Given proper treatment their intellectual faculties would be repaired and their behaviour rectified. Once cured, they could be restored to civil society. All the same, whether directed towards curing or merely securing, the rationales for confinement hinged upon a growing perception of the essential divide between normal reason on the one hand and delusion on the other.

It would be a mistake to regard this drive over the last three centuries towards institutionalizing insanity fundamentally as the brainchild of 'psychiatry'. In the first instance the sequestration of lunatics was primarily an expression of civil policy, more an initiative from magistrates, philanthropists and families than the achievement – for good or ill – of the doctors. Indeed, the rise of psychological medicine was more the consequence than the cause of the rise of the insane asylum. Psychiatry could flourish once, but not before, large numbers of inmates were crowded into asylums.

This is not to deny that there had long been medical interest in madness, boosted by the impetus to anatomy and neurology given by the Scientific Revolution. The old Greek organic explanations, which stressed the subtle unity of body and mind, soul and spirit, through the categories of the humours, temperaments and complexions, gradually lost their purchase. They were largely replaced by mechanical models of body and mind, and by growing attention to the role of the central nervous system in producing disturbances

17

of perceptions and behaviour. Some evidence of the growing explanatory importance of neuro-anatomy, and thus the concept of 'neurosis' in its original sense (a disease of the nerves), may be seen below in the discussions of George III and Daniel Schreber. George famously insisted that he was not truly mad but only 'nervous'; and a century later Daniel Schreber advanced an elaborate theory of how his own nerves were affected by rays emanating from the divine nerves. These medical investigations into mental disorder, from the late seventeenth century up to the present, have followed in the footsteps of the Greek doctors in endorsing 'medical materialism' – that is, expecting to find insanity rooted in organic, neurological or biochemical disorders.

Through such investigations a specialist branch of medicine – it may slightly anachronistically be termed 'psychiatry' – emerged from the late eighteenth century, anchored in the asylum movement. Its model was primarily organic. It set considerable store by drug therapies, some used to sedate maniacs, others to stimulate melancholics, and many designed to purge the constitution of its poisons through sweats, vomits and laxatives. Rival physicians pioneered their own quite distinct physical and mechanical treatments, including the use of electric-shock techniques, common from the eighteenth century, hot baths, cold showers and restraining chairs. With many such devices – as also of course with the use of manacles, strait-waistcoats or manual labour – treating the body was intended to have its impact upon the mind as well. Thus (to take one instance) the Englishman William Perfect, a late-eighteenth-century keeper of a private madhouse, deployed a veritable battery of physical techniques upon his patients, designed to tranquillize the frenzied and the frantic. He had recourse to drugs such as opium, solitary confinement in darkened rooms, cold baths, a 'lowering' diet, bloodletting, purgatives, etc. These would pacify the body. But in ending the agitations of the constitution, the ultimate aim was to calm the mind, and thus render it receptive to the blandishments of sweet reason.

Disciplining, strengthening and restoring the system through controlled courses of drugs and mechanical restraint played a large part in the techniques devised for the treatment of mental disorder from the eighteenth century onwards. But the segregative environment of the asylum ('far from the madding crowd') also proved a promising location for more explicitly 'psychiatric' techniques of mastering madness, by directly commanding the mind, the passions and the will, and thereby transforming behaviour. From the mid-eighteenth century onwards, innovators came to discount the routine deployment of medication as inefficacious. Radical critics also attacked mere mechanical restraint – the brutal manacles, whips and chains, but also the more subtle straitjackets – as cruel and even counter-productive. In the name of enlightened progress, new regimes were touted, placing an accent on 'moral' methods – kindness, reason and humanity – in the regeneration of the mad.

The 'moral management' movement prominent in late-eighteenth-century England made great play of reclaiming the deranged through the personal charisma of the mad-doctor, relying on force of character and the subtle deployment of inventive psychological tactics tailored to the needs of the individual case. First, patients had to be subdued; then they had to be motivated through the manipulation of their passions – their hopes and fears, their sensitivity to pleasure and pain, their desire for esteem and revulsion from shame.

This movement aimed in effect to revive the dormant humanity of the mad, by treating them as endowed with a residuum at least of normal emotions, still capable of excitation and training. It was taken several stages further at the close of the eighteenth century by the emancipatory visions of Chiurugi in Italy, Philippe Pinel in Paris, the Tukes with their 'moral therapy' at the newly founded Retreat in York, and, perhaps more ambiguously, by Reil and other Romantic psychiatrists in Germany. In their superficially different but fundamentally comparable ways, such reformers aspired to treat their charges as potentially curable human beings. Their 'French revolution' in psychiatry would free the mad from their chains, literal and figurative, and restore to them their suspended rights as rational beings. The mad might now be 'alien' but treatment would recreate the whole man anew. Brislington and Ticehurst asylums, where John Perceval was an inmate (see chapter 9), followed this philosophy.

Drawing upon John Locke's theory of the workings of the human understanding, such reformers characteristically stressed that the madman was not utterly bereft of reasoning power (such was the idiot); nor had his reason been totally destroyed by the anarchy of the passions. Rather he was a creature in whom the faulty associating of ideas and feelings in the mind had led to erroneous conclusions about reality and proper behaviour. Madness was thus essentially delusion, and delusion sprang from intellectual error. Mad people were trapped in fantasy worlds, all too frequently the outgrowth of unbridled imagination. They needed to be treated essentially like children, who required a stiff dose of rigorous mental discipline, rectification and retraining in thinking and feeling. The madhouse should thus become a reform school.

The psychotherapeutics just outlined – the idea that if you first isolated people from bad influences and then rigorously reprogrammed their minds you would positively work cures – generated noble optimism. Schemes for redeeming lunatics were put into action during the nineteenth century on a massive scale. If enlightened asylum psychiatry cured the insane, it was society's duty to put them in institutions. Throughout Europe and North

America, the new or reformed state accepted its duty to legislate and care for the mad, sad and bad. Increasingly the norm was for such people to be certified and compulsorily shut away in special institutions in the name of 'curing' as well as 'securing'. In Britain, perhaps 5,000 people were confined in asylums by 1800; this tally had leaped to about 100,000 by 1900, and to half as many again by 1950. By then, approximately half a million mentally ill or defective people were confined in psychiatric institutions in the USA. A new psychiatric profession, armed with a new psychiatric science, emerged in tandem to manage them.

The brute fact of the growing multitudes flooding into the asylums soon, however, gave pause for thought. On the one hand, the alarming idea struck many nineteenth-century doctors and magistrates that madness was, after all, infinitely more menacing than had been imagined. Early reformers had seen but the tip of the iceberg. No sooner were asylums built than they were filled to overflowing, and still the well-springs of lunacy gushed forth more maniacs, more suicidal melancholics, more senile dements in need of care and treatment. Whole new classes of the mentally ill seemed to appear: alcoholics, the criminally insane, sex maniacs, paralytics.

Furthermore, and even more distressingly, experience increasingly proved that the insane, even when placed in the much fêted utopian environment of the new asylums, did not recover as speedily, as certainly, as had been predicted. In fact most were not cured at all. In consequence, the asylum all too readily changed its character: from being the instrument of regeneration, it became the dustbin of the incurable. Indeed, even worse, radical critics alleged it might be the very machine tooled up for the 'manufacture of madness', and hence faith in the asylum might itself be a form of 'delusion'.

And so the optimism which created the asylum system left in its wake a new pessimism or fatalism. If the best that psychiatry could offer didn't work cures, the verdict which became increasingly plain to the profession from the mid-nineteenth century onwards was that most lunatics were obviously incurable. And this in turn gave a new boost to medical theories of insanity as an ingrained physical disease, perhaps even a hereditary taint, a constitutional diathesis, a blot upon the brain. To generations of psychiatrists whose daily occupation lay in watching the zombie-like living death of asylum recidivists and who familiarized themselves with the latest research into the neuropathology of sensory-motor disorders such as ataxia, epilepsy, aphasia and tertiary syphilis, sober realism demanded a 'degenerationist' theory, the mad seen as retrogressives, as throwbacks. This in turn matched the mood of a bourgeois socio-political elite anxious about the masses.

The degenerationist school of psychiatry in the late nineteenth century also readily saw mental disease in the decadent effusions of artistic and literary geniuses, from the *poètes maudits* to the Impressionists and Cubists. Some psychiatrists believed such painters were suffering from moral, mental and visual disorders – indeed, denounced the 'decadents' so vitriolically as to pose questions about their own mental balance. Creative figures such as Schumann, Virginia Woolf and Nijinsky, examined in later chapters, experienced traumatic relations with psychiatric doctors trying to restore them to normality.

But above all fear grew (one is tempted to call it hysteria) about the dangerous degeneracy of the masses, who were, many psychiatrists warned, wrecking civilization with their mental imbecility or savagery precisely when Darwinism was dictating that only fit societies would survive. Enlightenment optimism had culminated in the French Revolutionary aspiration that the mad could be freed from their mental shackles and restored to full reason. A century later, however – a century of depressing close encounters with the mad in the mental hospital – psychiatry had grown wiser or more pessimistic. A benchmark of this lies in the formulation by the German psychiatrist Emil Kraepelin of *dementia praecox*, soon to be termed schizophrenia.

The archetypal schizophrenic as depicted by Kraepelin was not straightforwardly stupid and brutal, a man without qualities; he might be frighteningly intelligent and astute. Yet he seemed to have renounced his humanity, abandoned all desire to participate in human society. He had withdrawn into a solipsistic, autistic world of his own. Describing schizophrenics, Kraepelin repeatedly used phrases like 'atrophy of the emotions', 'confused speech' and 'vitiation of the will' to convey his sense that they were moral perverts, almost a species apart. The Swiss psychiatrist Manfred Bleuler – the man who has perhaps done more than any other this century to investigate schizophrenia – was to speak of sufferers as 'strange, puzzling, inconceivable, uncanny, incapable of empathy, sinister, frightening'; all in all, he concluded, 'it is impossible to approach them as equals'. The schizophrenic was thus simultaneously psychiatry's prize exhibit, its double, yet also its Waterloo.

Most of the more lurid fantasies of degenerationist psychiatry – its egregious racism, its speculative hereditarianism, its sexual prurience – were wholeheartedly denounced by Freud and by the other leaders of the new dynamic psychiatries coming to prominence around the turn of this century. And of course the therapeutic innovation at the heart of psychoanalysis offered yet another optimistic new deal: the talking cure. Its promise was that if the patient simply 'told all', following the method of free association, the repressions which created neuroses would melt away like a snowball in summer.

Yet for all his 'new-faith' messianism, Freud felt an underlying pessimism which grew overwhelming with time. For one thing, he always insisted that it was only mildly disturbed people who could be treated by his methods – neurotics, not psychotics or schizophrenics – for psychoanalysis made demands upon patients which could be met only by those already possessed of a good sense of reality and a capacity for emotional interaction (or as the wags put it, you had to be pretty well to undergo Freudian treatment).

For another, Freudian psychiatry took a low view of human nature. People were selfish, aggressive and destructive: 'simply a wolf pack'. Freud's concept of the struggles between the unconscious and conscious minds which led to neurosis entailed a reworking of the old Platonic doctrine of the tripartite soul divided against itself, but one which took a particularly terrifying form. Whereas for his part Plato had optimistically concluded that true harmony would reign when reason ruled the passions, Freud saw the relations between id, ego and superego as generating ceaseless civil war, which took on a global character.

Moreover, Freud also endowed his concept of the unconscious with much of the deviousness traditionally attributed to the possessing Devil (the unconscious seemed to have the Devil in it). Both with the individual on the couch and with civilization itself, Freud programmatically took nothing at face value: his gloss on Cartesian doubt was a science of universal suspicion. And following this watchword, he suspected the whole charade of reason of being little better than a mask, a defence mechanism, a mystifying power of resistance. Reason might be the pinnacle of civilization, but it was also characteristically rationalization, the agent of false consciousness, primed to protect us from inadmissible desires and unbearable memories. Why else did mankind still live by such illusions as religion?

Worst of all, the drives of the self and the demands of society were forever at loggerheads. To make sense of the disasters of civilization, Freud suggested that it was founded upon parricide and animated by a death instinct. By the close of his career, his doubts even about the therapeutic potential of his own techniques were stated more publicly. His final word on that subject comes in a paper called 'Analysis Terminable and Interminable'.

What bearing has all this upon the central theme of this book, exploring how mad people themselves have come to think and write about their condition? To make a very basic point first, it is noteworthy that, over the centuries, two separate groups have emerged with an increasing sense of distinctive identity. On the one hand, there is the psychiatric profession, itself far from homogeneous of course. Psychiatrists have established their own rights to treat the disturbed over and against those of the laity, the clergy and, indeed, the medical profession at large. This has often been achieved at the cost of isolation and antagonism. Nineteenth-century psychiatrists (disturbingly they then called themselves 'alienists') often felt beleaguered in their asylum, rather like an army of occupation manning a network of castles. In the present century so acutely did Freud and his early followers feel rejected by society at large that he went to the length of forming his own 'secret committee', an inner cabal of the faithful whom he presented with their own secret rings.

On the other hand, the mentally and behaviourally disturbed were increasingly turned into a clearly identifiable group, typically locked by the nineteenth century in the bulging mental hospital, but also supplying a thriving traffic in office psychiatry. The more 'rational' society grew, and the more it prized 'normality', so the more visible the 'mad' became (or rather, in the end, invisible, since they were all shut up, out of mind, out of sight).

Obviously these two developments are linked, two sides of the same coin. The increased identification of a separate body of the mad proceeded as part and parcel of the emergence of the profession which identified and cared for them. As psychiatry has grown, it has staked greater territorial claims to 'discovering' mental disease where it had not been suspected before. For instance, nineteenth-century psychiatry newly claimed that its proper sphere extended to aberrant behaviour traditionally seen as vice or sin and once left to the bench or pulpit. Inordinate drinking became the mental disease of alcoholism, just as sexual abuses like sodomy were psychiatrized into the 'homosexual neurosis', and a whole range of other erotic 'perversions' were captured by psychopathology.

This point did not escape the eye of the mad. Their autobiographies often point out that psychiatry thus had a tendency to be grandiose but circular: it saw madness everywhere. For it created, or at least became fixated upon, those traits which it professed to cure. Thus mental medicine itself was infected by a sort of craziness, according to such asylum patients as William Belcher or John Perceval; it rendered others the victims of its own delusions, by conjuring up its own fantasy world of the mad. Once you had been forced to act out the role of patient in this fantasy, claimed Perceval, once you were confined in the asylum, you were allowed to escape only if you played your part to the letter. This perception of psychiatry as a theatre, in which the doctors wrote the script and directed the action, and press-ganged the mad as the actors – shades of Charenton! – stemmed of course from the peculiarity which made psychiatry unique in medicine: compulsory confinement in the asylum. For the great majority of the patients seen by mad-doctors or psychiatrists in the two centuries after 1750 had been excommunicated from their fellow men and set apart in special institutions, deprived of their legal rights and personality.

The whole business of identifying and isolating cohorts of people as mad, and then lumping them together in secluded 'total institutions', sometimes housing several thousand sufferers – what effect could it have other than to reinforce the basic contention of the psychiatrists, the supposedly fundamental alienness of the inmates? Thus the system became a self-fulfilling prophecy, by forcing those labelled as abnormal to live under circumstances precluding normal living. Deprived of any semblance of the choices, the freedoms, the self-determination of the world outside, mad people (claimed critics, some 'mad', some 'sane') of course lived down to the stereotype of craziness which psychiatry itself had formulated: what else could be expected?

Yet the behaviour of those cooped up in madhouses became tangible proof to their captors of the essential otherness of the insane. The fact that the mad did not, contrary to early hopes, recover in madhouses additionally proved the intractability of their condition. In a parallel way, the failure of neurotics to recover quickly on the couch seemed to many analysts proof of how deeply entrenched were Oedipal neuroses, how much analytic 'working through' was required.

The accounts contained in the succeeding chapters testify to the profound distrust, often antagonism, felt by mad people towards psychiatry. Such tensions are rarely seen in lay people's writings about doctors in general. The simple explanation, of course, is that the mad are mad. But it should be remembered that the special communication barriers which surface in so many of these narrations – the deafness, the indifference, the cross-purposes – inevitably follow from the path uniquely taken by psychiatry in compulsorily mass-confining patients.

This tendency to segregate the disturbed had another key consequence: a habit amongst doctors of putting the patient under the microscope in splendid isolation, and of probing exclusively within him, his own nature and life-history, for the roots of his disorder. The fact of removing the lunatic from his wider social context into the confines of the madhouse turned him into a clinical problem, a 'case'. Given that the asylum environment was officially 'benign', further failures of co-operation and conduct by the patient could only confirm further how the 'madness' lay within. Thus (as many of the mad writers discussed below perceive) institutional psychiatry put patients in a bind. On the one hand, they were deemed to be mad, and thus to be incapable of taking responsibility for their lives. At the same time they were habitually chided for their own delinquency. And if they rebelled against this 'no win' situation – or indeed attempted to point out the paradox – what did that amount to but further signs of trouble-making?

The discussions in later chapters suggest that modern psychodynamics similarly runs the risk of 'victimizing' the patient, by throwing upon him full responsibility for his own condition. Here the initial act of 'isolation' lies in putting the patient alone on the couch – it has no room for his parents, siblings, spouse, neighbours, employer, etc. – and then ruling normal human contact with the analyst out of bounds. The analyst professionally adopts the aloofness of the scientific observer, and analyst and analysand have a one-way contract. The radically distinct interpretations offered by Freud and by Schatzman of the *Memoirs* of Daniel Schreber underline these points. For Freud, Schreber's psychosis can be understood entirely in terms of his own inner drives. His web of fantasies can be decoded to reveal unconscious homosexual desires, the stifling of which creates disturbance. Those drives initiated in his infant desires for his own father and brother. Freud nowhere suggests that Schreber's persecution feelings might have arisen from intolerable family situations in which he had been placed as a child, or from impossible demands forced upon him by others – possibilities explored by Schatzman.

Thus psychiatry has its own blind spot. It may see only one dimension of the doctor–patient dialectic: the disease or demon within the sufferer. What patients' narratives particularly highlight are the demons without, amongst which the madhouse-keeping psychiatrist himself, his techniques and his milieux, may well all too readily figure as the final instance.

In short, a bird's-eye view of the history of psychiatry shows that profound developments have contributed over the centuries to 'constructing' the mentally sick person as a type, fit for treatment or at least for confinement. Society has progressively defined itself as rational and normal, and by doing so has sanctioned the stigmatizing and exclusion of 'outsiders' and 'aliens'. And the particular device of the walled and locked asylum – which after all ended up housing far larger populations than did prisons – backed by the medical specialty of institutional psychiatry, both underscored the differentness, the uniqueness, of those thus 'alienated' or 'excluded'. These facts combined seemed to so many mad writers a perpetual threat to their common humanity, a way (as Virginia Woolf put it) of 'penalizing despair'. The voice of the writers discussed below is one deeply conscious of having been made to feel different. Generally they complain that 'alienness' is a false identity thrust upon them, or indeed a non-identity, a sense of being rendered a non-person. And all too readily it forms an excuse for why they should not be heard.

Self and Identity

Mad people's writings often stake counter-claims, to shore up that sense of personhood and identity which they feel is eroded by society and psychiatry. Thus at the heart of psycho-politics a contest is waged over the sense of self: who defines it? who is its proprietor? And this throws us into the thick of a deeper history.

The rise of the West has involved the creation of ideals placing unique value upon the individual. Greek philosophy first declared man the measure of all things, and then stressed how each man must bear responsibility for his own fate. Socrates drank the hemlock, and Stoics later championed the autonomy of the rational will, nobly independent of all forms of outward dominion and enslavement to the passions. Thus models of self-knowledge and self-control established the superior worth of the individual.

From within its own very different scheme of values, Christianity further endorsed the uniqueness of the self. The picture presented by the Bible and theology of course was complex, in so far as for fallen, sinful man self-love meant the evils of pride and vanity; it was the Christian's duty to annihilate his self in pursuit of the love of God. Yet man alone was created in God's image, and God had guaranteed to each person an individual, immaterial and immortal soul. Unlike the other religions of antiquity, Christianity offered the promise not of a vague, depersonalized persistence after death, a commingling with the World Soul or a mere transmigration of souls, but the survival of the personal incarnate self intact through the resurrection of the flesh.

In a multitude of different ways far too complex to trace here, leading thinkers through the Middle Ages and into the era of the Renaissance and Reformation set ever greater store by a fundamental sense of the primacy of the individual self. Through meditation and mysticism, Catholic devotionalism probed the private soul for a closer walk with God. Protestantism too, with its priesthood of all believers and justification by faith alone, necessarily set the ultimate court of appeal in matters of conscience within the heart of every believer. As Max Weber emphasized, the ethos of Protestantism, by discarding Catholicism's institutional and quasi-magical sacraments of salvation, threw upon the individual Christian the immense burden of justifying himself before God. He had to scour and scourge his own soul, make confession to himself, and demonstrate to his fellows, by his own moral uprightness, his 'election' to salvation.

As Christendom fragmented, claims to theological tolerance grew, and these in turn became intertwined with political individualism. Liberalism invented the myth of the atomistic self born as a free agent in a state of nature, prior both to society and to the state. Capitalism produced a parallel myth, the notion of *homo economicus*, the sovereign individual producer–consumer pursuing his own private profit in the market. Such a person was given a local habitation and a name by Daniel Defoe: he became Robinson Crusoe, the isolated man on the island who – as if in defiance of John Donne – generated a whole economy and society from within himself.

A comparable sense of the intrinsic value of the unique self gained strength in traditions of introspective moral thinking (*nosce teipsum*) and autobiographical reflection (*que sais-je?*) from Montaigne onwards. Rousseau, whose *Confessions* turned self-revelation into an art form, offered an apology for himself as being if not virtuous at least different, and Romanticism soon embarked upon its odyssey of the moral education (*Bildung*) of the sovereign self as hero. And matching all these impulses to introspection there arose of course the exploration of the meaning of the self in the new disciplines of psychology and psychiatry.

The Scientific Revolution was important here. For it destroyed the old macrocosm – microcosm correspondences of the organic universe and imposed a vision of man standing alone in the cosmos. Cartesian dualism denied consciousness to any natural object except the human mind, and made man's awareness of self-existence a solipsistic projection of his sense of being. But Descartes' proof of self-existence did not long go unchallenged. Locke's empiricism showed that the individual character was itself the product of experience, of myriad atomized sense-inputs precariously coalescing in the sensorium: man thus made himself. And Hume took that perception of subjectivity one stage further by questioning the very continuity and integrity of our own perceptions of our identity: how could we be sure that we were from day to day the same person and not multiple personalities?

Thus the problem of knowledge led back to the problem of the knower, and how he could know himself. For Enlightenment sceptics, this became fundamentally problematic, a source of disorder and confusion. No wonder that Laurence Sterne could envisage his half-mad hero, Tristram Shandy, ever unsure of himself, of his self, dissolving under the challenge of a guard:

> And who are you? asked he.
> Don't puzzle me, said I.

Through Romanticism, through Germanic Idealist philosophy and its critics such as Schopenhauer, and later through Existentialism, modern philosophy and literature embarked upon the restless quest for ultimate authentic identity, and in doing so became caught up in an ever more incestuous affair with the categories and theories of psychiatry itself. The love–hate relationship between modern Freudian and Jungian psychoanalysis on the one hand and writers and artists on the other is too well known to need describing here.

I have been suggesting, in other words, that multiple thought traditions converged in modern Western thinking to place a premium upon the development and realization of the self. Individuality was prized. But it was problematic. It engaged its own psychiatric problems. The rise of the novel, with its exploration of the vicissitudes of the self as hero, experiencing moral education, offers a classic instance. But above all we see it in the development of distinct traditions of autobiographical writing.

In autobiography, religion paved the way. Indeed, St Augustine's *Confessions* provided the model and sanction for the later development of the genre. The communings of the self with God were widely recorded in the Middle Ages, and an introspective obligation was institutionalized within Catholicism through the practices of confession and penance. The keeping and publication of spiritual diaries then became common in the sixteenth and seventeenth centuries, directed towards auto-confession, making a clean breast of one's filthiness before God. A conspicuous theme of such spiritual autobiographies was the conversion experience. The sinner had first succumbed to temptation and was lurching blindly towards the jaws of hell. But God in His mercy engineered a profound spiritual crisis. Torment racked the soul, but grace saved the sinner and left him a thankful penitent. John Bunyan's *Grace Abounding* became, within the English-speaking world, definitive of this way of making retrospective religious sense of the wayward human tragi-comedy.

The most profoundly introspective instances of the *apologia pro vita sua* – some ostensibly private, some explicitly intended for publication – sprang initially from essentially religious protocols: the need to bare the conscience and confess one's sins beneath the All-seeing Almighty. They could serve as a way of redeeming others, help to convince the unregenerate world of one's own final hard-won worth, or essentially provide a way of casting up one's spiritual accounts before meeting one's Maker. In time, the language and values of the autobiography became more commonly secular, but the urge to self-lacerating revelations remained no less strong. The autobiographer might have little of virtue to reveal, except the ultimate virtue of 'honesty'.

But many other genres of autobiography also grew up, and it is relevant to take notice of one other here. This was proud rather than penitent, was bent less upon self-incrimination than upon self-justification. Often such soliloquies took the form of a vindication against the calumnies of the cruel world, or the 'objective' statement of one's achievements. Such versions of the self found their ways into print in many forms – as autobiographies proper, prefatory remarks, rebuttals, open letters and so forth, many of them celebrating the exceptional virtues of the subject. Burckhardt emphasized the individualism of the Renaissance; certainly from the Renaissance onwards, public figures felt little compunction about singing their own praises, or settling scores with their enemies, in the autobiographical mode.

The great and the glorious, from Benvenuto Cellini to Gibbon, and on to Freud and beyond, have felt the itch to put the record straight, to paint portraits of themselves as heroes. They have had droves of imitators amongst the unknown, demonstrating why they too would have been Cellinis, Gibbons or Freuds but for the machinations of their enemies and the malice of fate. Spurred on by duties to truth and a love of their fellow men, countless autobiographers have told their sad tales of neglect and vilification. Those who have undergone imprisonment, who have been deprived of their liberties, and who have battled for the Cause, have needed to tell their stories to set their own lives straight and put posterity in the picture.

Many turn autobiographer because they think themselves misunderstood. But it is of course a genre which cannot protect itself against misunderstanding. Autobiographers do commonly protest themselves too much, and the potentialities of the genre for pathos and unintentional self-parody were fully exposed in its early days by Jonathan Swift's modest invitations to enter into the monstrous self-deceiving egoism of the likes of the narrator of the *Tale of the Tub* and of Lemuel Gulliver himself. Are such 'unreliable narrators' telling the truth? Or are they offering no more than tales told by idiots, signifying nothing? It is precisely this radical ambiguity in the project of telling one's own story which renders autobiography liable to dissolve into a mad pursuit. That autobiographer is a fool who believes that his self-revelations will not be regarded as symptoms of psychopathology. Laurence Sterne nailed the autobiographical ejaculations of his enemy, Tobias Smollett:

> I'll tell it, cried Smelfungus [Smollett], to the world. You had better tell it, said I, to your physician.

Unsurprisingly then the autobiographies of mad people must prove a hermeneutic minefield. For the form itself demands a solipsism which might be seen as inherently pathological. To tell one's own story: what could better establish one's own veracity, or provide more conclusive symptoms of utter self-delusion?

Psychiatry and the Self

One of the tropes, one of the complaints, of psychiatry down the ages is that the mad have been so full of themselves. It is said to be a mark of their condition (paranoia, megalomania, etc.) that they believe that everything revolves around themselves (the problem of self-reference); they have the Ancient Mariner's ceaseless itch to talk about themselves or an unslakable thirst for writing (the *cacoethes scribendi*). Monstrous egoism of such kinds – initially the sins of vanity and pride – had long been of course definitive of the very state of madness itself. Such a form of auto-intoxication might manifest itself as despair (as with William Cowper, discussed below, whose *idée fixe* was that no one in the wide world could be so sinful as himself), or alternatively as inordinate self-importance, as in the claims of Daniel Schreber, Clifford Beers or perhaps Freud that through their own experience of psychoneurosis they were uniquely in a position to save the psyche through revealing to the world a new religion or a new science.

And it has certainly been true in actuality that mad people have tried to put their own plight on record. Clifford Beers tells us that his lifeline to sanity while in the asylum was often a stub-end of pencil secreted away somewhere in his cell. One may speculate that what kept him reasonably sane for the remainder of his life was his ability to tell his own story over and over again, thousands of times, to audiences at lectures and dinners. Nijinsky records that he sat resolutely writing his diary in Russian at the very time his doctors were trying to interview him. Many diaries of madmen are works of quite extraordinary length and detail: the journal of the late-seventeenth-century Whig politician and communer with the fairy world, Goodwin Wharton, runs to some half a million words – and that forms, he assures us, but a digest of his original jottings.

People in ordinary walks of life, under no daily threat to their mental control, no fears that no one would ever listen to them, have experienced profound needs to create versions of their selves which 'adjust reality' for the public or posterity. It should be no surprise then that those who have felt profoundly threatened by devils or by mad-doctors should have wanted to leave their own testament in order to achieve justice temporal or eternal, or simply as the only way to answer back.

What have society and psychiatry made of these tales from beyond? As noted above, traditional European culture, learned and popular, had been willing to entertain the conceit that madness might indeed have something to say, might possess, or be the vehicle for, mysterious truths. The jesting fool was allowed his privilege, the prophetic madman his converts. The possessed witch who incriminated her neighbours had her charges investigated. Early visitors to Bethlem, there to enjoy a spectator sport, took pleasure in the uncensored, unbuttoned rantings of the 'collegians' (as they were called), and toyed with the idea that there might be reason in madness, truth in folly, because at bottom it was all 'a mad world, my masters'. Bedlamites were reputed to bask in their unique freedom to curse the King, mock author-ity and unmask hypocrisy. They could speak their mind and ask: who were the real fools? Thus the lunatic (we might see him as pure id) might be the only free man.

Of course the joke was on the madman too. Commentators and psychiatrists alike made sport of the *soi-disant* poet, the inventor, the occasional inmate who believed he was Anacreon. In the tableau of Bedlam which forms the final scene of *The Rake's Progress*, Hogarth depicts himself as a crazy artist scribbling all over the walls. Returning the compliment, Paul Sandby drew Hogarth as *The Writer Run Mad*. Writing about mad people writing about ... It all so easily turned into a hall of mirrors.

Amidst all the cultural confusion, however, one truth seems clear. In the long run, the development of segregation through the madhouse system, and of a presiding discipline of psychiatry, served to silence the mad, or, perhaps more accurately, to render their voices inaudible to most and unintelligible to others, little inclined to listen. This occurred in a crude material sense. The more the mad were locked away, the more they were 'shut up' in every sense of the term. The weird or misfit person living within, though on the margins of, society obviously had more opportunity to express himself – and more of a chance of his rant being heeded – than his equivalent in the asylum. For example, the late-eighteenth-century Devonshire prophetess and mother-to-be of the New Messiah, Joanna Southcott – a woman widely believed to be quite crackbrained – was allowed to remain free, and she built up a following of thousands in London, founding her own church. By contrast, the contemporary and very similar prophet figure Richard Brothers largely faded from the public ear after he was confined on government orders in a madhouse.

Of course, the madhouse was itself an ambiguous institution, for it could be a sounding-board as well as a silencer. Till around 1770, London's Bethlem encouraged indiscriminate public visiting, and theatricals were put on at Charenton in Paris. But private madhouses had always been deeply concerned to keep those who were out of their mind out of sight, and secretiveness (justified as being in the interests of the patients) was to dominate the nineteenth-century public asylum and its legacy. Elaborate schedules of rules severely limited inmates' access to the outside world and *vice versa*. An early-eighteenth-century patient such as Alexander Cruden had no great difficulty in gaining access to the world beyond, receiving visitors and getting letters out. But that was to change. One constant complaint made in practically every patient autobiography from the nineteenth century onwards is of the communications barrier. The therapeutics of maximum environmental control, of psychiatric enlightened absolutism, seemed to demand the minimization of contact between the sufferer and society, almost as though the disease were contagious.

One of the greatest bugbears recorded by John Perceval in his *Narrative* was his isolation from his fellow men and the unremitting destruction or censorship of letters written by or sent to him. It was surely this enforced isolation which contributed to Clifford Beers's belief that those visitors who were allowed to see him in the asylum were actually frauds and stooges,

31

utterly unreal. Isolated in asylums, both Robert Schumann and Daniel Schreber believed their wives had died, having not heard from them for so long.

Other forms of communication or self-expression were equally prohibited as counter-indicated. The rest-cure therapy popularized by Weir Mitchell and others late in the nineteenth century denied patients access to pen and paper, for writing was believed to overexcite. Likewise it was thought therapeutically desirable that patients should not talk about themselves. The 'talking disease' was seen as a mark of a hysterical personality, forever craving attention. By listening to the hysteric's utterances the doctors would only exacerbate a morbid sense of self-importance. Even in today's enlightened age, patients' attempts to communicate or write are liable to be looked upon with suspicion. Some twenty years back, as part of an experiment, some American researchers had themselves confined in an asylum masquerading as schizophrenics. In the hospital, these pseudo-patients behaved normally, on occasion taking written notes of what they observed. This action was noted in their case histories as symptomatic of their schizophrenia: it was called engaging in 'writing behaviour'.

Thus, in rather abrupt ways, institutional psychiatry physically isolated the mentally sick from society, and put obstacles in the way of communication. As one Irish inmate complained to his superintendent: 'You have taken my language from me.' Schumann apparently almost lost the art of speaking through protracted silence. But psychiatry also tended to stifle mad people in a further, more subtle sense, by acting on the assumption that what they might say in any case had no meaning.

Heaven knows the mad were loquacious! But what they uttered (argued mainline views in psychological medicine) was the merest nonsense, was not in fact *communication*. This was certainly the verdict of doctors from the seventeenth century onward faced with witches and religious pentecostalists with their apparently diabolical or blasphemous utterances. Such words if taken literally were dangerous, even abominable. Hence it became standard to refer to what mad people said – their cursings, obscenities, insults and indecencies – through terms such as 'chattering', 'jabbering' and 'ranting', suggesting that the language of the mad was sub-human, communicating no more meaning than the sounds of wild beasts – to which, of course, lunatics were commonly likened. Lycanthropy, after all, was that form of lunacy which made a man howl like a wolf.

Behind all this was the assumption that what mad people said was devoid of signification: 'all cohaerance gone'. It did not form a proper and meaningful use of language, but was akin to a mere outpouring, a purge of the brain, a totally random, uncontrollable cry of pain or an infantile babble. After all, leading theories in mental medicine in the eighteenth and nineteenth centuries argued that the cause, the essence, of insanity did not lie in some primary conflict of the mind, but arose from a body lesion. Disturbance of the guts, a surplus of black bile, a taint of the blood, a tumour on the brain, the wandering of the womb – all such somatic disturbances produced agony, anxiety, hysterical seizures, hallucinations. The talk of the mad was thus merely a reflex reaction to that, like a rattle in a faulty car. It was secondary, symptomatic; it showed that something was amiss, but had no inherent truth. Such gibberish offered no clues to reality, personal, social or cosmic.

The view that the speech and writing of lunatics were best treated as sound and fury, as nonsense, was widely touted. Take the influential Dr Nicholas Robinson, a contemporary and follower of Isaac Newton. Robinson argued that the words and movements of the mad were just automatic spasms of the vocal chords. They did not follow from acts of mind, and so offered no insight to mental conditions, because madness was essentially the product of somatic disturbances. When a patient revealed his dreams of being ridden like a horse by a gentleman friend, Robinson construed this simply as symptomatic of an overheated imagination and recommended 'strong medicines' as a purge.

Psychiatry thus took speech peculiarities and defects as marks of madness, interpreted increasingly in the nineteenth century as caused by diseases of the central nervous system or the brain. But doctors were distrustful of engaging with what the mad actually said. That would merely embed their *idées fixes* yet more firmly in their minds, without providing the doctor with any significant information. The 'other minds' problem was solved in effect by their denial. Mad people's autobiographies habitually complain that their attempts to communicate are stifled, unheeded or wilfully misinterpreted. Their speech misappropriated, many have felt driven to protect themselves in silence or in invented lingo.

The culmination of this process lay in key features of *dementia praecox* as formulated by Kraepelin, shortly to be turned into Eugen Bleuler's incredibly influential 'schizophrenia'. Kraepelin was disposed to regard *dementia praecox* as organic in aetiology. Its striking symptomatic aspect, however, was that it was characterized by autism. The sufferer supposedly showed scant interest in the outside world, neither engaging nor communicating with it. He had thus made himself essentially *incommunicado*, alien from humanity. The schizophrenic was man as an island. Kraepelin saw the lack of will to communicate as typical of the condition:

33

The patients become monosyllabic, sparing of their words, speak
hesitatingly, suddenly mute, never relate anything on their own initiative.
. . . they enter into no relations with other people.

This designation of schizophrenia brought into focus one of the inchoate
tendencies of emergent psychiatry, the notion that madness's essence lies in
being alien, different, other. Critics of orthodox psychiatry such as R.D.Laing
and Peter Barham have observed that it is but a short step from there to
the notion that madness is essentially incomprehensible, inaccessible – which,
they claim, all too easily sanctions organized neglect. Laing has suggested
that Kraepelin's case notes with schizophrenics show that it was *he* who was
failing to communicate. The schizophrenic's muteness can be read, by one
attuned to listen to silences, as a very eloquent response.

From the nineteenth century onwards, organic theories permitted a deafness to what the mad said, a deafness ironically akin to that indifference
to communication which mad people themselves allegedly betrayed. Therapeutics present similar dilemmas. Thus even the advocates of 'moral therapy'
mentioned above were not interested in listening to what the mad had to
say for themselves, or in direct, person-to-person verbal communication. They
were preoccupied instead with what might be called 'behaviourist' techniques
of rendering their speech proper. At the York Retreat, no heed was paid
to hallucinations; that would have been pandering to patient egoism. What
counted was re-education in polite conversational patterns, for which taking
tea with the doctors would prove instructive.

Did these obstacles to communicating with the natives arise because no
one – at least, before Freud – possessed any skill in reading between the
lines, in decoding syllables and symbols? Surely not. For learned and
ingenious philological and hermeneutic skills had been the stock-in-trade
of traditional humanist scholarship. The words, symbols and rituals of one
text, or one culture, were habitually being translated into the language of
another by those who believed in universal mythology or universal religion.
Symbolic meanings formed the essence of the occult. There was no reason
in principle why the bending and stretching of language deployed by John
Clare or Daniel Schreber should not have been pretty intelligible to their
physicians as *façons de parler*. After all, in their different ways, both Freud
and Jung drew deeply upon these exegetical traditions of classical philology
and mythology. Philosophy, poetics and literary criticism all had pursued
hidden meanings with enormous skill at reading between the lines.

Moreover, the notion that some unconscious faculty was animating the
mind, whose workings might be mysterious but were nevertheless intelligible,
translating dark desires into words and images, was one with which Romantic

34

poets and philosophers were perfectly familiar: witness the conventions behind Coleridge's *Kubla Khan*. But amongst the pre-Freudian psychiatrists, listeners disposed to listen with a third ear were few and far between. Bethlem's John Haslam recorded James Tilley Matthews' fantasies, but solely it seems as proof that he was off his head.

In other words the deep disposition to see madness as essentially Other almost automatically dictated that what strange people said was denied standing as an authentic if broken form of communication, even by liberal and sensitive doctors. In his published account of his eight-year-long therapeutic relationship with 'Miss Beauchamp', the early-twentieth-century American psychiatrist Morton Prince identified many distinct fragmented personalities in his patient (BI, BII, BIII, etc.), each of which spoke to him in a separate tongue. He enumerated and labelled these separate splinters of the self (some were good, some bad), and tried to find the 'real' Miss Beauchamp (not surprisingly, she was the compliant one). Prince showed little interest, however, in what each of these selves was saying (although as we read his account it seems obvious to us that several of these selves were either mocking or displaying anger and confusion provoked by him).

This may sound like blaming Prince and his predecessors for not being Freud. That is, however, not a totally unreasonable complaint. After all, mad people's writings down the centuries have contained bitter complaints against the barriers and defences put up by doctors thwarting their own attempts to communicate. John Perceval and others admit that when distracted their speech was indeed strange. But (so Perceval subsequently claimed) the aberrations of his use of proper names and so forth were hardly so opaque as to defy understanding. Perceval concluded that authority had chosen to act deaf. He interpreted that as an aggressive gesture and retaliated in kind. Much of his spell in the asylum, he recorded, consisted of a wilful and mutual dumbshow.

But Freud's 'talking cure' is not of course without its own deep ambiguities, both in theory and in practice. If asylum life encouraged scenes of silence, with Freud we sometimes have dialogues of the deaf, conversations conducted in different languages (in which 'no' typically means 'yes') and with an interpreter suffering from *idées fixes* about the meanings of certain words. Freud was evidently both an extremely good and an extremely bad listener. He was totally selective, and his appropriation of his patients' stories for his own theoretical purposes was arguably more aggressive and insensitive than the stone-deafness of his predecessors, as the cases of the 'Wolf Man' and of 'Dora', examined below, suggest.

The Return of the Repressed

One function – or at least by-product – of the rise of institutional psychiatry and psychiatric theory has been a habit of not listening to the mad; less perhaps the great silence about which Foucault wrote than a great deal of talking past each other. Some of the mad, nevertheless, have certainly had their say. Many hundreds of mad people have *published* their life stories. (Who knows how many have written them?) The accounts which follow in the next nine chapters offer a drop in the ocean of what they have wanted to communicate.

Broadly, we can schematically fit their writings into the chief genres of autobiographical writings discussed earlier. On the one hand, there is the tradition of spiritual autobiography. Those who have gone through madness, precisely like those suffering religious crisis and conversion, have commonly retailed their experiences: often the two amount essentially to the same. Publishing after the event forms a way of making sense of a former condition, and of telling the world that reason has been recovered. It was not a foolproof project of course, and it could backfire. For example, to Daniel Schreber's doctors, it was his very desire to publish his memoirs which seemed proof positive of the persistence of his madness.

In this confessional genre the early accounts are religious in the literal, Christian sense. Several authors I discuss below, such as Margery Kempe, George Trosse and John Perceval, regard themselves as totally orthodox in religious terms. Others such as Schreber write overtly religious accounts of their own psychoses, but their religion is a hotchpotch of their own making. Still others (such as 'Barbara O'Brien') write accounts of being possessed by superior and inferior powers, which clearly echo the religious scenario, but from which the formal elements of religion are absent.

And then there are some spiritual autobiographies (all the ones I discuss are modern) whose concerns continue to be those elements of despair – temptation, the dark night of the soul, the road to recovery – which draw on the *de profundis* confessional genre but whose authors think essentially within a secular framework. Jim Curran's account of his work and drink crisis offers an instance; the 'mythical' framework he draws upon is that of the American dream.

Several of the accounts analysed below, however, fall into the second genre of autobiographical writing touched on above: they are aggressive works of self-justification, which expose foes and vindicate the author's own actions. To a large degree, such works constitute a wail of protest against the treatment of madness itself, against the persecutor which was purportedly their protector.

Many writings from the eighteenth century onwards indict mad-doctors and their henchmen. In these it is often alleged – as for example by Samuel Bruckshaw – that a perfectly sane victim has been improperly confined. Alternatively, the autobiographer may be more disposed to admit to a degree of former mental incapacity. But then his charge is levelled not against confinement *per se* but against the evil or sinister regime of the madhouse. The institution and its staff are exposed as inept, exploitative and counter-productive. As William Belcher and others contended, the madhouse becomes an evil engine for making men mad rather than mending their madness. In this book I have chosen not to give a very copious account of this genre of writings, because it is very fully represented in Dale Peterson's excellent anthology of protest writings, *A Mad People's History of Madness*.

It would be misleading to try to string all these autobiographical accounts together into a single chronological line, and expect that they would thereby tell a progressive story. Each narrative is unique, and I have merely bunched them loosely around themes. But some developments are conspicuous. What is particularly noteworthy down the centuries is a growing rapport, even convergence, between the consciousness of the mad as expressed in their own writings and the lore and language of psychiatry. Unsurprisingly of course the earliest autobiographical accounts are untouched by psychiatry in any shape or form. In the fifteenth century Margery Kempe accepts the fact that she had been out of her mind, but thereafter all her contacts are with the clergy; likewise somewhat later with Christoph Haitzmann and his possession experiences. George Trosse recovers in a madhouse but thinks, moves and has his being in the idiom of religion; and so forth.

Eighteenth-century writers such as Alexander Cruden, Samuel Bruckshaw and William Belcher certainly came under the power of the mad-doctor to a greater degree. But they respond to it essentially as a negative and oppressive force, alien to themselves, and lacking insight into their plight. That cannot be said so simply for John Perceval in the nineteenth century. He regarded the asylum regimes to which he was exposed as essentially alien, but became concerned in a practical, indeed a constructive, way to formulate criticisms of asylumdom with a view to its rectification. Perceval was also eager to train a proper psychiatrically informed gaze upon himself. Standing back, he wanted to know in psycho-philosophical terms how he had actually come first to be mad and then to recover. And he explored what kind of asylum would have been effective in handling a patient like himself.

But the spectacular transition to a novel *entente* between disturbed patient and psychiatric doctor comes with the twentieth century. A good marker of this is the fact that so many volumes of mad people's memoirs in this century have been published replete with introductions, apparatus and conclusions penned by psychiatrists, thereby giving the memoirs a professional seal of approval: the writings of 'Barbara O'Brien', discussed in chapter 10, form a good instance. Moreover – a totally new feature – many now have a tale to tell of salvation through psychiatry, albeit certain works (as for example those by Curran and Balt discussed below) tell a tale of two psychiatries: one bad and the other good.

This growing positive interplay, coalescence or symbiosis between the voice of the madman and the voice of his doctor might be interpreted in many different ways. It may simply show that what we might call the psychiatric-cum-psychoanalytic empire has become more ubiquitous this century, that today's neurotic or psychotic falls under the psychiatric gaze much more ineluctably than did his predecessor of one or two centuries ago. It may simply mean that twentieth-century psychiatry is truly experienced by sufferers as being more sympathetic. Where once we had protesters wishing to denounce mad-doctors from the rooftops, modern patients are much more inclined to sing psychiatry's praises. But it may also suggest that it has become more seductive. Being abnormal in certain approved ways is accepted in twentieth-century trans-Atlantic culture as a form of normality in itself; and not a few modern patients have either 'changed sides', turning (like Clifford Beers) from patient into prophet or practitioner, or have chosen to portray their own odysseys into inner space as dedicated to the discovery of the truths of the psyche.

Thus an element of assimilation – madness may have moved towards psychiatry. But all motion is relative; we may be witnessing yet another mode of *folie à deux*, madness and psychiatry as doubles.

3 · Madness and Power

A patient in a Parisian asylum early in the nineteenth century used to cry out:

> I am man, God, Napoleon, Robespierre, altogether. I am Robespierre, a Monster. I must be slain.

The history of madness is the history of power. Because it imagines power, madness is both impotence and omnipotence. It requires power to control it. Threatening the normal structures of authority, insanity is engaged in an endless dialogue – a monomaniacal monologue sometimes – about power. This is partly due to the irresistible analogy drawn ever since the Greeks between microcosm and macrocosm, the body natural and the body politic. Plato explicitly developed the analogy between the hierarchical ordering of the healthy soul (in which reason lords it over the base and unruly passions) and the organic social order, in which rational guardians possess true authority, disciplining the anarchic multitude, who have no potential for self-control, but are slaves to their own appetites.

For two thousand years afterwards, healthy minds, healthy bodies and healthy societies were associated with the rule of reason, and disturbance with the tumult of base and vulgar desire. Echoes of this pattern, transformed to his own uses, survive in Freud's tripartite division of the psyche and in the role he mapped out for the controlling superego and the anarchic id.

The analogy was not just descriptive but prescriptive as well. Good order required that reason should reign. When it was overthrown, the political madness of civil war followed, as happened when King Lear gave away his kingdom and lost his mind in the storm on the heath. In other words something particularly evil had occurred when reason, that rightful instrument of government, both personal and political, ceased to fulfil its proper office. When princes abused their office and turned tyrant, substituting base urges for higher duties, they disturbed the order of things. The fates or nature, or God, would wreak revenge, fittingly by driving them mad. Greek legend

39

and history teem with rulers driven insane by way of nemesis for their own frenzied ambitions or lawlessness. Often such madness was seen to be positively therapeutic through producing a cathartic effect. Rage or folly is purged; the hero is restored – to health if not to his kingdom – or can die a wiser and better man than before. The loss of reason in time makes King Lear wise, just as the loss of his eyes gives his old crony, Gloucester, insight.

Alongside these essentially Greek ideas, Judaism and Christianity embraced similar views. When the mighty abuse their power and are humbled, madness is the apt symbolic fate. The despotic Nebuchadnezzar, who commits atrocities against God's people, is reduced to bestial madness. Medieval chroniclers and artists imagined him naked and hairy, banished from society, on all fours, eating the herbs of the earth. Within Christian theology, the visitation of madness upon the powerful is sometimes interpreted simply as a punishment. Often it is a trial (a humiliation to be followed by exaltation), and occasionally it is a straightforward blessing, ecstatic direct communication with the divine will.

All such associations between, on the one hand, individual psychic order and disorder and, on the other, the constitution of the commonwealth itself, resonated powerfully down the centuries. But they took on a markedly new nuance perhaps from the eighteenth century onwards. For alongside and challenging the age-old link between ruling and rationality, the idea was increasingly floated that there was actually something *pathological* about the exercise of power itself.

It was, of course, a notion which lent itself readily to the language of opposition and radical political discourse, eager to expose all monarchs and generals as power-crazed banditti. In his *Tale of a Tub*, Jonathan Swift ironically eulogized madmen as the authors of all that was great in empires and kingdoms, and throughout the eighteenth century British political cartoonists never tired of portraying supposedly ambition-mad politicians such as Charles James Fox or Edmund Burke as raving mad or straitjacketed. The Bedlam scene in Hogarth's *The Rake's Progress* predictably includes a mad king (presumably, punningly, a 'pretender').

Astonishingly, this idea that the high might actually be highly unstable appealed to the ruling orders themselves. They eagerly adopted the notion of an 'English malady', a sort of constitutional disorder of the nerves which picked up the high-born and high society. Being not quite normal or rational, prey to moodiness and melancholy, became a mark of talent and superiority, the price of genius or the pressures of power, rather than a disqualification from the exercise of power. No one was too surprised when Pitt the Elder underwent a terrifying breakdown, or believed that such an episode should put a terminus to his career in public life. The suicides of Robert Clive and Lord Castlereagh were taken in the nation's stride as symptomatic of the burdens of office.

The medical profession was influential in popularizing this new ideology which 'gentrified' mental disturbance, in particular the cadre of what we may anachronistically call 'psychiatric doctors' emerging across Europe during the eighteenth century. Mad-doctors – especially those who kept madhouses – became acutely aware of the psychopathology of the ruling passion through personally having to deal with large numbers of lunatics suffering delusions of grandeur and believing they were popes or emperors, omnipotent, immortal or immensely rich. The pioneer of American medicine, Benjamin Rush, extended the diagnosis: within his taxonomy of mental illness, radicalism and revolutionary fervour themselves became mental diseases, just as being black became a physical disease. In early-nineteenth-century Paris, Esquirol had scores of patients who thought they were Napoleon. Clearly links were being forged within emergent psychiatry between the power-crazed delusions of the common-or-garden lunatic and the fantasies of real kings, politicians or preachers. From the French Revolution, through to Adler and to Wilhelm Reich's inquiry into the psychological roots of Fascism – the need of the little man to ape the big man – the will to power was to become a central doctrine of psychiatry, rendered clinical in megalomania, etc.

In this process, the focus of the debate about madness and power shifted towards the authority – which was ever increasing – of the mad-doctor himself. Physicians in general may not have wielded much power in pre-modern medicine. Their lack of provenly effective curative techniques and need to submit to client control left doctors without any independent power-base to dominate in matters of general health. But the situation was rather different for physicians handling the mad, especially in the context of the privately owned madl.ouse. It stood to reason that the insane had forfeited their rights to govern themselves, to exercise a voice or veto in their own detention or therapy. Commanding, even manhandling, the mad often formed part of the treatment. Mad-doctors were often portrayed holding the whip.

Moreover, during the eighteenth century mad-doctors all over Europe started to believe that they held madness in their power: they could cure it. (A few regarded this in itself as a delusion.) Traditional medical views had been quite pessimistic. In his *Anatomy of Melancholy* (1621) Robert Burton had concluded that, beyond prayer, there was little that could be done for serious melancholy and mania: it was part of the human condition, almost a pandemic. And traditional madhouses such as Bethlem had gone in for no more than the most routine schedules of medication. But growing numbers of mad-doctors began to argue that, hide-bound pessimism notwithstanding, madness was amongst the more curable maladies. There were two modes of madness, argued William Battie in the mid-eighteenth century: original madness, which, like original sin, was beyond cure, and consequential madness, which was generally curable.

But insanity would not yield to universal remedies or general medication. Management would achieve more than medication, claimed Battie, and his slogan was taken up and applied by a score of doctors who aimed to develop new and more effective techniques of management: early institutionalization, solitary confinement, pacifying medicines, new mechanical therapies such as shock treatment, and above all 'moral management', or what we might call psychological control. For doctors such as William Pargeter, Joseph Mason Cox, William Hallaran and others, what really counted was the exercise of *mental* dominion by the doctor over his patient, by deploying the manipulation of emotions, pleasure and pain, hope and fear, by commanding the environment, by anticipating responses, by outsmarting the low cunning of insanity. Mad-doctors had to be generals; they themselves thus had a taste of power. By the early nineteenth century they were beginning to formulate grand – even grandiose – designs for the ideal asylum as a sort of therapeutic utopia, more rational than society itself.

And it seemed to work. One of them, the Rev Dr Francis Willis – a man who notoriously subdued his charges through the charismatic, fascinating force of his eye – told a parliamentary committee that nine out of ten of his crazy patients recovered. It was Willis who was called in to treat George III in 1788 when the regular court physicians proved powerless to handle his disorder.

Traditional accounts of George's royal malady drew heavily upon the old moralistic stereotypes of reason overthrown. Contemporary Whig politicians and critics saw it as a classic case of nemesis. The monarch who had jeopardized the free constitution by his crazy ambition for personal tyranny was now reaping the whirlwind in his mind. Recent historians' pop-Freudian character judgements have essentially adopted the same framework, adding a few refinements. George, according to modern biographers, was less of a despot than a fusspot, a tidy-minded, Teutonic bureaucrat. He became overconscientious and subjected himself to a self-punishingly obsessional regime of administrative detail – he personally wrote all his own letters. Furthermore, married to the ugly Charlotte, he must (historians suggest) have become a hotbed of festering sexual frustration. Eventually he exploded, succumbing to bouts of insanity perhaps in 1765, but certainly in 1788–9, 1801, 1804 and 1810 (from the last of which he never recovered but sank into senile dementia).

The psychiatrists Macalpine and Hunter have argued, however, that this psychodynamic interpretation amounts to little better than saloon-bar speculation. The evidence for deep and lasting psychic conflict stemming from infancy and childhood is flimsy. The arguments for it are essentially *ex post facto*. Generally sceptical of the validity of psychoanalysis, Macalpine and Hunter have proposed an alternative explanation of George's malady: that he was suffering from porphyria, an inherited metabolic disorder producing intense irritation and delirium. George was primarily physically diseased; his mental disorders were essentially secondary and symptomatic.

Leaving aside these 'power struggles' between the neurological and the analytical camps, the psychodynamic interpretations of George's condition raise far more questions than they solve. They must necessarily remain guess-work, for we lack adequate records of George's own inner consciousness, both over his lifetime as a whole and particularly during his bouts of illness. Some psychiatrists might find it revealing that the King typically referred to himself in the third person; but that was characteristic of the office not the person, and third-person reports are hardly likely to plumb the depths of consciousness.

We possess various other reports of the King's mind while it was unhinged. But those which are probably reasonably trustworthy – for example, the daily case-notes written by his physicians, Sir George Baker and Dr John Willis, Francis Willis's son and assistant, are terse and stereotyped, while those which are rich in anecdote were mainly written by tittle-tattling scandal-mongers, many of whom were not eye-witnesses, and whose veracity must be doubted. One day in February 1789, the King, then on the mend, was allowed to stroll around the grounds at Kew. Spying Fanny Burney, then a lady-in-waiting, he ran after her. She panicked and fled. Commanded by the Willises to stop she was buttonholed by the King, who poured out all his troubles to her. 'What a conversation followed!' she confided to her diary:

> Everything that came uppermost in his mind he mentioned; he seemed
> to have just such remains of his flightiness as heated his imagination
> without deranging his reason, and robbed him of all control over his
> speech, though nearly in his perfect state of mind as to his opinions. . . .
> What did he not say! – he opened his whole heart to me, – expounded
> all his sentiments, and acquainted me with all his intentions.

So what did the King say, what was the secret of his heart? Burney does not tell *us*.

It is thus not realistic to expect to penetrate to the heart of the King's disturbance. What can be explored, however, is the dizzying dialogue of power which the royal insanity set in motion.

When George fell sick at Cheltenham in the summer of 1788 with what was termed 'bilious fever', he responded – as his contemporaries typically would have done – by consulting his trusted physician, Sir George Baker. He obeyed medical authority in some respects (he took a purge by which he was 'well disciplined'), and followed his own whim in others, persisting in heavy riding despite medical advice. In mid-October, a similar complaint returned and worsened. He suffered stomach pains, cramps, spasms and swollen feet. He grew costive, quite probably the result of medication. People talked about 'gout' and 'rheumatism'.

His condition worsened. His spirits grew agitated. He became vehement, voluble, hoarse. He fell into a fever, becoming confused and suffering distortions of vision and hearing. He was overcome by great 'hurry of spirits' and started talking nonstop, becoming 'incoherent', 'trifling' and 'childish'. Before the end of the month, delirium had set in. The regular royal physicians, above all Sir George Baker, Sir Lucas Pepys and Richard Warren, had him cupped and purged. 'Blisters' were applied as a counter-irritant. George resisted. He displayed 'noted aversion to physicians', insisting that 'the Queen is my physician, and no man need have a better'. He reassured Fanny Burney, 'I am nervous – I am not ill,' but by early November she believed he was in a 'positive delirium'.

Through November the King's condition grew more serious. He got weaker, occasionally lapsed into coma, and people noted a growing 'derangement of his faculties'. Soon it was feared that he might actually die. As early as the 8th, taking refuge in the decent obscurity of a learned language, Warren wrote in his diary: '*rex noster insanit*', adding, 'there is little reason to hope that his intellects would be restored'. Other medical attendants reluctantly concurred. And though official bulletins continued bravely to talk of 'fever', the nation read between the lines and recognized the true meaning behind the euphemisms. The new admission that the King was suffering from what Baker called 'alienation of mind' and 'deluded imagination' (or, not to mince words, that he was now 'mad') transformed the situation.

Nationally, it opened a Pandora's box of troubles. Kings could rule if sick in body; but what if they were out of their mind? The Whig Opposition – headed by Sheridan and Burke in the absence of Charles James Fox, holidaying on the Italian Riviera with his mistress – were soon pressing for a regency which would confer full regal powers on the Prince of Wales. The King's minister, Pitt, by contrast, began to indulge in masterly Fabian prevarication.

Quickly, the King's condition became a political football. The daily health bulletins were read as gnomic oracles. Was the King sleeping? Was he agitated? Was he mad? Whig rumour-mongers such as the Duchess of Devonshire spent the winter spreading stories that the royal insanity was total and appalling – the King, rumour had it, had reduced himself to the childish condition of wrestling with his pages and snatching off their wigs. Moreover,

Whigs argued that the lunacy was settled and incurable. Inevitably, these party-political battles involved the King's physicians in mimic bouts of medical politics. The most blatant irritant here was Dr Richard Warren, a man who publicly insisted on being looked upon as first physician to the King, but whose Whig sympathies and familiarity with the Prince of Wales were notorious. Warren's political loyalties put him in the bizarre position for a doctor of being adamant that, despite the best treatment he could offer, the King was not mending and indeed could not recover. George was certainly sane enough to recognize that his physician was a rat: 'Richard Rascal' he would call him.

The royal delirium created anarchy at the bedside. Normally, when kings were sick with physical maladies, Court etiquette prevailed. Physicians did not speak unless spoken to; they received, rather than gave, orders. Such bedside protocol was indeed observed in the early days of George's illness. When on one occasion George refused Warren admittance, the physician had to form a diagnosis by listening to the royal ravings through the keyhole. George himself attempted to stay in command. As the loyal equerry Robert Fulke Greville reported, 'The King certainly did not feel Himself got the better of in the late struggle, and therefore He still aimed at Authority, which He seemed conscious He had not lost, tho' it had been impeded.' But the idea of a mad king, sometimes so violent as to need manhandling, ordering the conduct of his own cure was obviously too paradoxical to last. But who was to take charge? The Queen, though well-meaning, was herself often 'hysterical'. The Prince of Wales was too obviously an interested party, running for a regency, to command respect. Pitt could hardly manage George's bedside from Westminster. Would the physicians assert clinical control?

The senior doctor was Sir George Baker. A mild man, he suffered a case of total funk when faced with the traumatic prospect of having to take charge of the King. Let us not minimize how daunting the prospect must have been. To command a monarch was hardly conduct proper for a gentleman. In any case, the physicians must have feared for their futures, if they had to use violent remedies and then were the King – thanks to their own efforts! – to recover.

All the same the doctor failed to cope with the dilemma (he grew 'half-crazed' himself, reported the Whig gossip Jack Payne). When the two Georges confronted each other, it was not Baker but the King whose will triumphed. On one occasion the royal George pinioned Baker against a wall and let it be known he was no better than an old woman, taunting him with being too 'nervous' even to speak to him. In the equerry Greville's judgement, Baker's constant state of being 'undecided' merely left the royal bedchamber in chaos. Increasingly, as Greville saw it, the King became a lord of misrule;

he *would not* do this and *would not* do that. Once he refused a warm bath and created such a scene that eventually he had to be forced into a strait-waistcoat.

People saw that this bedside confusion was exacerbating the King's confusion. He took to playing one doctor off against another. Yet it must all have been very confusing for His Majesty. Philip Withers claimed that while in the King's presence he and other attendants were under orders to preserve strict silence, for the sake of the King's health. On one occasion, the King inquired of Withers if he had been out hunting. Following instructions, Withers merely bowed. George repeated the question, Withers repeated his bow. Not surprisingly, the King grabbed him by the scruff of the neck and 'attacked with such vigour and alacrity' that Withers had at last to break silence and call for help. Clearly, the bemused King thought everyone else had gone crazy. As the trusted Greville summed up the situation,

> The general conduct of the physicians has not been so decided or firm
> as the occasion of their attendance has required. They appear to shrink
> from responsibility and to this time they have not established their
> authority, though pressed by every attendant.... The task becomes more
> difficult from the intricacies of various controls and various interferences.
> We ought not to be embarrassed by fluctuating decisions nor puzzled with
> a multitude of directions from other Quarters.

At this low point, at the beginning of December 1788, Lady Harcourt suggested calling in the Rev. Dr Francis Willis, the celebrated (or notorious) mad-doctor who owned a private madhouse at Greatford in Lincolnshire; Willis had treated her mother there. It was a crucial juncture. For to summon a specialist mad-doctor (one widely regarded as little better than a mountebank) would be both an unmistakable admission that the King was indeed insane and also a vote of 'no confidence' in the King's regular physicians. The Queen agreed with great reluctance. Willis arrived on 5 December accompanied by his son John and a posse of his 'men', i.e. trained heavyweight attendants. Once the King recognized the enormity of what had happened, he confessed that he would never dare show his face in England again, and would have to retire to Hanover.

Willis – a beneficed clergyman, an Oxford MD and, not least, at seventy-three, a generation senior to the King – did what no one before had dared to do. He took charge. By virtue of his unshakeable confidence in his powers to cure the King, he won the grudging support of the Queen and the loyal courtiers (Fanny Burney became a particular admirer of both Willises). He encountered icy and unremitting hostility from Warren and to a lesser extent from the other court physicians. Warren still looked upon himself as first physician, and regarded Willis – who was not even a member of the Royal College of Physicians – as no more than the King's keeper. Warren liked to say that he spoke to Francis Willis 'with authority', and he hardly even deigned to speak at all to Willis's son, John.

Greville made note of 'jealousies among the medical corps' – in other words, the physicians fought. Even the wording of the daily medical bulletin became the subject of heated exchanges: had the King passed a 'very good night', as Willis often claimed, or merely a 'good night', Warren's habitual emendation? Parliament grew greatly exasperated with these medical games. But Willis proved more than a match for the regular physicians. Warren in fact made one particularly fatal *faux pas*. On one occasion, he entered the King's chamber. George begged him to remove the strait-waistcoat which Willis had applied. Warren did so, whereupon George at once tore off all his plasters, scratched his medicinal blisters and worked himself up into a fury. The strait-jacket had to be reapplied. Warren did not interfere again. Soon after, Willis pinned up a notice that the King was to be approached only with the Willises' own permission. In fact, it was not too difficult for the Willises to achieve ascendency in the sickroom. For they or their men were in constant attendance, whereas Warren, Sir Lucas Pepys and the other physicians rode down to Windsor or, at a later stage, Kew, just for a few hours daily, while keeping up their London practices.

In turn, that gave Willis authority in the wider politics of the regency crisis. Willis was a crusty Tory and a supporter of Pitt. His unwavering confidence in the King's speedy restoration heartened Pitt in maintaining his delaying tactics. Pitt now had medical authority with which to trump the Whigs when they recited Warren's pessimistic prognoses. The Whig zeal to prove the King irremediably mad rebounded against themselves.

Above all, Willis showed himself every inch a psychiatrist and fearless towards the King. He possessed no fancy advanced psychiatric theory. His key idea was simplicity itself. Madness was overexcitation. The paramount priority was calm. Madness was anarchy. The desideratum was to combat confusion with control. Here medical authority must exceptionally supersede the authority possessed by rank and majesty. Willis explained:

As death makes no distinction in his visits between the poor man's hut and the prince's palace, so insanity is equally impartial in her dealings with her subjects. For that reason, I made no distinction in my treatment of persons submitted to my charge. When therefore my gracious sovereign became violent, I felt it my duty to subject him to the same system of restraint as I should have adopted with one of his own gardeners at Kew. In plain words, I put a strait waistcoat on him.

(In this view of madness as the great leveller, Willis broke with the common psychiatric practice of bowing to rank, though ostensibly for therapeutic purposes. Thus his contemporary Dr John Monro explained to Parliament that his charges at Bethlem were manacled, but the paying patients at his private asylum were not; the latter were gentlemen, and would 'resent' being clapped in irons. This 'resentment' would hinder recovery.)

The King had to become Willis's subject and accept his word as absolute. This, in turn, was backed by the sanction of the strait-waistcoat. Sometimes the mere threat was enough: when George rattled on, Willis would warn the obstreperous King that he was talking himself into restraint, or would command that he 'must control himself otherwise he would put him in a strait Waistcoat'. Often it had to be applied in reality. Restraining chairs were also used. George complained that the Willises beat him, but it is unclear whether they actually used more than the necessary quantity of force required to overpower a bull-like fifty-year-old man when he grew frantic.

But threats and force were not Willis's royal road to recovery. He had twenty-eight years' experience of handling the deranged, and understood how much could be achieved by character, sensitivity to mood, and a commanding tone of voice – in fact, by majesty. Greville – no great friend to the Willises, for they were largely responsible for turfing him out of the King's chamber and installing their own men – saw how effective this could be. On one occasion, the King became agitated while abusing Warren and the other doctors:

> Dr Willis remained firm, and reproved him in determined language, telling him he must control himself or otherwise he would put him in a strait-waistcoat. On this hint Dr Willis went out and returned with one in his hand.... The King eyed it attentively and, alarmed at the doctor's firmness, began to submit.... On Dr Willis wishing him good night and recommending composure and moderation, he retired.

It was all a bit like lion-taming. Yet Greville was impressed.

> [I] was much struck with the proper manner and the imposing style of the authoritative language which Dr Willis held on this occasion. It was necessary to have this struggle. He seized the opportunity with judgement and conducted himself with wonderful management and force. As the King's voice rose attempting mastery, Willis raised his and its tone was strong and decided. As the King softened his, that of Dr Willis dropped too.... The King found stronger powers in Dr Willis ... gave way and returned to somewhat of composure.... This seems to have been the first solid step leading to permanent recovery.

Willis did not rely merely upon a certain adversarial boldness. He gradually succeeded in building a relationship with the King (he would for example play backgammon with him to aid his powers of attention). Sometimes he would grant the King his wishes, permitting him to see the Queen on occasion (they would play cards and sing catches) and encouraging walks. And he aimed to build up trust. He would allow the King to read (perhaps it was through Willis that George got hold of *King Lear*, though he hardly needed the play to make the identification, since the by now blind former Prime Minister, Lord North, paid him a visit and the pair would have been for all the world like Lear and Gloucester on Dover Beach). Above all, Willis permitted the King to shave himself and gave him a penknife to pare his nails; the Whigs professed the risks involved in this quite scandalous. But all such privileges were to be permitted only within a framework of absolute power.

Within two months of the arrival of the Willises, George was on the road to recovery. From time to time he relapsed, the Willises laying the blame on the irritating therapeutic blisters applied by earlier physicians. By the middle of February 1789, he was, to all intents and purposes, back to normal, in the nick of time to forestall the passing of the Regency Bill. The Willises claimed full credit, and were handsomely rewarded by Pitt (Francis received a pension of £1,000 per year, John half that amount).

But did they really cause, or even speed, his recovery? It is impossible to say. Clearly, if Macalpine and Hunter are right to argue that George's ailment was porphyria, then nothing the Willises did could possibly have helped; his recovery was spontaneous. But in terms of the management of the symptoms, their arrival was surely effective, by restoring a settled atmosphere to the sickroom. And eye-witnesses noted how effective they were in pacifying the King's moods. Greville perceived this very clearly.

> Whenever Doctor Willis was out of the room, he rambled wildly on various subjects, but when the doctor returned he turned the subject, played his cards better and talked more cautiously.

Even Warren had to admit this (though using the point to confirm the King's continuing underlying insanity):

> When Dr Willis or his son are present, His Majesty is under great awe; when they are absent, he talks and acts quite differently.

But what did the King make of being turned into a subject of psychiatry?

The pity is we little know. His Majesty of course kept no journal, nor did he later write memoirs. For what passed through his mind during his crisis, we are dependent on the scrappy snatches recorded by his doctors and attendants. These are highly biased politically, Warren routinely stressing alienation of mind long after the Willises were recording marked improvements in his capacity for attention. But they are also heavily censored. Thus fragments of the record indicate that George frequently fantasized about Lady Pembroke, the former Elizabeth Spencer, one of his early sweethearts. He serenaded his 'Eliza', addressed 'Queen Esther' and 'Queen Elizabeth', and in an utterly Shakespearian moment declared he would have the dissolution of all marriages. In one stormy exchange with Queen Charlotte, conducted in German which (diplomatically?) no one present properly understood, His Majesty apparently told his wife that Eliza was his true love. On another occasion, however, George was contrite and ashamed of revealing his 'wrong ideas', and expressed the hope that nobody had heard them. But what precisely George fantasized about and let slip we know not. The discreet Greville merely repeatedly recorded that the King spoke 'indecently' or used 'improper conversation', and even then felt the need to justify his boldness by stating that all information about the King's health might be valuable. Francis Willis of course engaged in no proto-Freudian analysis of the King's erotic desires, but rather 'gave him a severe lecture on his improper conversation'.

In his final bout of madness, George (by now Shelley's 'sad, mad and blind' whitebeard patriarch) increasingly held conversations with the dead, and believed the nation was about to be inundated in a great flood. Dr William Heberden the Younger recorded, 'he appears to be living . . . in another world, and has lost almost all interest in the concerns of this'.

In each of his bouts, the King never denied that he was disordered. When he sketched new designs for Kew House, he quipped, 'not bad for a man who is mad'. But all the time he seems to have retained a perception that what lay at the crux of his condition was a struggle for authority. When, playing cards, that game so symbolic of royal power, he scribbled on a knave 'Sir Richard Warren Bart First Physician to the King', it was his way of making clear who was still the King of the pack: indeed, he begged Willis to carry Warren off to Greatford. When a regency seemed inevitable, George himself drew up his own choice of regency cabinet, with the Archbishop of Canterbury at its head and the Prince of Wales relegated. He knew that political chaos was anathema. 'The English Constitution is the best in the world,' he remarked in his ramblings, 'if it has a fault, it is that of not being fit for a king.' And he was well aware of a delicate balance of power between himself and his physicians.

Probably, right from the first, he detested the Willises, for they made no bones about treating him as a madman. He expressed his loathing of them in no uncertain terms when they were called in during his next bout of insanity in 1801. Then Dr John Willis, assisted now by his younger brother,

Robert Darling, and their clergyman brother, Thomas, exercised their power with even less restraint than before. They could do this partly because they knew they had the weak Prime Minister, Addington, in their pocket. John Willis records Addington giving them permission to 'take him again into our power' if the need arose.

Sometimes during this bout they secluded him completely from the outside world, and refused admission to the Queen. They furthermore insisted on scrutinizing state documents placed before the King to save him from anxiety. And on one occasion, during his convalescence and after he was formally freed from their control, they actually hijacked him physically in an extra-ordinary cloak-and-dagger operation as he was driving to Kew, and he literally became their prisoner for nearly a month. Yet the King acquiesced in their regimen because he needed to recover, and he was well aware that the Willises had no less a stake in his recovery, whereas Warren's interest lay in a perma-nent insanity and a regency. Thus, mad patient and mad-doctor needed to pull together. Sometimes therefore George was glad to co-operate with the Willises, as when he blithely and rather joyously dismissed his other, non-plussed physicians on 7 February 1789 ('Poor man, how mad he is!' whispered Warren, audibly, as he shuffled out). But at other times, he was able to outwit the Willises, as when in 1801 he effectively went on strike and refused to sign state papers or documents until the Willises backed down over his demand to visit the Queen. Throughout the King's reign, mad or sane, politi-cal manoeuvring went on as usual.

Perhaps they ordered these things better in Denmark. The Scandinavian monarchy was ruled between 1766 and 1808 by George III's brother-in-law, Christian VII (Christian had married George's sister, Caroline Mathilde). For practically the whole of this span, Christian was agreed to be more or less out of his mind. Effective power lay in the hands of a council led by the King's brother; but, in the absence of a formal regency, Christian continued to go through the motions of majesty, an authentic mad king. Thomas Malthus on his travels records the mindless monarch holding reviews of his troops during the Napoleonic wars.

All contemporary Danish sources were extremely circumspect about dis-cussing the royal 'condition', and it is thus hard to ascertain its exact form and the timing of its onset. Christian – by all accounts a sharp and sophisticated young man – seems to have celebrated his accession in 1766 by imitating the rake's progress. There are hints of drunken binges, of frolics semi-incog-nito on the town, and of sexual indulgences. As the historian Reddaway put it, Caroline Mathilde 'failed to captivate' her husband (allegedly, on his wedding night, Christian bewailed the fact that *he* had to bed her when there were so many other men around who could perform the job). Christian took to mistresses, especially the strapping aristocratic 'Booty Catherine', and there was talk of whippings and other deviant practices. But none of this would have seemed so irregular in an *ancien régime* court, and certainly would not have been deemed a mark of madness. Yet as early as 1768 a certain volatility in his emotional make-up was being noted, and in a wonderful parody of *Hamlet* he was sent on a royal visit to England for the sake of his health. Conversations with his brother-in-law and sightseeing apparently did the trick, for he was said to have returned to Denmark a more sober man.

It is then hard to explain the sudden events of the next two years. For the staid and slow-moving autocracy underwent a dramatic palace revolution. Within months a helter-skelter programme of reform was initiated, modernizing the bureaucracy, abolishing privileges, attacking inefficiency – all clothed in the trappings of Enlightenment ideology. It may have been the King's work – and certainly it was later seen as a symptom that he had lost his head. Quite likely it was the doing of the charismatic royal physician, the German Struensee, who had won the ear of Christian, and more than the ears of Caroline.

Whoever was responsible for these whirlwind months of reform – Struensee was later to insist that they were all the King's work – the traditional political establishment was affronted. They took their revenge. In January 1772 they carried out a *putsch*. The Queen was held, Struensee clapped in jail and put on trial. The official charges spoke of improperly arrogating powers to himself, but it was universally known that Struensee had been carrying on an adulterous liaison with the Queen (even Christian had been jesting that his second child had been fathered by the Holy Ghost), and that was quite enough to seal his fate. Struensee met his end on the scaffold, hung, drawn and quartered. Caroline was kept under tight security, and Christian was allowed his puppet existence, dreaming his life away lost in another world:

> When he is dressing he may sit whole hours and more quite quiet, with
> eyes fixed, mouth open, head sunk, like a person who has no feeling.
> I know him [wrote Prince Charles of Hesse] and I have not forgotten that
> attitude, which always foreboded some violent scene and some revolution
> which is then brewing, and it is at these times that his mind, by nature
> very active and lively, but much depressed by a thousand causes, of which
> the chief is physical, works with most force, makes new plans, takes
> violent resolutions, which however possess no stability, nor danger even
> for those against whom they are formed.

What precisely was wrong with Christian is unclear. Around the turn of this century, the Danish psychiatrist Christiansen tried to prove he was suffering from *dementia praecox*, suggesting that masturbation was the exciting cause. We have, however, little to go on, beyond some evidence of his occasional violence (he would smash dinner tables and windows), of a delight in multilingual wordplay ('Ich bin confus'), and of the deluded belief that he was a foundling, an orphan, and that his navel was disappearing. What is significant is that the kingdom should have endured for a generation under a lord of misrule.

Quite early in his delirium, when he started speaking in the third person, King George III quipped that he was doing it to curb his loquacity, fearing 'I am getting into Mr Burke's eloquence, saying too much on little things.' George thus became his own Court jester. His Majesty did not need the special insight of madness to perceive that his old foe himself betrayed many of the symptoms of insanity. Indeed, after one parliamentary debate on the King's health, Burke found a bulletin left on his own Commons bench: 'Very irritable in the evening, no sleep all night and very unquiet this morning'.

The emotional and obsessional Burke was widely believed to be heading for madness. Boswell recorded him 'foaming like Niagra'. Gibbon called him 'the most eloquent madman that I ever knew', and the diarist Wraxall portrayed him quite out of control:

> His very features, and the undulating motions of his head . . . on some occasions seemed to approach towards alienation of mind. Even his friends could not always induce him to listen to reason and remonstrance, though they sometimes held him down in his seat, by the skirts of his coat, in order to prevent the ebullitions of his anger or indignation.

Burke personally admitted to deep 'melancholy', and so intense did his brooding terror of a universal Jacobin revolution become that he wanted to be buried in an unmarked grave, lest the sacrilegious French should invade and desecrate his bones.

It was Burke of course who fixed the notion in the minds of right-thinking English people that the French Revolution was one public act of madness. The so-called rationality of the age of reason was in reality delusion. The blind faith that the legislative *fiat* of *liberté*, *egalité et fraternité* would at a snap of the fingers redeem the world was the kind of hideous delusion entertained by Swiftian anti-heroes. And sanguinary revolution itself was sheer Terror, a crazy paroxysm.

Many, however, subscribed to a very different interpretation of the psycho-politics of the French Revolution. The Fall of the Bastille seemed to symbolize the release of the human mind from its traditional manacles, both physical fetters of iron and those which were 'mind-forg'd', the bugaboos of superstition, ignorance and error. In revolutionary Paris, Dr Philippe Pinel struck off the chains from the lunatics at the Salpetrière in a gesture of psychiatric liberation, a new dawn in the treatment of the mad. And almost simultaneously the Quaker Tukes essentially banished physical constraint in favour of moral therapy at their new asylum, the York Retreat. Everywhere shifting political power-relations found echo in the new-regime language of psychiatry, and psychiatric relations were discussed in the idiom of politics. In this situation of flux, it appeared that power – the power of mastery and that of madness – resided in the mind: a perception marked in France by the coining of the term 'ideology' and in Britain by the cant phrase, the 'march of mind'. For many contemporaries, this new empire of the intellectual over the physical – what psychiatrists called 'moral therapy' – seemed the hallmark of progress. As the French philosopher Michel Foucault has stressed, however, it had – and, indeed, was seen to have – its more sinister dimension, a potential for subtler and more masked mastery, for brainwashing, and later for the political abuse of psychiatry. The career of James Tilley Matthews exemplifies this well.

Matthews was a London tea-merchant, who, like Wordsworth, flushed by the new dawn of the revolutionary era, was lured to Paris in 1793 where he picked up a knowledge of Mesmerism. Deploring the outbeak of hostilities between England and France, he got it into his head to mount a peace mission, captivated by the Mesmeric doctrine of harmony. Following an audience with Lord Liverpool, Matthews prepared to start negotiating with the French authorities. The Jacobin seizure of power, however, wrecked his plans. The Jacobins clearly distrusted him, for he had Dantonesque sympathies, and, in any case, they were hostile to Mesmerism, seeing it as fashionable aristocratic decadence – indeed they were to confiscate Mesmer's own assets.

Matthews found himself coming under suspicion. As he put it in a later letter to Liverpool, 'I became equally the subject of intrigue . . . letters were fabricated . . . discovering plots centred in me.' Luckily for him, 'I am not afraid soon by a whole Jacobin army !' Nevertheless, the Jacobins had him clapped in jail in 1793. He was eventually released, and he made his way back to England in March 1796, convinced that it had fallen to him to be Britain's saviour. He alone was privy to a dastardly French plot for:

> surrendering to the French every secret of the British government, as for the republicanizing Great Britain and Ireland, and particularly for disorganizing the British Navy, to create such a confusion therein, as to admit the French armaments to move without danger.

The secret weapon the French were mobilizing to gain this dreadful end was Mesmerism. The notion that Mesmerism had a great potential for mischief was one widely pointed out from the beginning. Franz Anton Mesmer himself, the Viennese doctor who had first developed the 'hypnotic' technique, had been driven out of Vienna and Paris because of fears that his hypnotic powers gave him absolute command over his patients, young women in particular, who fell 'under the influence'.

Even before the French Revolution, Mesmerism's dangers were highlighted in England. Hannah More warned Horace Walpole in 1788 against this new 'demoniacal mummery' which had taken such a hold in France and was beginning to put down roots in England. The subversive political implications were spelt out by another English anti-Mesmerist writer, John Pearson. Perhaps ministers of the Crown, in pursuit of absolute power, might themselves abuse Mesmeric 'influence':

> If the minister fears opposition in some favourite motion from a turbulent orator, he may by the eloquence of his fingers, consign the troublesome member to sleep; or if the gentleman be already on his legs, thundering out invectives against mal-administration, he may find this Demosthenes other employment, by throwing him into a crisis.

The threat was real, according to Pearson: 'You may say that this Power may prove a dangerous engine in the hands of a corrupt administration.' Luckily remedy was to hand, in the guise of counter-measures:

> But remember, Sir, the Patriots may avail themselves of the same weapon, so that on a day of public business, St Stephens would exhibit a motley scene of members sound asleep or rolling in convulsions. This would form a new era in the history of ministerial influence.

Suddenly we are back in the world of the Whig, Burke, with his hypnotic oratory, and the Tory, Francis Willis, with his capacity to fix a madman with his eye. Indeed, they had confronted each other in a House of Commons committee, when Burke was sceptical about the old quack's ability. What, thundered Burke, made Willis so sure he could control the King?

> 'Place the candles between us, Mr Burke,' replied the Doctor, in an equally authoritative tone – 'and I'll give you an answer. There, Sir! By the EYE! I should have looked at him *thus*, Sir – *thus*!'
>   Burke instantaneously averted his head, and, making no reply, evidently acknowledged this basiliskan authority.

The authority of the eye, of the voice, or indeed of Mesmeric rays – all formed part of that new apparatus of 'mind control' flourishing around the time of the Revolution. It was specifically the Mesmeric rays which perturbed James Tilley Matthews.

55

Teams of what he termed 'magnetic spies' had been infiltrated into England. They were stationing themselves in strategic positions 'near the Houses of Parliament, Admiralty, Treasury, etc.', armed with machines (called 'air-looms') for transmitting waves of animal magnetism. Thereby they would Mesmerize members of the administration, rendering them 'possessed', as under a 'spell, like puppets', able to plant thoughts and read minds. Above all, the Prime Minister himself was especially subject to their influence, for (Matthews had heard it from the conspirators' own mouths):

> Mr Pitt was not half able to withstand magnetic fluid in its operative effect, but became actuated like a mere puppet by the expert-magnetists employed in such villainies.

Because of his earlier associations with Mesmerism, Matthews was privy to all this, and so he became number one on the conspirators' hit-list. A 'gang of seven', led by one known intriguingly as 'Bill, or the King', had been sent to wipe him out, enabled by their hypnotic 'science of assailment' to deploy torture-at-a-distance which included such atrocities as 'foot-curving, lethargy-making, spark-exploding, knee-nailing, burning out, eye-screwing, sight-stopping, roof-stringing, vital-tearing, fibre-ripping, etc.'. Worst of all were their 'dream-workings', mind control during sleep. These threats to his life explained the urgency with which, on his return, Matthews sent warning letters to the administration and the Speaker of the House of Commons. In particular, he wrote to Lord Liverpool reminding him of their previous meeting, divulging the plots and hinting that he could do with a financial reward. Liverpool must have been silent or sceptical, for Matthews tried a follow-up letter to him on 6 December 1796, which opened:

> I pronounce your Lordship to be in every sense of the word a most diabolical Traitor. – After a long life of Political and real iniquity, during which your Lordship by flattering and deceiving, and more than anyone else contributing to deceive your King, who believing your hypochritical [sic] Professions, has to the detriment of many of the Countries Friends loaded you with Honours, and Emoluments, you have made yourself a principal in schemes of Treason founded upon the most extensive intrigue.

Matthews revealed that he had rumbled that Liverpool was actually in league with revolutionary France and the Mesmeric conspirators, and informed him that he knew 'you did actually effect the Murder of the Unfortunate Monarch', Louis XVI. Indeed, it had become clear to Matthews that the British and French governments were in league to keep up the war and cause 'both nations to be assassinated' in order to 'deprive me of existence' and 'sacrifice me to popular fury'.

Having discovered the treachery of the closet regicide Liverpool, Matthews proceeded to the House of Commons, where he accused the ministry of 'perfidious venality'. Hauled before the Privy Council and examined, he was committed to Bethlem in January 1797, his family's protests of his sanity being overridden by Lord Chancellor Kenyon. Yet what did his committal do (Matthews later argued) but corroborate his own accusation, that the government was indeed the puppet of a gang of Mesmeric assassins sent to silence him? Still further proof was the fact that, soon after his detention, it proved possible for the gangs – now untroubled by his counter-efforts at jamming them – to Mesmerize the British navy and spark off the Nore mutiny.

Confined in Bethlem – where by a splendid irony another patient, Urbane Metcalf, believed he was heir to the throne of Denmark – Matthews felt utterly at the mercy of his persecutors, for the French Mesmerists were now somehow aided and abetted by the mad-doctors of the institution itself. Assailed by an unholy league of the French, the British government and of Bethlem itself, Matthews began to turn to the universe for redress. Napoleon-like he penned a document beginning 'James, Absolute, Sole, Supreme, Sacred, Omni-Imperious, Arch-Grand, Arch-Sovereign . . . Arch-Emperor', and offering rewards beyond the dreams of avarice to those who would assassinate his foes. But he remained in Bethlem.

In 1809 his family pressed for his release, and two distinguished physicians, Drs Birkbeck and Clutterbuck, testified that he was sane. They were opposed by the medical staff at Bethlem, who argued that he was as obsessed as ever, 'sometimes an automaton moved by the agency of persons . . . at others, the Emperor of the whole world, issuing proclamations to his disobedient subjects, and hurling from their thrones the usurpers of his dominions'. To corroborate his craziness, the testimony of further physicians was adduced, including (the irony is masterly) both Robert Darling Willis and Sir Lucas Pepys – old adversaries in the treatment of King George himself. The best way to prove Matthews' continuing delusions, believed John Haslam, the Bethlem apothecary, was to let Matthews speak for himself: and he simply published Matthews' own story, taken from documents penned by Matthews himself, in a mischievous but delightful volume entitled *Illustrations of Madness: Exhibiting a Singular Case of Insanity, And a No Less Remarkable Difference in Medical Opinions: Developing the Nature of An Assailment, And the Manner of Working Events; with A Description of the Tortures Experienced by Bomb-Bursting, Lobster-Cracking, and Lengthening the Brain. Embellished with a Curious Plate* (1810). Here, as Haslam's title hinted, was yet another case in which the mad-doctors had no rational common ground between them, a case of medical madness. Haslam added with a sneer, 'madness being the opposite to reason and good sense, as light is to darkness, straight to crooked etc., it appears wonderful that two opposite opinions could be entertained on the subject': were Clutterbuck and Birkbeck in their right minds?

It is not clear whether Birkbeck and Clutterbuck had been initially unaware of Matthews' theories of French conspiracy, or knew about them, and thought they were utterly rational, as perhaps Burke might have done. Certainly, many men around the turn of the century, notably the Abbé Barruel and John Robison, advanced full-blown conspiracy theories on the nature of the Revolution. Far from being committed to the madhouse, they were widely fêted as public heroes. Indeed, just like Matthews, Barruel thought that Mesmerism was implicated in revolutionary plots.

Matthews spent several more years in Bethlem. He whiled away his time drawing up architectural plans for the new Bethlem building; some of his designs were incorporated in the new building which survives in Lambeth appropriately as the Imperial War Museum. On his eventual release, he was transferred to Mr Fox's madhouse in Hackney, where he found employment as 'advising manager' on the conduct of the lunatics, a splendid instance of poacher turned gamekeeper, or, maybe, 'automaton' turned 'emperor'.

Haslam too was 'released' from Bethlem. When Parliament inquired into the state of madhouses in 1815, Bethlem was discovered to be riddled with corruption (Haslam himself testified that the recently deceased surgeon to Bethlem, Bryan Crowther, had for some years himself been so insane as to require constraint by a straitjacket). Haslam was made into a scapegoat and was dismissed in 1816. Perhaps this experience soured his mind. Certainly, later in life, he seems to have come to see the whole of society as crazy. Testifying in court on one occasion in an insanity plea, he contended that not only was the accused mad, but so too was everyone else in court – indeed in the nation – and that perhaps the only exception to this universal insanity was Almighty God Himself (he had been reassured of God's soundness of mind, he respectfully added, on the authority of eminent Church of England divines).

Matthews' fear of the political use and abuse of Mesmerism was no singular paranoid delusion but a common perception of threats of danger from without. We might choose to interpret Matthews' sense of persecution by external mind control as indicative either of his political awareness or of his delusional state. It certainly registered his authentic experience of being under the arbitrary control of the staff at Bethlem, the English Bastille. He was surely not deluded to believe these were times of torture and conspiracy. The irony of his particular case is that his voicings of these fears led to his being locked up as a lunatic for his pains – a neat demonstration that in the political use or abuse of psychiatry it was not only the radical left who found their liberty in jeopardy.

Yet it remains a nice irony that Mesmerism proved a medium through which people believed themselves to be persecuted, bedevilled no longer by demons or by Satan, but by that very instrument which has often been hailed as the forerunner of the psychoanalysis of Freud (Freud, in his early career, it will be recalled, tried to make extensive therapeutic use of hypnotism, but proved inept). Of course, Matthews' mind-raping 'gang of seven' (pumping him full of Mesmerism) was all 'imagination', just 'in the mind'. A world of kings and subjects produced a mimic lunatic world of the omnipotent and the impotent, emperors and automata (one remembers that *robot* is Czech for 'drudge'). The world of revolution erupting at the close of the eighteenth century was one in which kings lost their heads, literally or metaphorically, and new-dawn *citoyens* such as James Tilley Matthews swung violently from liberty to reaction, unsure whether there was reason in the revolution. No wonder the Parisians flocked to watch De Sade's dramatics at Charenton.

4 · Madness and Genius

Virginia Woolf was extremely wary of Freud. Having been personally subject to childhood sexual abuse, she can hardly have applauded Freud's interpretations of such memories as essentially 'hysterical', the marks of infantile wish fantasies.

But she certainly suspected his hunger for anatomizing creativity. Sometimes Freud could be disarming ('Before the problem of the creative artist analysis must, alas, lay down its arms'). But no one could take that disclaimer seriously in the light of his staggeringly reductive explanations of artistic meanings in his analyses of Leonardo, Hamlet, etc. Woolf was very dismissive of the supposed hidden meanings psychoanalysis found in literature: 'these Germans think it proves something – besides their own gull-like imbecility'.

Moreover, she also distrusted the doctrine that creative people were neurotic. Possibly she did not want to be reminded of her own history of mental instability or want her 'art' to be thus medicalized. Certainly she feared that psychiatric treatment would rob her creative well-springs of their powers. She had already heard too many meddling doctors telling her '"you shan't read this" and "you shan't write a word"'. What she never denied was that there was a frenzy, which could be called madness, that fired the imagination. She wrote to Ethel Smyth in 1930 of her own bouts of insanity ('my brain went up in a shower of fireworks'):

> As an experience, madness is terrific I can assure you, and not to be sniffed at; and in its lava I still find most of the things I write about. It shoots out of one everything shaped, final not in mere driblets, as sanity does.

Woolf was in this respect a latter-day and metaphorical Platonist. Plato had argued, in the *Symposium*, in *Phaedrus* and elsewhere, for the existence of a mystical heaven-sent spirit or *furor*, through which a select few could be 'inspired': 'The greatest blessings come by way of madness, indeed of madness that is heaven sent.' Possessed thus of transcendental visions or knowledge, such people enjoyed a 'divine madness' which elevated them above the worldlings.

Freud's construal of genius was rather different. It was not a gift of the gods but an outworking of the processes of the unconscious; it came not down from above but from within, up from the depths. When the psychic traumas of infancy and childhood were not successfully negotiated, Freud argued, the consequence was adult neurosis. Repression typically bred neurosis which simply tended towards incapacitation. In some cases, however, the repressed found sublimated expression of a highly creative kind. Thus art and neurosis were cousins if not twins. In so far as he saw artistic and literary talents emerging from particular temperaments, Freud was more an Aristotelian than a Platonist. For Aristotle, and the whole tradition of classical medical thinking about man associated with his name and with Hippocrates', had argued that 'melancholy' was both a disposition and, almost, a disease. Melancholy people were anxious, jealous, depressed, solitary. They were difficult or even dangerous. In a few, that moody, broody, pensive streak proved highly creative in images and ideas; it was the humour of genius.

These conceits about the uniqueness and vocation (gifts) of the artist were widely put around. Particularly when strengthened by the kind of Neo-Platonism advanced by Renaissance philosophers such as Ficino, with their idea of cosmic mind, they offered an ideology which ennobled the poet to prophetic wisdom. But they commonly also had a sting in the tail. When Montaigne went to visit the great Italian poet Tasso, who had gone mad and had been confined, it was not the elevating alliance between great wits and madness that struck him but their antithesis. Tasso had become mindless.

Montaigne's own sceptical strategy was the reverse, to depict the literary man as a rather ordinary – if at the same time, individual – fellow. And Shakespeare was clearly dabbling in ironies when he had Theseus declaim, in *A Midsummer Night's Dream*, that

> The lunatick, the lover and the poet
> Are of imagination all compact.

The relations between art and madness were thus complicated. Scores of authors in the Renaissance and Enlightenment made use of mad or foolish characters in their plays and novels as masks or mouthpieces for themselves – Cervantes' Don Quixote, possibly Laurence Sterne's Tristram Shandy, possibly Diderot's Rameau's nephew are all, to some degree at least, their author's double, albeit distanced. Yet it is not easy to find many who clothe their own selves in the mantle of madness. 'Art' and artistry more than inspiration were seen as the hallmark of the writer or artist, and the patronage structures of the traditional world of letters offered strong arguments in favour of social conformity rather than eccentricity in the artist.

This is not to say that 'imagination' and visionary 'genius' were at a discount in critical quarters. But classical theory, as modified by Enlightenment empiricist psychology, insisted that imagination should not be wayward, idiosyncratic and visionary but should abide by the solid information of the senses and be tempered by judgement. True genius was a healthy organic impulse for combining the raw materials of the mind. The pathology of imagination or genius gone wrong – of Parnassus perverted by Bedlam – was explored in the merciless satires of Swift, Pope and the other Augustans through their device of the mad scribbler.

Not surprisingly then, the laurels of the mad poet were sometimes specifically rejected. Not much is known about James Carkesse, beyond the fact that he once worked in the Navy Office under Samuel Pepys in the reign of Charles II, and after a series of rows ended up confined in Bethlem and in a private madhouse at Finsbury kept by Dr Allen, the physician to Bethlem. While confined and thus officially certified as mad he penned a series of poems which he published on his release under the title *Lucida Intervalla*, that is 'lucid intervals', in 1679.

As verse they are unmemorable. As autobiographical *apologiae* they are intriguing because they play a double game. As news from inside, they draw upon the traditional prerogative of the mad person to be a licensed fool, to rail and pronounce the whole world mad (he borrows Burton's *semel insanivimus omnes* as his epigraph). Yet at the same time he wants to vindicate his own reason, and to use his capacity to versify as proof of his sanity. He is utterly sane, he asserts – or at least would be were he not being mistreated by a physician in a madhouse:

> Says He, who more *wit* than the *Doctor* had,
> Oppression will make a wise man Mad ; . . .
> Therefore, *Religio Medici* (do you mind ?)
> This is not Lunacy in any kind :
> But naturally flow hence (as I do think)
> Poetic Rage, sharp Pen, and Gall in Ink.
> A sober Man, pray, what can more oppress,
> Than force by Mad-mens usage to confess
> Himself for Mad ?

The delusion that the world labours under is to mistake pcetic inspiration – which he possesses – for madness, which would possess him :

> Doctor, this pusling *Riddle* pray explain :

> Others, your *Physick* cures, but I complain
> It works with me the clean contrary way,
> And makes me *poet*, who are *Mad* they say.
> The Truth on't is, my *Brains* well fixt *condition*
> *Apollo* better knows, than his *physitian*:
> 'Tis *Quacks* disease, not mine, my poetry
> By the blind *Moon-calf*, took for *Lunacy*.

The real priority, Carkesse insists, is to distinguish poets like himself from madmen, and to put an end to the sinister doctrine of '*nullum magnum ingenium (absit verbo invidia) sine mixtura dementiae*' – there is no great wit without it being mixed with madness:

> It goes for *current truth*, that ever some madness
> Attends much wit, '*tis strange in sober sadness:*
> Hence they are call'd, by *Plot* of *poor* and *rich*,
> *Madmen*, whose *wit's* above the standard pitch
> But sure, when *Friends* and you me *Mad concluded*,
> 'Twas you your *senses* lost, by th'Moon *deluded*.

Carkesse alleged that Dr Allen (whom he dubbed 'Mad-Quack') had informed him that 'till he left off making verses, he was not fit to be discharged'. Yet what did that prove but the doctor's folly? For true poetry was neither the source nor the symptom of madness, but was properly medicinal – why else was Apollo god of both song and healing?

Once the popular association of madness and poetry carried the danger of actually leading to the madhouse, it is not surprising that poets should have been chary about espousing it. Georgian poets such as William Collins and William Cowper had their paroxysms of madness, but there is no hint that they saw insanity as a source of inspiration. The failure of strong poetic feeling may actually have contributed to Collins's decline into morbid melancholy.

Eighteenth-century 'sensibility' and the rediscovery of the Gothic and its bards prized the solitary with his inner feeling (the minor poet Edward Young spoke of 'the stranger within'). In elegaic writers like Thomas Gray, melancholy once more became the midwife to art. But it is with Romanticism, of course, that the indissoluble link between madness and artistic genius comes into its own as an autobiographical experience, even as the armorial bearings of talent. Sometimes what is stressed is that madness (or, more generally, great torment) is the anvil of noble art. Sometimes the message is the Promethean one that madness is the price to be paid for creation.

Art is thus a demon, an exterminating angel; it exacts a terrible toll; it burns you out. To produce great art, the artist is sapped of health, mental or physical. Either way, this Romantic doctrine which saw genius and madness as doubles elevated art into ecstasy and the artist or writer into an aesthetic analogue of the prophet gifted with otherworldly powers.

The Romantic belief in creative madness found ebullient expression in the outlook of William Blake. Blake presented art as 'visionary'. Repudiating the 'single vision' empiricism and materialism of Bacon, Newton, Locke and (in painting) Sir Joshua Reynolds, he insisted that 'mental things alone are real'. Art was not, after all, despite the orthodox doctrine, a matter of imitation. The typical Lockean Enlightenment concept of imagination as the building of images out of sensations was false, as was Dr Johnson's reduction of the 'visionary' to the 'imaginary'. By contrast, Blake regarded imagination as the power which gave form to visions. As such it was the *sine qua non*, the living spirit, of art. Imagination was the prerogative of the mad. 'This world is all one continued vision of fancy or imagination.' Blake rejoiced in his madness. For him it was an enviable state of artistic fecundity and health. In a dream or vision, he imagined William Cowper soliciting his aid:

> Cowper came to me and said: 'O that I were insane always. I will never rest. Can you not make me truly insane? . . . You retain health and yet are as mad as any of us all – over us all – mad as a refuge from unbelief – from Bacon, Newton and Locke.

To some degree, of course, Blake's 'madness' should be seen as metaphorical, a device which allowed him to estrange himself from worldly rationalism and commercial artists. Blake needed his own world: 'I must create a system, or be enslav'd by another man's. I will not reason and compare: my business is to create.' He needed a persona permitting him to perturb people with proverbs of hell. Thus when he writes:

> What, it will be questioned, when the Sun rises do you not see a round Disk of fire somewhat like a guinea? O no I see an Innumerable company of the Heavenly host crying Holy, Holy, Holy, is the Lord God Almighty

he is being provocative, while also making a serious point about the inescapability of the subjective. He liked to accept the world's 'aspersion of madness'; it made him other, beyond the pale, it gave him licence to rail, to denounce the true craziness of the 'mind forg'd manacles' of a life-denying civilization. But it would be wrong to imply that it was just a pose, a self-dramatizing rhetoric. The religious Romantic Blake believed in the literal sense that he often wrote under 'immediate dictation'. He conversed familiarly with the prophets as also with his dead brother; and he and his wife sat around naked in their garden recapitulating paradise. Blake was an odd cove.

He never came under psychiatric care, however, nor was he ever put away in an asylum. There are doubtless many reasons for that; not least, that Blake had enough sympathetic patrons to ensure that his undoubted eccentricities kept him out of real mischief. But he was also fortunate to live just before the mythology of Romanticism, with its celebration of the nuptials of genius with madness, ceased to be a conceit, a *jeu d'esprit*, and became conscripted within the expanding discipline of psychiatry. Aspects of the ideology of Romanticism made their mark upon doctors of the mind as well as upon artists and aesthetes. By that means they became dangerous.

First Pinel in revolutionary France and contemporaneously the Tukes in England with their moral therapy echoed revolutionary liberationist optimism by freeing the mind from the tyranny of iron fetters. But then slightly later, particularly in Germany in the ideas of Reil, psychiatry increasingly represented insanity itself as a dark night of the soul, a perversion of the will, an almost Byronic waywardness. And by the mid-nineteenth century, late Romanticism's own Byronic or Bohemian self-image was being transformed by the psychiatrists into the new diagnostic category of decadent degeneration. As such it was increasingly linked (albeit speculatively) with a presumed organic aetiology: the Romantic flight was brought to earth as a somatic disease, or at least as one of the leading symptoms of degenerative disorders such as consumption, neurasthenia or indeed syphilis. Genius itself came to be seen by doctors not just as a demon, but specifically as pathological, and a swarm of books appeared exposing *The Infirmities of Genius*, or the illnesses of *The Great Abnormals*. The Romantics liked to tell the world that they were mad. Little did they understand how the world would take its revenge.

In the mid-nineteenth century, Dr Franz Richarz, owner of a private asylum at Endenich, just outside Bonn, shared the views of degenerationist psychiatry. He believed that 'almost all great artists' – he included Mozart and Goethe – were beset by 'spontaneous melancholic moods'. Their frenzied bursts of creativity involved 'over-exertion' and 'immoderate mental, especially artistic productivity', and this in turn 'exhausted the substance of psychically active central components of the nervous system', leading to 'slow, but irreversible and progressive deterioration'.

Precisely this had happened, Richarz believed, in the case of Robert Schumann, who had been admitted into his asylum in 1854, remaining there till his death two and a half years later.

Schumann was the quintessential Romantic. He was born into a family disposed to cherish the ideal life of art, ideas and passions above mere worldly advancement. His father was a bookworm and an author, with a very characteristic Germanic love of myth and fantastic folklore. His highly emotional mother was musical. Schumann grew up charged with feelings, sensitive, full of ardour, and with an intense longing to lose – and find – himself in the kingdom of culture. For long, however, he remained unsure whether his prime gift lay with words, like his father, or with music, like his mother; his highest aspirations were to unite both in lieder, in oratorio, in opera.

From 1828 he spent his student days at Leipzig in an atmosphere aquiver with Romanticism. Nominally he was studying law; in reality he gave his time to the piano. Disciplined and dissipated by turns, Schumann explored, refined and abused his senses with alcohol, coffee and cigars. His binges sometimes left him unconscious or semi-delirious, and precipitated auditory disturbances. He flung himself into passionate and beautiful friendships with a succession of highminded fellow students. He read, idolized and imitated the canonical Romantic authors – above all, Jean Paul Richter and E.T.A. Hoffmann, from whom his circle borrowed their ideals of artistic brotherhood and their *noms de plume*. In the time-honoured way of young love, he became infatuated with unapproachable and unavailable women.

True young Romantic as he was, Schumann became a dreamer. He cultivated an intense and overwhelming theatre of fantasy around him, partly shared, largely private. The power of imagination was to be a proving ground for his talent. What first drew attention to him as a musician was his astonishing gift of improvising at the piano, especially his capacity to conjure up music which perfectly captured someone's mood or character. This he called 'fantasizing' or 'mad improvising'.

He would often describe such elation as a form of madness. As such it was a hallmark of his genius. This was not merely an affectation, an adolescent self-indulgence. Rather it was a crucial milepost in the attempt to establish an identity which would advance his career, win acceptance and recognition, and fulfil his 'promise'. Battling against a parental wish that he should initially play safe and train to be a respectable lawyer, he needed constant proofs that he really possessed superior powers. Aged twenty, he penned a remarkable self-analysis of the artist as a young man, in which he emphasized his own 'unique individuality' and 'melancholy temperament'.

But Schumann's cultivation of an intense inner life was more than youthful elation or a poet's apprenticeship. It was a way of coming to terms with a deep unease towards the world. He yearned to achieve. He set his sights high, often too high. Not surprisingly, he was racked with doubt, indecision, insecurity. He was shy, self-conscious, impressionable, unsure of his own future; his 'letters home' show how anxious he was to please his mother. Above all, life itself often seemed precarious. There was 'a thunderstorm hovering' over his life.

Why this insecurity? Life itself was insecure. When he was sixteen, his father died; his eldest sister committed suicide a few months later. He remembered his father as a semi-invalid, hypochondriacal, self-preoccupied. His mother too was often depressed. The deaths of other family members affected him profoundly. When his brother Julius died of consumption in 1833, the event precipitated terror: 'I was seized with a fixed idea of going mad.' Some of his best friends while he was a student also died young. Throughout his life, separation from those he loved caused him terrible distress, and provoked fears of abandonment. He cried all night when Schubert died. Under emotional stress, he quickly panicked and went to pieces. As early as 1828 he was writing, 'It seems to me that I'll go mad one day.' He had a superstitious belief – he carried it with him all his life – in the self-fulfilling nature of prophecies.

Schumann frequently became moody. He was deeply introspective, and committed his endless self-reflections to a journal. He was haunted for much of his life by 'loathsome dreams'. He gained a reputation from his student days onwards for being self-contained, distrait, lost in his own thoughts when in company. Maladroit, he would make scenes over trifles. He often smarted under the dart of failure. 'If only I could be a genius.'

Schumann's supersensitive temper and his frequent feelings of dread led to abnormally powerful episodes of depression. His first sight of Colditz Castle, then used as a lunatic asylum, gave him a premonitory terror. He was prone to sudden fits of panic, associated with confusion and guilt. A sense of his complete inability to cope with death led to an abortive suicide attempt in 1833, when he tried to throw himself out of a fifth-floor window. It left him with a lasting horror of heights.

In some ways, sketching in these details of Schumann's early career amounts to saying that he was dramatizing himself in a rather adolescent way as the mad genius in the making. Apprenticing himself for the role, he began to hear noises in his head. Then voices began to address him. He personified two of these and gave them proper names. On once engaging in self-recrimination, 'My genius, are you going to abandon me?', he was answered by the arrival of a disembodied voice, 'Florestan', who over the years became the confident, extrovert and manly alter ego. Schumann liked to see 'Florestan the Improviser' as his 'bosom friend . . . my own ego'.

The other voice that haunted him came slightly later, and was to be christened 'Eusebius'. This was Schumann's more sensitive, withdrawn, passive, feminine part. Of course, the advent of these figures reflected fashionable

Romantic thinking about *Doppelgänger*, derived largely from Jean Paul. But, once they appeared, the solitary Schumann was often to be found talking to his selves.

But if Schumann's Romantic quest thus made him increasingly quirky, what primarily needs to be stressed is his capacity to harness and exploit these strange forces his imagination had conjured up, his success at putting them to work for him. Florestan and Eusebius were to become the mythic subcontracted authors of much of Schumann's musical journalism, polar personae which allowed him to explore different points of view in print. His inner dialogues thus released in him a literary voice.

Above all, the sounds he heard in his head led him to compose at the piano. He often wrote music under 'dictation': 'gods were coming out of my fingers'. At a later, mature stage in his career, he believed his inner voices dictated to him his Spring Symphony and his *Manfred* Overture. These noises formed one of several psychic aids which helped guide him towards, and convince him of, his true vocation: being a composer. For, from early on, he was faced with an objective decision. If he were to pursue a successful career as a musical genius, what precisely was he to do? Schumann never felt the slightest desire to make his mark on the world as the great music teacher of his generation. For long he hoped to become a virtuoso concert pianist. But he developed a mysterious injury to one of the fingers of his right hand, which impaired his playing (it may well have been psychosomatic). And he progressively became the victim of stage-fright. These were wise handicaps to develop, for his pianistic technique was far from impeccable, and in an age of Liszt, Mendelssohn, Chopin ('a genius', according to Schumann's own journalism), and child-prodigies like his own wife-to-be, Clara Wieck, an attempted career as a concert pianist would surely have been all rebuffs and humiliation. At a later stage, awkwardness and self-consciousness in public likewise meant that his conducting career was unsuccessful. His heart had never really been in that, however, for on-stage he could never compete with Clara. The promptings of all these forces meant that it was composing that became his destiny.

In his prime, Schumann could certainly be a difficult man, prey to dramatic mood swings, and subject above all to black melancholy. In particular, he passed an abysmally depressed year during and after Clara's concert tour to Russia in 1844. He was jealous of her success. While they were travelling, her career made it impossible for him to pursue his own. His composing ground to a standstill. Far from home, he grew even more morbidly fearful for his health. He developed phobias about being poisoned (it is at least possible that the multiple medications he was prescribed were producing quite serious toxic side-effects). He became withdrawn.

Over the years, however, Schumann's edgy and erratic behaviour is surely less a foreshadowing of the progressive brain and personality deterioration which doctors have often ascribed to him than a quite understandable response to insecurity and pressure. For many years he had wooed the gifted Clara apparently hopelessly, in the teeth of her father's diehard opposition: Friedrich Wieck remained hostile even after the Schumanns' wedding in 1840, and to his death kept a hold over Clara. Once Robert had won her, he clearly found her a stronger personality than himself, and more successful in the quest for fame. Robert's capacity to provide for his growing family was never very secure. He gained a steady income only by accepting posts as concert master or musical director – first in Dresden, then in Düsseldorf. But such jobs irked him, and his unsuitability for them caused his anxiety and irritation. Moreover his family responsibilities steadily grew (the Schumanns ended up with six children). The wonder is that he – and of course Clara too – coped so well, while turning himself into a fertile and prolific composer.

Schumann entertained a Romantic notion of the creative act and the holiness of art. His doubts about his own genius often left him in despair. There is no sign, however, that he wallowed in the morbid idea that profound misery was necessary to great art. Indeed his most productive creative periods were precisely when he was most joyous, above all in the years immediately following his betrothal to Clara. A remarkable flow of compositions, including all his symphonies and concertos, poured out within the span of little more than a decade. Certainly, he worked at times with a manic fury. But there is no convincing evidence that in doing so he truly burned himself out. His later compositions betray no sign of powers in decline. As Ostwald notes, however, in his enveloping hypochondria Schumann may have imagined himself spent. After all, one of the texts he had put to music was Byron's arch-Romantic *Manfred*:

> Look on me! there is an order
> Of mortals on the earth, who do become
> Old in their youth, and die ere middle-age
> Without the violence of warlike death;
> Some perishing of pleasure, some of study,
> Some worn with toil, some of mere weariness,
> Some of disease and some insanity,
> And some of wither'd or of broken hearts.

The year 1853 proved particularly difficult for Schumann. The appointment as *Kappelmeister* at Düsseldorf which he had accepted three years earlier caused him to hit rock-bottom. His conducting failures led to his being ousted from that post. He and Clara made friends with two young geniuses, Joachim and Brahms, and it is likely that their presence made Schumann feel a spent force and reminded him of his mortality. At some point, Schumann may have become aware of the mutual attraction between Brahms and Clara.

At the beginning of 1854, Schumann began to suffer further hallucinations. He heard music in his head. At first it was divine: 'music that is so glorious, and with instruments sounding more wonderful than one ever hears on earth'; 'angels' would 'sing the melody'. Later the angels turned to 'demons', and his head became a torture box. His mind experienced 'exquisite suffering' as fresh voices told him he was a 'sinner'. On 27 February 1854, he hurled himself into the Rhine. Rescued, he felt shame and humiliation: 'O Clara, I am not worth your love.' It was Schumann himself who insisted on being hospitalized in an asylum. Clara resisted: asylums were stigmatizing. Robert assured her that a short period of peace would prove recuperative and lead to the resumption of normal life.

In thus imagining, Schumann fell victim to the deluded idealism about life in lunatic asylums so common in that age of psychiatric optimism. He dug his own grave. At Endenich asylum, several hours' drive from where Clara was living, he was isolated, rejected, dejected. His pathetic letters to his friends plead for them to send him writing paper, so that he can compose. Following Richarz's common practice, he was presumably put under heavy medication. When, early on, Brahms visited Endenich, he was not even allowed to see his fellow composer. Clara did not visit. She had almost certainly been advised by the doctor that contact would be damaging to the patient. For possibly complex reasons, she obeyed. Indeed, she did not see him again until he was known to be on the brink of death.

Brutally isolated, and feeling more abandoned than ever, Schumann withdrew into himself. Asylum life forced this Romantic inner journey upon him. He hardly spoke. Such friends as Joachim, who paid him occasional visits, noted that he seemed to be losing the power to communicate. There is not the slightest proof, however, that he was actually and irredeemably undergoing rapid deterioration of the brain or indeed passing into a dream-world of delusions. His last agonized letters to Clara are perfectly lucid. Achingly, they look forward to reunion with his family and a better future. He received no replies (Richarz doubtless thought letters would overexcite him). When Brahms visited, Schumann inquired if Clara were dead.

As long as a year after his incarceration, Schumann evidently still seemed quite *compos mentis* to some who came to see him. The writer Frau von Arnim reported:

He told me, in words which could only be articulated with effort, that it has gotten to be difficult for him to speak, and now that he hasn't spoken to anyone for over a year this ailment has gotten worse. He conversed about everything of interest that he had encountered in life, about Vienna, about Petersburg, and London, about Sicily, about works by Brahms. . . . In short he talked uninterruptedly about all the things that had ever pleasurably excited him.

At some stage Schumann clearly recognized that he was to be allowed no future. Life in the asylum had turned him into a case who to the eyes of psychiatry looked irreversibly mad (Frau von Arnim commented sourly that Dr Richarz was himself 'a hypochondriac' who 'regards Schumann as a symptom of illness, rather than understanding his noble mind'). The one piece of verse he set to music in the asylum was a clear premonition of death. It was the old chorale:

> When my final hour arrives
> To depart from this earth
> I beg thee Lord Jesus Christ
> To help me in my last suffering.
> Lord, my soul at the end
> I commit into thy hands
> Thou knowest well how to protect it.

Mad Schumann took his own life in the only way possible: he starved himself to death. He died on 29 July 1856. Alone.

Towards the close of the nineteenth century, the German psychiatrist Paul Möbius, a man morbidly fascinated by the psychopathology of genius, looked back upon Schumann's case. He found the medical evidence advanced by Richarz on the basis of the autopsy less than satisfactory. Möbius came up with what seemed to him a more up-to-date and satisfactory diagnosis of Schumann's malady. He had suffered from *dementia praecox*, a 'disease' newly identified by Möbius, Kraepelin and other contemporaries. This condition was soon to be renamed schizophrenia by the eminent Zurich psychiatrist Eugen Bleuler. It was typified by flight from reality; its prognosis was universally poor. Bleuler was to diagnose another Romantic genius as schizophrenic, with results even more poignant than Schumann's tragedy. He was the Russian dancer Nijinsky.

Born in 1890 of poor parents with dancing in their blood, Vaslav Nijinsky trained from the age of nine at the Imperial Ballet before embarking upon a spectacular career under the impresario Serge Diaghilev. He became the leading dancer of the age. Moreover he played an active part in conceiving and choreographing the new ballets which took Europe by storm: *The Rite of Spring, The Firebird, Prélude à l'Après-midi d'un Faune*, and so forth.

Diaghilev had taken Nijinsky as his lover (he assumed it as a *droit de seigneur*). 'I hated him but pretended,' Nijinsky later wrote. By the mid-1910s Diaghilev had become more attracted to younger dancers. Nijinsky himself felt distanced and displaced. The outbreak of the First World War disrupted tours and performances. Nijinsky sought to break away, hoping to form his own company and create his own ballets. Above all, Nijinsky married. With his Hungarian wife, the ballerina Romola de Pulszky, he began a family. The relations between Diaghilev and Nijinsky ended sourly and with mutual recriminations. The last years of the war found the Nijinskys at St Moritz in Switzerland, their funds running low, and with no definite engagements for the future. All that was certain was Nijinsky's unshakeable belief in his divine dancing.

Nijinsky did not exactly see himself as a genius. He rather believed he was gifted or possessed by genius. In a way which surely reflects his own adoration of Tolstoy, he saw his art as holy or sacred.

Inactive and cooped up in a St Moritz hotel, Nijinsky exhibited increasingly odd behavior. He went for long solitary walks, wearing a large cross. He grew irritable, impatient, moody. He drew macabre Goyaesque drawings of the calamities of war. He was rude or even violent to his wife, or he withdrew from her. A servant who recalled the insane Nietzsche thought Nijinsky had begun to wear the same face. Nijinsky said he wanted to go and become a peasant; do that, and I'll divorce you, Romola threatened. He started to keep a diary which he refused to show her. Towards those he loved, he wavered between defiance on the one hand and guilty abjection on the other. Terrified, Romola called in medical aid.

Nijinsky distrusted doctors. As his diary shows, he felt contempt for their misunderstandings and was fearful of their power. When they wished to inspect his diary, he refused. For them, the fact that he continued to scribble his thoughts in their presence was proof positive of what they suspected. He resented his wife collaborating with them: 'I can no longer trust my wife, as I feel she wants to give this diary to the doctor.' He saw them as spies and tried to distance himself from them. All this they interpreted as symptomatic of mental pathology. Nijinsky saw the science of the doctors as profoundly antithetical to the genius of art. The doctors' reasoning understood nothing. 'They want to examine my brain, but I want to examine their minds.'

As his diary unfolds, we read Nijinsky expounding an extremely lucid, and often witty, vision of the holiness of what the doctors even then were diagnosing as his madness. The world, as he saw it, is an out-and-out hypocrite. It worships at the shrine of reason. But this reason is crazy. Worldly reason sanctions greed, materialism and violence. It divides people because

it is enamoured of the distinction between mine and thine. The love of property and the abuse of power go hand in hand. Avarice for possessions has
turned art into a commodity, has reduced it to an object of consumption.
Art is thereby degraded to become the plaything of the rich, emasculated
and prettified within polite society. Love too is turned into a commodity,
given cash value. It takes the forms of lust and lechery. It is symbolized
by meat-eating, the slaughter of innocents to support carnality. The collective
expression of these values and actions spells annihilation. 'Politics are death,'
politicians are the real criminals. It is a world at war, a world of war. Nijinsky
presents us with an analysis of civilization and its discontents, of reality as
a hollow lie, an analysis which is Tolstoyan rather than Freudian.

Nijinsky vowed to have nothing to do with life as anatomized by doctors.
Theirs was the taint of death. Their shibboleth was science. Science was
the disease of thinking too much. Science understands nothing. Darwin saw
nature all at strife. He was wrong: 'all nature is alive'. The patron saint
of this sick society was the doctor. 'I am against all drugs.'

Repudiating all this, Nijinsky (like Nietzsche) does not pin his hopes upon
revolution, upon radical political solutions. Why hate the rich? He does not
hate them, he insists; they have as much right to live as all the other living
creatures they exploit and slaughter. Nor does he romanticize the poor: 'Life
is not poverty.' Nor is he a Bolshevik: 'my party is God's party'. He would
like to explode the illogic of degenerate civilization and its doctors in more
subtle ways: he will, for example, under divine instruction, find a way of
breaking the stock exchange, which is death to the poor.

Above all, he advances a totally transformed set of priorities. True life
must be built upon feeling: 'I am simple, I need not think.' Feeling is love.
God is love. Love is the expression of God. Feeling is the holy fire. Fired
by God, Nijinsky the dancer becomes the divine in motion. Dance is the
divine in the world, the Dionysian religion. 'Without energy there is no
life,' writes Nijinsky, sounding for all the world like Blake, though without
his taste for satanic paradox.

'God is in me.' Through his dance, states Nijinsky, he is the bringer of
God, of divine fire, into the world, for I am 'God in a body', possessed
of 'grace, which comes of God'. Civilization is built upon history; all that
is just dead weight. 'I am God's present.' For God is life, God is movement.
'I am a man of motion,' 'I am God in flesh and feeling.' So much is revealed.
Like Blake, he writes at divine dictation: 'I write everything He tells me.'
'People who write a great deal,' he remarks perceptively, 'are martyrs.'

'I am the Saviour.' Like Christ he will redeem; but he will redeem through
dance. Inevitably, he will be persecuted, he must be 'a martyr'. 'I suffered
more than anyone else in the world.' Why? Blinded by reason, the world

cannot, will not understand. In a cruel world, racked by war, how can a saviour survive? How can God live?

Nijinsky downgrades Nietzsche's demon in contrast to Tolstoy's. 'I was sorry for Nietzsche,' for he became 'frightened of people'. Nietzsche had gone mad because he would 'think too much'. By contrast he acknowledges his boundless debt to Tolstoy ('Stop imitating that old lunatic', Romola chid him). Like Tolstoy, his madness is divine.

Nijinsky enjoys playing with the paradox of his own prophetic madness. Sometimes he denies point-blank that he is mad (i.e. mentally sick as diagnosed by the doctors). For pathological madness as they define it is a disease of thinking. Joyously spoofing Descartes, he writes, 'I do not think, and therefore cannot go mad.' The label of insanity is what foolish, envious people pin on him. They all sneer and say, 'Why does Nijinsky always talk of God? He has gone mad.' But not so! 'A lunatic does not realize what he is doing. I understand my good and bad actions.'

Sometimes, however, he claims merely to be acting mad, performing another stage part. By 'playing the part of a lunatic', he can test the sincerity of those he is with. He would like people to think of him as a 'harmless madman'; no one need fear *him*, unlike the terrifyingly dangerous madmen who are running amok and ruining the world. 'I will pretend to be a clown, because they will understand me better.'

But often he glories in his full-blooded madness, identifying with Dostoyevsky's *Idiot*. 'God is the fire in my head.' Such madness is life indeed: 'I am alive as long as there is fire in my head.' He is ablaze with the flames of love: 'I am a madman who loves mankind. My madness is my love towards mankind.' 'I want to inflame people.' People may not find him intelligible, but that is because they are mentally blinkered, one-dimensional men. 'I like to speak in rhymes, because I am a rhyme myself.'

Yet, deeply understood, his madness is reason as well as rhyme. 'I am a madman with sense.' Hamlet had put one over on Horatio. Now Nijinsky out-Hamlets Hamlet. 'I do not like Shakespeare's Hamlet because he reasons. I am a philosopher who does not reason – a philosopher who feels.' Nijinsky's genius tells him: 'I am God in you. I will do everything to make you understand.'

Nijinsky consented to be seen by a doctor, just to humour him. Poor fellow! 'He is a nervous man. He smokes a lot.' He knew medical examination was all part of the silly charade of this stage of fools. 'Scientists think about me. They are stupid.' He was sure that his wife would 'betray me to the doctors'. Yet he owed compliance to her.

She consulted Eugen Bleuler, director at Kreuzlingen Asylum ('an old man with infinite understanding in his eyes', she said). In the stilted but insidious clichés of Romanticism he told her: 'genius, insanity, they are so near'. Initially he was reassuring: 'the symptoms you describe in an artist and in a Russian do not in themselves prove any mental disturbance'. To be on the safe side, however, he should see the patient himself. Nijinsky agreed to an appointment with Bleuler ('it will calm my wife'). His forebodings were grim. 'They will put me into a lunatic asylum. ... I am not afraid of anything, and want to die.'

Bleuler informed Romola that 'your husband is incurably insane'; he is a 'schizophrenic': 'you have to get a divorce'. Nijinsky must be confined. Romola agreed: 'The doctors were right.' The ambulance came for him. Nijinsky struggled, resisted and became violent (apparently for the first time); he was bundled off and locked up.

He remained in Kreuzlingen for four years. Once there his condition rapidly deteriorated. He suffered 'catatonic attacks', withdrew into himself and went on hunger strike. His behaviour was interpreted as symptomatic of his disease. Seeking further advice, Romola took Nijinsky to see Jung and Forel. Apparently Freud declined to see him, saying that he could not help schizophrenics.

In 1923, Romola removed Nijinsky from the asylum. By then he was a broken man: almost mute, shuffling, haggard, numb, frightened. Isolation and, presumably, medication, had killed his fire. Romola looked after him. She understood how the institution destroyed her husband ('he became a human wreck'). In 1929, however, Nijinsky was returned to Kreuzlingen. Romola wished to go on a lecture tour to the USA; Nijinsky of course was not allowed in. He remained institutionalized until the outbreak of the Second World War, when Romola took him back to her native Hungary. In 1938 insulin therapy briefly reanimated him.

But only once more in his life did he come alive and dance. The pair spent Hitler's war in Hungary. In 1945 it was liberated by the Russian army. Nijinsky came face to face with his countrymen, peasants all, for the first time for over a generation. Some of them remembered the legend of the dancer. They treated him as a normal human being. Romola recorded:

> For the first time since 1919, people did not stare at him, did not shrink
> from him because he had suffered a mental illness. They spoke to him
> in the same nonchalant manner as they did to us. At first I warned them:
> 'Leave Vaslav Fomitch alone, don't talk to him. He might get annoyed
> and impatient, he is afraid.' But they just laughed. 'He won't be afraid
> of us,' they said. 'Let him alone to do what he wants.'

The encounter brought him back to life. He danced with the soldiers.

Schumann, Nijinsky and many other great artists and performers were trapped in a collective mythology, partly of their own creation, the idea that madness and genius were doubles, soulmates. They were particularly the victims of that mythology, in that their final confinement in a mental hospital did not provide them with *asylum*, that release from the extraneous and footling cares of the world which would allow the fountain of their genius to play freely. Rather it spelt silence, paralysis. That cannot be said of John Clare, the Northamptonshire 'peasant poet'. But the Romantic myth trapped him all the same.

Born in 1793, Clare conformed easily enough to the popular Romantic cliché of the poet possessed and destroyed by his writing demon. At the height of his fame he would put down in his letters such sentiments as 'my Muse is a fickle hussy who stilts me up to Madness and then leaves me as a beggar'; ominously he wrote that to his sympathetic publisher, the well-meaning man shortly to be responsible for his first confinement. Clare confided much in the medical profession, and medical authority put its own gloss on such auto-diagnoses. Dr Fenwick Skrimshire, a local practitioner whom Clare had been consulting for years, inaugurated Clare's second period in the asylum with the diagnosis that he was lunatic, 'by years addicted to Poetical prosings'. Clare was to spend the last twenty-seven years of his life under sequestration.

Yet for practically all that time he continued to write. As Geoffrey Grigson has demonstrated, his asylum output contains some of his best verse; indeed confinement as a lunatic released him from much of his earlier self-censorship as a poet. Plans were made by well-wishers to publish a (doubtless censored) volume of his asylum poetry, and, though these fell through, a dribble of his verses continued to find its way into print. Clare offers a distinctive case of the mad genius with a difference, one to whom clinical insanity gave a new voice.

It would be pure Romantic myth-making, however, to see Clare simply as a man maddened by his muse. For many complex strands contributed to the tragedy of his life. He was locked up for around thirty years, but all his days he was held on a social chain which sometimes appeared to be loosened or lengthened but from which Clare never had more than the simulacrum of freedom. What made society applaud him as a poet also made him a prisoner.

Clare was born in the tiny village of Helpstone in Northamptonshire, the son of an agricultural labourer. His mother was illiterate. As a child he began to take that passionate interest in the living natural world all around him which sustained him to his grave. He was always to look back upon idyllic childhood days spent outdoors, talking to the animals and communing with the fields. He recalled himself as a solitary ('the Crusoe of the lonely fields'),

76

though this may simply show a retrospective mythologizing of the poet as hero–victim. He loved the oral lore of country people, with their songs and tales of ghosts and goblins, before which he felt 'fearful ecstasy'. But a sound village schooling also filled him with 'a thirst after knowledge'. He pored over books; the village thought him 'no better than crazy'. His first two purchases were Isaac Watts' *Hymns* and Thomson's *Seasons*. His oral heritage and his book-learning between them led him from an early age to be forever making verses of his own. From his teens these were entered into an expensive copy book.

Clare grew up with the local lads. Rejecting 'the confinement of apprenticeship', he obtained work as a gardener, and nearly joined the militia. But his muse (or as he often fearfully and guiltily put it later, his 'foolish pretensions') gradually set him apart from his fellows. At the end of his teens he made a first attempt to publish some of his verse by subscription, and, when that failed, was overcome by the profound mortification of feeling like one who had had no business to be fired with 'ambition', no right to transgress his station. It was ominous.

Soon, however, he was 'discovered' by well-meaning local men of letters who acted as patrons. They made him known to the metropolitan literary and publishing scene. By 1820, John Taylor in London – Keats' publisher – had brought out his first volume of verse, *Poems Descriptive*. It was a sizeable success, going through three editions and selling 3,000 copies in its first year.

Clare's muse was everything literary London thought a peasant's poems should be: direct, lyrical, uncorrupted by artifice. He was a natural poet, warbling his native woodnotes wild, almost a character out of Wordsworth, a leech-gatherer penning sonnets on the side. When Clare made his first trip to London in the same year, he lived up in person to the image of a good peasant. He was honest, bluff, fresh-faced, handsome, manly. He was unspoilt and rough-hewn without being coarse. He spoke from the heart. His heart was in the soil. Clare was a very gratifying version of pastoral.

In an age which (as Cobbett thundered) was seeing the relentless destruction of the countryfolk and countryside by agricultural capitalism and enclosure – it came to his native soil during his lifetime – and when men of letters were deploring the evils of towns, industry and commerce, a rustic genius such as Clare was an endangered species. Steps were taken to preserve him. A subscription was raised which guaranteed him financial support (albeit of a slender nature: too much would have debauched him). He was given *entrée* to literary circles. He was urged to spur his muse. Not least, he was exposed to constant pressures to improve himself, to reform his speech and manners, to become a more polished peasant poet. He should improve his diction (literary friends suggested), drop his dialect words, cut out his barbs against the landlords – in short, delicately deracinate himself.

The pressures proved contradictory and crushing. To survive and thrive, the demand was 'publish or perish'. Clare drove himself (he was, he wrote, 'all madness for writing') and overburdened his mind. Moreover, he was forced to be several men at once. A peasant true to his roots and his folk (he still needed to work the land for money as well as for inspiration); a forelock-tugger who could defer gratefully to the great who were showing him such condescension and generously affording him such valuable critical hints. But also a natural, manly, independent poet, who should prove himself a worthy successor to Thomson, an East Midlands equivalent of the Lakers.

Kept company by those boon 'companions of genius, Disappointment and poverty', Clare was soon to crack. During the 1820s he fell prey to a downward spiral of distress, depression and anguish. He became, he wrote, a 'half mad melancholy dog'; he had 'the horrors', suffered 'numbing pain', 'blue devils', 'black melancholy'. Occasional escapist drinking binges made things worse. His longstanding organic disorders worsened – above all, chronic pains in his guts and his genitals.

Physically, it is unclear precisely what he was suffering from. Possibly his indispositions were initially psychosomatic; certainly he developed a dread (probably unfounded, the child of guilt) of having been venereally infected. Quite possibly it was medicine itself which provoked his deteriorating physical condition, for Clare became an insatiable swallower of pills and potions. What is beyond doubt is that he turned into a hypochondriac. He knew this was the poet's fate: 'I fancy, which I believe to tell truth is the whole of my complaint.' A childhood experience of seeing a man fall off a hay waggon and break his neck had led him to have a fit. He suffered subsequent seizures. They may have been epileptiform. Certainly, they stoked a morbid fear in him of destiny, incipient madness and death. Clare began to feel doomed.

The relative failure of his next volume, *The Shepherd's Calendar*, and subsequent collections made things worse. He had married a local girl, Patty, in 1820. His family grew. Debts mounted and Clare turned from despondency to despair as the future grew darker. His letters of the early 1830s recite a litany of anguish. He began to lose control of his mental processes. He always had been suggestible, his head ringing with the bogeymen of rural life. When depressed in London in the 1820s, he had feared walking alone at night, terrified of spooks that haunted the shadows. Now a terror of madness sometimes overtook him, with its spectre of decay both physical and mental.

He began to take refuge in an imaginative escape of his own making. The haven of hope was the figure of Mary Joyce, a childhood sweetheart who, advised by her father, seems to have resisted Clare's advances because he was socially inferior. Clare started to weave fantasies about her. As background to this, he increasingly fantasized about the good times of the past, of his childhood, a golden age when the countryside was free (free of enclosure, free of tyrant farmers) and he was free in it. He came to identify imaginative power with childhood, and thus poetry with the past. 'There is nothing but poetry about the existence of childhood. ... there is nothing of poetry about manhood but the reflection and the remembrance of what has been.'

His mental condition worsened. In the early 1830s his letters echo with dread: 'greatly disturbed today', 'fear of Decline', 'great distress'. Eventually 'I am at the world's end.' His patrons once again came to the rescue. In his days of promise they had set him up as a peasant poet. Now, in his time of need, they would save him as a lunatic poet. One day in 1837, there was a knock on the door. A man with a letter. It was from John Taylor, his publisher:

The bearer will bring you up to town and take care of you on the way. ...
The medical aid provided near this place will cure you effectually.

As always, Clare obeyed.

Clare was escorted to High Beech. It was a very special private asylum in Epping Forest, run on the progressive principles of moral therapy – kindness and sympathy – by the highly enlightened Dr Matthew Allen. Clare was allowed to wander in the grounds and was encouraged to write: Allen believed it therapeutic for him. Initially, Clare felt released from care and content, and produced some of his most characteristic songs to nature. In time, however, it came to seem to him a nature increasingly stamped with decay: 'nature to me seems dead and her very pulse seems frozen to an icicle in the summer sun'. His own mood turned to despair:

My mind is dark and fathomless and wears
The hues of hopeless agony and hell;
No plummet ever sounds the soul's affairs
There death eternal never sounds the knell.

During Clare's four years under Allen, there is little sign that he was seriously deluded, suicidal or dangerous. Yet no prospect appeared of his release. His patrons feared that a return home to family responsibilities would mean a return to the pressures and poverty which had racked and wrecked him before. It seemed best to protect him by making him a poet in residence. There was something picturesque about the mad author ensconced in the benevolent asylum, rather like a holy hermit in a grotto. The *litterateur* Cyrus Redding – a man who published some of his asylum verse – put it thus after visiting High Beech: 'I never before saw so characterized personally the *Poeta Nascitur* ... which lifts men of genius above the herd.' William Hunt came and painted him as a 'Self Taught Genius'.

Over the years, Clare himself grew more distraught. He felt alien, a foreigner, severed from love, affection, friends, family. Increasingly he viewed the asylum as a prison. It was a 'hell of a madhouse'; it resembled a 'slave ship from Africa'. Cut off from reality, the world of appearances became deceptive. He was surrounded by 'mock friends and real enemies'. He wrote pleadingly to his wife Patty: 'there is no place like home'. He was trapped in the English Bastille. His fantasies about the world he had lost – the world stolen from him – possessed him with urgent intensity. In particular, in poems and in unsent letters, he transformed Mary Joyce into his first wife (he still wrote passionately about Patty).

At the same time he also erected himself into a warrior against the system of oppression, Old Corruption, Cobbett's 'Thing'. He personified himself as a prize fighter, a new Tom Spring. It was a role he carried to his grave, one which all his dumb contemporaries saw as proof of his delusions. Above all, he came to see himself as Byron reincarnated. His *Don Juan* and *Childe Harold* resumed where Byron had left off. Byron–Clare was the despised hero waging war against cant and lies. Society pretended to be so rational, civilized, polite, genteel. What hypocrisy! In reality it was lust, greed, envy, deceit and malice that made the wheels go round. Morality was just a veneer, an illusion:

> 'Poets are born' – and so are whores – the trade is
> Grown universal: in these canting days
> Women of fashion must, of course, be ladies,
> And whoring is the business that still pays.

Impersonating Byron, Clare became the disillusioned poet, stripping the world of its illusions. As he later wrote to his son, 'never act hypocrisy, for Deception is the most odious Knavery in the world'. Byron would have enjoyed the irony of the role he had pioneered as aristocratic bitter fool now being filled by a certified lunatic.

Confinement surely released something in Clare. For years his verse had had to mind its Ps and Qs. He had written looking over his shoulder at his patrons and public, his collective superego. Now, amidst his continued outpourings of love for nature and for his two wives, there was a new strain. The pent-up anger, resentments and frustrations of the years came out in satire, in bawdy, in a cynicism which would never have become a proper peasant poet. Clare had never stopped being an alien. Now, once officially alienated of mind, he could give vent to his deeper identity and sing of the bittersweet experience of being an outcast from someone else's world.

In 1841, inspired and helped by gypsies, Clare escaped. He walked the hundred miles home. *En route*, no one it seems mistook him for a lunatic. He lived at home for some months, till, after further ructions, his long-time trusted doctor, Fenwick Skrimshire, had him carried off to the Northamptonshire General Asylum, to be paid for by Lord Fitzwilliam. He was never released. Its superintendent, Dr Thomas Prichard, boasted that Clare 'enjoys perfect liberty here'. It did not seem that way to Clare: 'I am in fact in prison' – indeed, 'I am in this damned madhouse and can't get out.' He found it a 'hell', a 'Bastille', a 'Sodom'.

Almost up to the time of his death, his letters home reveal a man in control of powerful intellectual faculties, demonstrating tender and loving devotion to his family ('think Fred – for yourself', he advised his son). He was visited by his sons, but never, it seems, by his wife. Twenty more years of poetry lay before him. Its quality deteriorated, but no more so than Wordsworth's. Well-meaning *litterateurs* visited him, like anthropologists about to lay before the civilized world their tales of their encounter with the mad poet (by then assumed by many to have been long dead). Clare, tired of the ghouls, no longer had to defer to this condescension, as the writer Agnes Strickland found when she visited Northampton in 1860:

> I told Clare I had been much pleased with his lines on the daisy.
> 'Ugh! It is a tidy little thing,' replied he, without raising his eyes or appearing in the slightest degree gratified by my praise.
> 'I am glad you can amuse yourself by writing.'
> 'I can't do it,' replied he, gloomily; 'they pick my brains out.' I enquired his meaning.
> 'Why,' said he, 'they have cut off my head, and picked out all the letters of the alphabet – all the vowels and consonants – and brought them out through the ears; and then they want me to write poetry! I can't do it.'
> 'Tell me which you liked best, literature or your former avocation?'
> 'I liked hard work best,' he replied, with sudden vehemence. 'I was happy then. Literature has destroyed my head and brought me here.'

As the riddling Clare knew, it was not literature as such which had picked him up, cast him down and brought him there. Rather it had been a set of cultural fantasies associated with the place and powers of genius, initiated by other people but shared by himself. These had been overlaid in Clare's life, but not so evidently in the cases of Schumann, Nijinsky, Virginia Woolf and many others, with parallel mythologies about the madness of storming the social order. And the coming of institutional psychiatry had invented peculiarly destructive nurseries of genius.

5 · Religious Madness

'One half of the Christian world', reflected the embryo poet William Cowper in 1766, 'would call this madness, fanaticism and folly: but are not these things warranted by the word of God?' He was referring to his own new-found religious faith. He had recently become an adherent of the Evangelical movement then rapidly gaining converts in England.

True religion, as 'brands plucked from the burning' such as Cowper saw it, was not a matter of intellectual assent to an established, authorized, well-documented programme of proofs, principles and practices (that was 'pretended belief'). It was an ardent embracing of lively faith shooting out of the heart, a spiritual quest, an inner certainty. As such it was subjective, personal or (the term the Evangelicals preferred) *experimental*, that is, grounded upon individual *experience*. But what actually redeemed, what saved the individual sinner from the sentence of eternal perdition he so richly deserved, was not, in fact, his own faith, but the spontaneous (and quite unmerited) gift of divine atonement; salvation by grace. Conversion was that experience of being overwhelmed with grace.

Evangelical Christianity thus required not merely a pure and zealous emotional conviction, but the total commitment of the believer's conscience to a framework of beliefs which were, ultimately, transcendental, mysterious, beyond reason: a theology enshrining the cosmic battle between God and Satan for the soul, the radical sinfulness of mankind, the reality of eternal hellfire punishments for the damned and of eternal bliss for the saved, the special interventions of Providence in guiding the pilgrim's progress.

It was, in consequence, easy to call a true Christian of this stamp 'mad'. Many Christians themselves had traditionally welcomed the label. After all, God himself had been mad to send His Son to be crucified for man's sake, and the 'madness of the cross' had been echoed in the Patristic idea that the spiritual 'ecstasy' of the true believer was itself a form of going out of one's mind or senses, through literally 'standing outside' oneself, being 'beside oneself'. 'Good' madness of this kind had a long and noble pedigree in Christian theology. Erasmus had drawn upon it in his *Praise of Folly*. And in the England of the Reformation and the Puritan revolution, the godly and the pious – in particular the more antinomian of the 'Saints' – were widely reputed to be in touch with divine voices, to witness visions in dreams, utter prophetic truths, and above all to see the hand of God in everything.

Of course, there was 'bad' religious madness too. Satan was always striving to take possession of weak and tempted sinners, and those possessed by the Tempter duly manifested their own marks of senselessness: they cursed, blasphemed, got drunk, whored, committed idolatry, broke the commandments, or fell into despair and took their own lives (suicide was both a deadly sin and a crime). Being wily, the Devil would insinuate himself into souls under pretence of being the word and will of God Himself. Many authors of penitential diaries or of 'spiritual autobiographies', like Christoph Haitzmann in seventeenth-century Austria or his contemporary George Trosse in England, recorded their encounters with the Devil and his temptations. Typically such people explained how they had languished under the fatal conceit that they were receiving divine commands, in their head, in their dreams, in signs and manifestations – only, finally, usually in the nick of time, to be disabused, to have the Devil discovered to them. Though thrown headlong into crisis, they would eventually come to differentiate between the diabolical and the divine.

Haitzmann and Trosse provide illuminating points of comparison and contrast. Both underwent terrifying spiritual crises assailed by visions and temptations, yet recovered to present happy endings. But the process of crisis and cure for the German Catholic is revealingly different from that experienced by the Puritan from Exeter.

Haitzmann was probably born in the 1640s or 1650s. He came from Bavaria, he was a painter and he was poor. Almost nothing else is known about him until he presented himself in the autumn of 1677 to the pastor of Pottenbrunn in Lower Austria drowning in despair.

He told the pastor that while in church on 29 August he had succumbed to terrible 'fits'; these continued over the next days. He went as a supplicant before an ecclesiastical official who asked if he had had any connection with the Devil. He broke down and confessed. Haitzmann revealed that nine years previously, just after the death of a 'parent', he had become depressed, despairing of making a livelihood. Strolling one day in a wood, he had been accosted by the Devil in the guise of a burgher walking his black dog.

The Tempter lured Haitzmann with a pact. Nine times he refused, but eventually he succumbed. At the end of nine years, Haitzmann was to resign himself, body and soul, to Satan's power. Those nine years were almost up. Awaiting his doom, Haitzmann was in Faust-like agony of mind. His only hope, he believed, lay in going to the famous pilgrim shrine of the Blessed Virgin Mary at Mariazell, in hope of inducing Satan to yield up the pact. He was given a letter of introduction.

Arriving at Mariazell at the beginning of September 1677, Haitzmann submitted himself to three days of continuous exorcism, expiation and prayer. At midnight on 8 September, while praying at the holy shrine, the Devil finally appeared to him in the form of a dragon. Haitzmann made a flying leap and snatched back the pact. Rescued by this 'miracle', his melancholy ceased; he was cured. The penitent seems to have made some pledge to join the monastic community at Mariazell. Out of gratitude for his cure, he painted a series of nine pictures, setting out his satanic temptations. These survive.

Shortly afterwards he went to stay with his sister in Vienna. Within a month he was once again molested by the Devil, undergoing fresh seizures which racked him with great physical pain and induced paralysis; and these continued until early into 1678. During this period, Haitzmann was assailed by a series of apparitions. Initially these presented him with the worldly temptations of the deadly sins. In trance-like states he would see himself fêted in lavish halls surrounded by 'cavaliers' and seductive ladies dressed in all their finery. These dream people tried to lure him into the lap of luxury, promising him power and wealth beyond the dreams of avarice, persuading him to renege on his religious undertakings. Faced with these devils in disguise, Haitzmann summoned up the strength to call upon Holy Mary and Joseph, thereby banishing them and awakening him from his trances.

Soon the apparitions changed. He would be shown visions of blessed austerity, simple ascetics and hermits leading pious existences, designed to torment him as a backslider. He would be commanded to forswear the paths of wickedness. He was reminded of his unfulfilled religious vows and told to do six years' penance in the desert. He saw himself confronted once again by damnation, the flames of hellfire engulfing him as punishment for continuing to walk the ways of the flesh. Evil spirits reviled him with ropes. Under such agonies, he collapsed. The sinner returned in May 1678 to the convent at Mariazell and made yet another confession. He now at last revealed that all along there had been a second pact with the Devil, this one written in ink (the first had been signed in blood). Once again the Holy Fathers conducted exorcism. It was successful. Haitzmann remained at the convent, becoming known as Brother Chrysostomus, until his death in 1700. Now he was assailed by the Devil only when he was in his cups.

Many contemporaries would have called Haitzmann mad. That term, however, would have carried markedly different meanings for different people. For an out-and-out sceptic in these matters such as Thomas Hobbes, all claims to immediate personal contact with God or the Devil were by definition either frauds, fictions or crazy delusions, marks of diseases of the head. They lacked scientific plausibility; they had no authentication. The majority of educated men of that period might well have called Haitzmann religiously deranged, which was a diagnosis meaning otherworldly powers – in this case the Devil – had taken possession of his will, understanding or soul. In his immense and influential *Anatomy of Melancholy* (1621), Robert Burton had interpreted the religious despair and strife prevailing in that age of Reformation and Counter-Reformation in precisely those terms (though as a good Protestant, Burton believed that all Roman Catholics were *ipso facto* infected with that kind of madness).

What is noteworthy is the utter absence of the term 'insanity' and similar language in the testament of Haitzmann and the written commentaries on the case offered by the Mariazell churchmen. Haitzmann, it is true, had admitted to 'melancholy'. But nowhere was it suggested that his visions of Satan were a form of sickness, were unreal hallucinations, or even were diabolically induced madness. Rather Haitzmann was simply possessed. God and Satan visited him with contending good and bad visions. And he was 'treated' not by doctors, not by confinement in a madhouse, but by the formally sanctioned ecclesiastical ritual of exorcism – the casting out of devils – whose success was seen as a 'miracle'.

This is, as we shall soon see, in marked contrast to the beliefs surrounding the crisis suffered by Haitzmann's English contemporary, George Trosse. For Trosse's episode – which nevertheless bears many points of resemblance – was seen by all parties in terms of madness, albeit, of course, not organic but devilishly originated. It is, furthermore, utterly at odds with the gloss which would inevitably be put upon those events in Lower Austria by any modern psychiatric commentator. Freud, possibly intrigued by the Vienna connection, examined Haitzmann's case in 1923. And he was to underline this very point, how fundamentally the interpretation of such experiences had been transformed down the years.

In the eighteenth and nineteenth centuries, Haitzmann's despair would typically have been viewed as hypochondriacal, the symptom of a victim of organic malady, causing auditory and visual disturbances. Freud thought that that unsatisfactory resolution had itself been superseded in his own day, and psychological explanations, relating the consciousness to the unconscious, had at last taken their rightful place. By one of the ironies of fate, Freud added, the ancient demonological interpretations actually shared much in common with psychoanalytical accounts. Indeed, Freud noted, aware of further ironical possibilities, it could be said that 'the demonological theory of these dark ages has in the long run justified itself'. For both demonology and psychoanalysis stressed the priority of turmoil in the consciousness, rather than resting content with lazy suppositions of mere organic disease. The 'superstitious' theory of the 'dark ages' had presupposed maleficium, forces possessing from without, from above; modern psychiatry saw disturbance as triggered by forces within, welling up from below. For that reason, the religious neuroses of several centuries back were – just like the neuroses of children – easier to 'crack' than the complex organically disguised neuroses of latter days.

Freud thus believed that Christian demonology had stumbled upon, yet ultimately mystified, the true nature and cause of disturbance. But he could lay that mystification bare, by showing how the theological language was a sort of code, recording all the hieroglyphic clues in a strange tongue which would succumb before the right translation device. Freud had no hesitation in labelling Haitzmann a case of 'neurosis'.

The key to understanding this neurosis lay in Haitzmann's attitude towards the Devil. For Freud, Haitzmann's Devil was a father-substitute. Haitzmann's unconscious had fantasized the notion of the pact with the Devil; doing so had been for him the only legitimate means of expressing what must have been his profound passive-homosexual longings for his own father. The death of the father had caused Haitzmann's melancholy and inability to work. Haitzmann's compact with the Devil offered him an outlet, a kind of marriage with his father. It was for nine years because (if one read 'years' as a screen for 'months') that was how long it would take for his father's baby to gestate in him.

Freud anticipated resistance to his reading (it was, after all, devoid of any supporting evidence) and was ready with answers. If Haitzmann truly had erotic longings for his father, why (sceptics would ask) did he not express them openly? It was because they were too terrible to contemplate, for to imagine a homosexual tie with one's father necessarily entailed the retribution of castration. It was thus, Freud contended, 'impossible' for Haitzmann to confess consciously to his father-longings. The ramifications of that had been proven in the case of Daniel Schreber's *Memoirs* (discussed in chapter 8). For these reasons, not the father but the Devil had embodied Haitzmann's wish which, once displaced, had become a dread.

But wasn't it peculiar to pick the *Devil* as a father-substitute, as a love-object? Not a bit of it, argued Freud, and for several good reasons. For one thing, the Devil, as portrayed by Haitzmann in his paintings, actually possessed many of the macho features which a sexually desirable father should have. For another, the Devil served admirably as a symbol of the deep 'ambivalence' which a son would feel towards his father, mingling 'fondness and submission' with 'hostility and defiance', and so creating tensions between 'longing' and 'dread'. Supporting these ambivalences, Haitzmann's portrayals of the Devil had shown him with prominent female secondary sexual characteristics – in particular, large breasts. Freud claimed that this was most 'unusual' in representations of the Devil, and hence a psychologically significant way of representing Satan. It probably meant a 'projection' of Haitzmann's own feelings of femininity. Moreover giving the Devil the attributes of 'tenderness' would further help to defuse his fear that his father/the Devil would prove a castrating threat.

Clearly, Freud's is a bizarre fantasy to spin (it makes true demonology seem like sweet reason). For one thing, it is built upon evidential sand. We don't even know – despite Freud's confident supposition – that Haitzmann compacted with the Devil soon after the death of his *father*. The Latin text says *'parens'*, which could just as easily mean 'mother' or indeed another close older relative. We have not the slightest scrap of independent evidence about Haitzmann's relationship to his father. Furthermore, Haitzmann's depiction of an ambisexual Devil was not in reality an aberration of the painter, but conformed to longstanding artistic conventions. The Devil was commonly presented as a double-sexed monster, part man, part woman, part bird, part fish, a creature whose ability to terrify lay precisely in transgressing all the proper boundaries.

Moreover, what is especially peculiar about Freud's account is the ambiguity of its presentation of demonology as neurosis. Freud had earlier argued in his analysis of Daniel Schreber that it was precisely when Schreber's unconscious came to insist upon its longing for the object of its homosexual desires that Schreber collapsed, because of the irresolvable conflicts such desires set up. But just the opposite seems to happen with Haitzmann. His diabolical pact with his father-substitute does not make him guilty but makes him prosper; yet for some peculiar reason he falls into crisis just when, at the end of nine years, he is finally about to give birth to his father's baby. Even within the rules of Freudian theory, the implausibilities, discrepancies and proliferation of saving-clauses invoked here are surely a bit much.

A thorough critique of Freud's interpretation has been mounted by Ida Macalpine and Richard Hunter, psychiatrists of a very different school. They had substituted a quite distinct set of psychiatric postulates, in place of Freud's Oedipal concerns. They are diagnostically at odds, for whereas Freud put the word 'neurosis' in his title, his critics labelled their book *Schizophrenia 1677*. For them, the root cause of Freud's mistakes lay in seeing the Oedipal phase (father–son rivalry) as cardinal in generating the conflicts which erupted in neuroses such as Haitzmann's. As a result, Freud sought father-figures and suffered father-induced crises; and of course, finding them in himself, he found them everywhere. Hence, in this case, he read the Devil as a phallic 'superman', a projection of Haitzmann's father, and saw Haitzmann guiltily in love with the Devil. Macalpine and Hunter note that Freud's own theories of ambiguous father–son relations developed soon after the death of his own father; maybe Freud's tale about Haitzmann tells us nothing at all about Haitzmann and everything about Freud.

But what is remarkable, Macalpine and Hunter point out, is how unlike a 'superman' Haitzmann's Devil actually is. Contrary to the simple expectations set up by Freud, in none of the nine paintings does he have any genitals of any kind (Freud disingenuously notes that this Devil has no *female* genitals but does not point to absence of a penis). Indeed, Haitzmann's devil is as much female as male. What this truly signifies, they argue, is that Haitzmann's neurotic fantasy derives not from repressions stemming from the Oedipal phase but from pre-Oedipal psychic stirrings produced long before the infant is aware of gender differentiation, produced at a time when the child might see ambisexuality as normal. At this stage when the infant consciousness is pre-sexual and pre-phallic, it is primarily concerned (they contend) with the problem of life and its origins, and sees new life (babies) being engendered not by the successful resolution of sexual conflict but out of oneself or quasi-magically. Hence the androgynous nature of the devil; hence also Haitzmann's fantasies of feeding and being fed, and the clear importance of mother-figures to him, not least the fact that he goes to be healed at the shrine of the Blessed Virgin Mary.

Macalpine and Hunter's reading respects the evidence more than Freud's does. But their own preoccupations with Haitzmann's alleged fantasies of gestation, with the repetition of the concept of 'nine', and with the breasted devil are no less *parti pris*. And above all, the very attempt to throw shafts of light upon Haitzmann's own psyche by the analysis of such tiny and inconclusive scraps of evidence seems a forlorn and foredoomed enterprise. Haitzmann was worried about temptation, being evil, being doomed. Saddling Haitzmann with gender ambiguity, gestation fantasies and dilemmas over creativity tells us no more about him than does the claim that he was fixated on his father.

All these psychiatric techniques of isolating figures like Haitzmann, putting them on the couch and diagnosing their problems can indeed become positively perverse. For doing so withdraws attention from the social, cultural, institutional and linguistic environments which gave all their actions meaning. And what Haitzmann's life-story does reveal very clearly is not his personal psychopathology, but rather the assumptions and procedures routinely deployed in that society to make public sense of the trials of life: the notions of God and the Devil, of the Church, of heaven and hell. In their own practice, psychoanalysts do not believe that they have to show why their patients have a need – indeed, a neurotic need – to fantasize the very institution of psycho-therapy as a defence–displacement–projection of their own troubles. It is simply there as a cultural 'given' of modern society. No more do we need special explanations of Haitzmann's own 'therapeutic' resorts, such as the Devil. Haitzmann simply subscribed to the 'givens' of his own times.

Freud throws down a challenge. 'If a person does not believe in psycho-analysis, nor even in the Devil, he must be left to make what he can of the painter's case.' True. But does that pose any great problem? For what Haitzmann did, and said he did, was not that uncommon. Isolated 'poor folk' like Haitzmann were widely believed to commune with the Devil to provide them with a source of strength, albeit an ambiguous one: the female equivalent was the witch's resort to diabolical powers. The idea of selling your soul to the Devil – the Faust myth – was in one way or another a story familiar to all, a tale, a spiritual diagnosis Haitzmann could present to the Church authorities knowing that they would then be able to make sense of his troubles and his needs. The battles which Haitzmann saw in his visions between the temptations of the world and the duties of renunciation were abolutely central to Christianity itself.

The best sense that we can make of Haitzmann's case is thus to say that it should be seen not as one of individual psychopathology, but as one reflect-ing collective mythology embodied in institutions such as the Church. He is not a great personal puzzle but rather a representative figure in a standard scenario. It is not unlikely that one of the factors which made Haitzmann's 'rescue' possible was precisely the fact that he was not labelled 'mad' ('neuro-tic', 'schizophrenic'), and thus not treated as a parlous case. Rather by being seen as bedevilled by alien evil forces outside himself, he was readily absorbed within structures of remedy. It may be noteworthy – if we choose to follow through Freud's own comparison – that Haitzmann ended up happily in the convent, tormented by the Devil only when drunk, whereas Schreber endured nine terrifying years in the asylum, suffering acute isolation partly at least because none of the psychiatric authorities would give the slightest authentication to the terms (religious persecution) in which he himself exper-ienced his 'psychosis'.

The effectiveness of religion as a set of beliefs and practices for handling grave personal crises shows clearly in Haitzmann's case. It is also visible in the practices of the seventeenth-century parson–physician, Richard Napier, as studied by Michael MacDonald. Napier personally called upon the angel Raphael for medical advice. It surfaces also in the life of George Trosse. Trosse, who grew up in Exeter at the time of the Civil War, wrote his life story in 1692–3 when he was in his early sixties. It was in the classic mould of Puritan spiritual autobiography, as best epitomized by John Bunyan's *Grace Abounding to the Chief of Sinners*. The genre told a story of youthful indifference or sinfulness, an unthinking rebellion against God, leading to satanic temptation and even possession, culminating in crisis. The providential outcome of this was, however, eventual conversion, and a mature life spent walking in the paths of righteousness.

As Patricia Spacks has stressed in her *Imagining a Self*, the Puritan spiritual autobiography is by definition a success story. What made Trosse's *apologia* distinctive, though not unique, is that his crisis took the form not merely of an acknowledgement of sin, wickedness and debauchery, a traumatic emotional experience, the rebirth of a regenerated person, the sinner reformed, but rather of a full-blown episode of insanity, involving medical treatment and confinement. Trosse regarded his religious madness not (as fashionable theorists of his time – the age of the scientific revolution – increasingly did) as a physical disorder, producing wild symptomatic delusions, but rather as a literal psychomachy, a fight between God and Satan for possession of his soul.

Born in Exeter in 1631, Trosse came from a wealthy and prominent family of lawyers, Anglican in its confession and royalist in its politics. Looking back from the standpoint of a Presbyterian patriarch ripe in years, Trosse denounced his youth as a veritable Sodom of sin. Once he had been, he tells us, a 'very Atheist', an 'enemy to Puritans', who had followed every 'cursed carnal principle' that had fired his lusts.

Pricked by 'a Roving Fancy, a Desire to get Riches, and to live luxuriously in the World', he chose to travel abroad as an apprentice merchant, so that he could enjoy to his fill the pleasures of the 'unregenerate World, the Lusts of the Flesh, the Lusts of the Eyes, and the Pride of Life'. In thrall to 'a blind Mind, a foolish Fancy, and a graceless Heart', he was led into 'great Sins and dangerous Snares'. Living amidst the abomination of popery in France and Portugal, he neglected all religion, and instead followed the paths of drunkenness and sexual dalliance (he had indulged in 'the most abominable Uncleannesses' short of 'compleat Acts of Fornication'). A spell of business working in London led him to toy with a relative who was betrothed to a merchant abroad. So lost was his life that even bouts of near-fatal illness had not led him to think on death and perdition, or on the merciful Providence which had spared him. Eventually he returned to his home town, as a notorious and persistent sinner against all the Commandments, suffering above all from a drunkenness and wantonness which had blinded his mind and hardened his heart. He sinned, he recalled, 'as a Devil and a raging Furie', though of course he had given no thought to his own abominations.

At last, in the lower depths, a crisis arrived. After one particularly gross bout of drunkenness, after which he was put to bed 'more like a hog than a man', he awoke the next morning hearing 'some rushing kind of noise' and seeing a 'shadow' at the foot of his bed. 'I was seiz'd with great Fear and Trembling'. He heard a voice asking 'Who art thou?' Sure it must be the voice of God, he contritely replied, 'I am a very great Sinner, Lord!' Trosse fell to his knees and prayed. The voice proceeded: 'Yet more humble; yet more humble.' Trosse pulled off his stockings, to pray upon his bare knees. The voice continued. He pulled off his hose and doublet. Warned he still was not low enough, he found a hole in the floor where a plank was missing and crept within, praying there while covering himself in dust and dirt.

The voice then commanded him to cut off his hair, and he anticipated it would next tell him to cut his own throat. At this point spiritual illumination suddenly dawned. The voice was not God's but the Devil's. He knew he had 'greatly offended', and finally heard a voice, which he took to be the Holy Ghost, telling him 'Thou Wretch! Thou has committed the Sin against the Holy-Ghost' – the sin which Bunyan feared he had committed. Falling into despair (knowing that the sin against the Holy Ghost is unpardonable) he wanted to do nothing but curse God and die. His head became filled with a babel of clamouring voices, making a 'Torment of my Conscience', and he took a fancy in his wickedness to a peculiarly sinful thought, induced by his 'malicious will' – the notion that in his own hopeless, wretched, damned state, he could himself actually 'torment the Almighty and Unchangeable God' through 'this Blasphemy and desperate Enmity against God'.

Possessed by further voices and visions – gremlins, great claws appearing on the wall and so forth – he fell into an utterly 'distracted condition'. His friends, fortunately, knew of a physician in Glastonbury who was 'esteem'd very skilful and successful in such cases'. They carried him there by main force, strapped to a horse. He resisted with all his might, believing he was being dragged down into the 'regions of hell'. On the journey voices taunted him by saying 'What, must he go yet farther into hell? O fearful, O dreadful!' The Devil, Trosse later recalled, finally took full possession of him.

They reached the madhouse. He identified it with hell, and quite literally regarded its chains and fetters as satanic torments and torture, seeing fellow patients as his 'executioners'. Eventually, however, though long seeking 'revenge and rebellion' against God, he began to grow more tranquil, resigned, composed. This was largely thanks to the doctor's wife, Mrs Gollop, 'a very religious woman', who would soothe and pray with him. At first this comfort was no better than 'water spilt upon the rocks' but gradually it took effect, and his 'delusions, distractions and blasphemies' began to subside. Eventually 'I bewail'd my sins', and he was thought to have recovered enough to return to Exeter.

Alas! He proved to be no better than the proverbial dog to his vomit, returning to his old ways with 'aggravated Recidivations'. This time, however, the fight with the Tempter was at least more in the open. On the one hand, he pursued 'lewd and lascivious actions'. On the other, he applied to godly ministers, such as the Presbyterian Thomas Ford, for guidance for removing his 'great load of guilt'. Self-trapped in this renewed torment, he was carried to the Glastonbury physician once again. There Trosse 'rag'd against God' and 'thought myself in Hell', believing again that he had sinned against the Holy Ghost. But the doctor 'reduc'd [me] again to a Composedness and Calmness of Mind'.

Even then, his regeneration and conversion were not complete. Trosse now possessed religion, yet his faith was but 'Pharisaical'. He backslid into unspecified folly and licentiousness. He was persuaded to return for a third time to Glastonbury. Finally, and this time permanently, 'God was pleas'd, after all my repeated Provocations, to restore me to Peace and Serenity, and the regular Use of my Reason.' On reflection, the main source of his cure and conversion had been Mrs Gollop: 'she has been the prime Instrument both of the health of my Body and the Salvation of my Soul'.

Trosse was a man reborn. He went off to study at Oxford. He was now powerful enough to overcome dreams which were the Devil's temptations. With God's assistance, he assured himself that he was called to the ministry, and at the great Ejection of 1662 – the expulsion of old Puritans from the Church of England – became a Nonconformist. The rest of his career was spent as a Dissenting minister in Exeter, sometimes undergoing a measure of persecution – such as occasional imprisonment – for his convictions.

The Trosse who looked back on his life and penned his autobiography had a very clear-cut concept of the religious significance of madness. Reason was walking in harmony with God. Madness was that state of mind when the soul, possessed or obsessed by the Devil, railed and blasphemed against the Almighty. Trosse seems to have had no concept of positive holy madness. Madness was thus a desperate, negative condition, but it played a vital function in the redemption of souls, because it brought a sinner's evils out into the open, into a state of crisis. It provided at least a prelude to recovery.

Trosse, one might say, was a fortunate man, supported by friends and a helpful asylum. He came to believe himself redeemed, being finally assured of his ability to distinguish the true voice of God from the temptations of the Devil. He never looked back. But for many sincere believers, seeking after a sign, God's voice and providential finger remained more obscure. They were uncertain whether the dreams they dreamed and the voices they heard were God's, Satan's or merely their own sick fantasizings.

These dilemmas over what were true and what were merely deceptive inner experiences created immense chaos – chaos for the individual, but also for whole congregations and for society at large, uncertain whether those smitten by the outward marks of religious madness were truly saints, the worst of sinners or just sick. Partly for this reason, for many the whole concept of Christian madness – ever ambiguous – came under a cloud. Surely divine wisdom would not use such an uncertain and dangerous medium for revealing His Word and Will to His people? Surely God in His mercy would not subject believers' consciences to such excruciating torments and allow the Devil to delude? Increasingly, so opinion-leaders argued in the rational and tolerant eighteenth century, it seemed more likely that such tormented souls were truly possessed neither by God nor indeed by Satan, but rather by misconception, disorder or malady. Those who ranted and raved in the name of God, who wailed out in church or fell into fits while listening to sermons, were increasingly seen as objects of pity. They were sick; they needed treatment. They were in the grip of 'religious melancholy'.

That was a diagnosis commonly pinned on those Methodists and Evangelicals who formed a rising force in mid-eighteenth-century England: the phrase 'Methodistically mad' became something of a catchphrase amongst those who, feeling sorry for the simple serving maids all too commonly thrown into fits by Wesley's hellfire preaching and sometimes driven to suicide, were contemptuous of the canting Wesleys and Whitefields who fanned such hysteria. Little wonder that William Cowper – as quoted at the opening of this chapter – suspected that his own mode of faith would have been thought to be mad. For not only was he a close friend of John Newton, one of the most emotionally volatile of all the early Evangelicals (a man, noted Southey, notorious for 'preaching people mad'). Not only had he undergone a full-blown conversion experience. But he had actually undergone it, rather like Trosse, while in a madhouse, recovering from what even he admitted was a terrible bout of insanity.

Cowper's immensely sad existence was stained with mental disturbance of the melancholy kind (as he put it, the thread of his life had a sable strand woven into it). He suffered five distinct severe breakdowns, during some of which he tried to take his own life. The first came early in his twenties; the last set in when he was sixty-three and dogged him to the end of his days. And even in between these episodes, the black mark of despair was rarely very far away, sometimes kept at bay only by enforced sociability, application and activity (for Cowper, writing verse was quintessentially occupational therapy, to stave off the idleness which led to melancholy).

Cowper's disturbance was never a poetic fiction; it never smacked of the modish *penseroso* persona so common amongst super-sensitive artistic souls suffering from the 'English malady' in that age of syrupy sensibility. Rather it communicates itself, through his letters, poems and autobiographical recollections, as the most terrifying and crushing burden, eventually culminating in a profound desire never to have been born. It overwhelmed him with anguished feelings of hopelessness and abandonment, a cast-iron certainty of being damned in Samuel Johnson's sense of the term (being 'sent to hell and punished everlastingly').

Attempts have been made from various twentieth-century viewpoints to diagnose Cowper's condition. James Hendrie Lloyd resolved the whole problem in a few words. 'The case is probably best described as a form of circular insanity, with alternating phases of profound depression and mild hypomanic reaction, but without distinct intervals of complete sanity. . . . It was a constitutional psychosis.' Good to know. R.R.Madden thought that the answer lay in the guts. He speculated in particular that Cowper may have suffered from some organic disease, akin to dyspepsia – why else would Cowper have complained so much about his digestion? If only some doctor had put Cowper's stomach to rights, thought Madden, he would have been spared the agonies of the soul.

Others have puzzled whether some embarrassing physical defect perhaps created that shyness and solitariness which so plagued Cowper and made him feel like a lone tree on a hill. Early in the nineteenth century the diarist Charles Greville obliquely recorded that Cowper had apparently been a 'hermaphrodite' (but what exactly did that term mean to Greville?). And it is well known that Dr William Heberden reported a case of a man who castrated himself, the facts of which fit Cowper. The hypothetical presence of some abnormality of the sexual organs (possibly self-inflicted) could perhaps account for the fact that on the one occasion when Cowper became engaged to be married, he rapidly plunged into another of his insane episodes, and the engagement was called off. But this seems destined to remain no more than speculation.

More convincing amongst these attempts, perhaps, are psychodynamic hypotheses. Cowper's enduring sense of isolation and abandonment may well have been connected with his childhood distance from his parents. His mother, whom he remembered as 'most indulgent', died when he was six. He was soon sent away to school, and never seems to have been emotionally close to his parson father. Indeed Cowper specifically recorded an anguished childhood episode in which his father got him to read the arguments contained in Montesquieu's *Lettres Persanes* in favour of the legitimacy of suicide; and when Cowper junior attempted to refute them, his father did not back his efforts. One may surmise that Cowper perhaps feared this meant that his father would not object if he were to kill himself.

Cowper's stepmother hardly receives a mention.

Cowper seems to have found close attachments hard to make. This was possibly as a result of a lack of close early bonding. When he fell in love as a young man, it was, possibly significantly, with his cousin Theodora; and then he had the mortifying experience of her father vetoing the relationship – it is not certain why. It must have confirmed to Cowper the fragility of aspirations to intimacy – and confirmed this to Theodora too, who grew melancholy herself and, evidence suggests, ended up, almost as in a maudlin novel, confined in the very lunatic asylum which Cowper himself had once occupied. Cowper was grief-stricken: 'Oh that the ardour of my first love had continued!' When later he became engaged, in his early forties, to the widowed Mrs Unwin, it was to a woman he habitually likened unto a true mother to himself.

Did Cowper *himself* see any connection between his later griefs and some childhood want of intimacy with his parents? There is no final answer. There is not the slightest evidence that Cowper, unlike say John Perceval, ever *blamed* his parents or relatives for his morbid melancholy. His own relationship with his elder brother John grew close and supportive, and his *Adelphi*, his memoir of the two brothers, told a pious story of how John had been the agent of his rescue and ultimate conversion when he had run mad, while he, William, had succeeded in converting John when *he* was approaching his deathbed. One particular letter, however, loosely suggests that some link existed in Cowper's mind between family emotions and his mental illness. Looking back in a letter written in 1788, he recounted the deaths of his father and stepmother, and immediately went on to say that these losses had been followed in short order by his own loss of spirits.

Be that as it may, Cowper himself overwhelmingly understood his own sea of 'troubles of mind' in terms of his religious life, a believer's quest for assurance of salvation in a world of sin ensnared by Satan. Cowper's insanity is a tale of two quite distinct, chronologically sequential, spiritual experiences: the first an account of ultimately 'good' religious madness, the second a saga of 'bad' madness. The first we are familiar with from a memoir Cowper wrote in the late 1760s, almost at the halfway stage of his life. (It was not published until after his death.) This was a narrative following the pattern of the classic spiritual autobiography. It portrayed the hero sinking ever deeper into the slough of sin, falling into Satan's clutch, undergoing crisis and finally becoming a convert to the truth thanks to saving grace. For the Cowper of this tale, madness was a providential medium, an instrument of 'regeneration'.

He had no idea that within just a few years of his conversion, all his confidence would evaporate, for ever. The terrors and despair of his earlier crisis returned, multiplied and deepened in a series of further crises from 1773 onwards, as inky depression and conviction of indelible doom took possession of his whole existence. We know about the mad bouts of these years from letters he wrote at the time (and even more so, if frustratingly negatively, from letters he didn't write: for example, for four years, between 1773 and 1776, the normally almost garrulous Cowper seems to have written no letters at all). A brief spiritual journal – a descent into hell – survives from towards the close of his life, though the last five years of all but unremitting depression are almost wholly marked by silence.

There are thus two madnesses for Cowper. There is madness mastered, a madness with a meaning in a providential scheme. And then there is a madness insupportable and incomprehensible.

Cowper's first madness was a prelude to his Evangelical conversion. Despite having a clergyman for a father, despite going to Westminster School, he grew up, he tells us in his *Memoir*, little better than a pagan. God made continual attempts to show young Cowper the path of true religion. When he was terrifyingly bullied at school, he learned to cope with affliction through having a text from the Psalms leap into his mind: 'I will not be afraid of what man can do unto me'; but the divine lesson was soon forgotten. When as a youth he had proud and profane rebellious intimations that he might be immortal in the flesh, God smote him – but smote him mercifully with smallpox and with a consumptive disposition, as manifestations of His power and of man's frailty. But (Cowper recalled) the lessons were lost on him: he grew up in 'total forgetfulness of God'.

When Cowper fell into his first profound bout of melancholy in 1753 – he was then in his early twenties – his shallow companions warned him off religious exercises, lest they make him morbid. He took a trip to Southampton and recovered. No wiser than a heathen, Cowper attributed his cure to the change of scene and the sea air. In reality, he recalled in his *Memoir*, it was the mercy of Providence which worked his recovery. Cowper then frittered away his time and his talents in his twenties as a young man-about-town, living at the Temple, going through the charade of the study of law. Further Providences were revealed to him – he narrowly escaped injury in a shooting accident, débris from a building just missed his head – but he took no heed at the time, remaining hard-hearted and indifferent.

Eventually, in 1763, a crisis loomed. Cowper needed employment and income. His uncle, Major Ashley Cowper, controlled some patronage in the appointment of the clerkship to the journal of the House of Lords. Cowper solicited the post. He secretly wished for the present incumbent's death – and the man died! Cowper was overcome by remorse and guilt. As he retrospectively saw it, 'It pleased the Lord to give me my heart's desire, and in it, and with it, an immediate punishment for my crimes.' As a result of office politics, it then transpired that Cowper could not after all be appointed to the post unless he underwent an examination *viva voce* before the Lords. He studied to acquire the skills needed for the post, but grew ever more convinced of his own utter incapacity. Increasingly trembling at the prospect of the examination (which he saw as a 'judgement'), Cowper became paralysed with fear. He had to escape, but how could he? Madness, he says, was 'the only chance remaining'.

But at this point Satan stole upon the scene. The Tempter insinuated the idea of suicide into his head. He recalled how his father had never dissuaded him from suicide; an apparently chance conversation with a stranger in a tavern further helped convince him that suicide was a legitimate course of action. That the act might be sinful never crossed his mind. He bought laudanum, but when on several occasions he attempted to swallow the lethal drug, he became paralysed thanks to the intervention of an 'invisible hand' acting beyond his control (today we would of course say his unconscious took a hand). Abandoning poison, he decided to drown himself in the Thames. He arrived however at low water, and found himself observed by lightermen. He changed his mind, decided to hang himself, rushed home and strung himself up by his garter. As he lapsed into unconsciousness he heard a voice say, ''Tis over'; but later he awoke to find himself sprawled on the floor, his neck swollen and bruised. The sash had snapped at the crucial instant. His uncle was called in. He pronounced his nephew unfit for the post. Cowper was off the hook.

It was at this moment, for the first time, that Cowper, having gained his desire, was seized with religious guilt. Not till then had the element of ungodly rebellion in suicide struck him. Now he was consumed with an overwhelming sense of 'God's wrath' directed specifically against himself. Surely he must be uniquely the worst of sinners? He paced up and down in his room, repeating to himself, 'there never was so abandoned a wretch; so great a sinner'. He hardly dared go out. When he did, he fancied that 'the people stood and laughed at me, and held me in contempt'; the 'eyes of man I could not bear'. He felt deserted, rejected, a monster. He combed theology convinced that he had probably committed the unpardonable sin, that unique blasphemy against the Holy Ghost which, biblical scholars agreed, put a sinner beyond the bounds of forgiveness and mercy. (Cowper seems initially to have thought the sin lay in the pharisaical act of ascribing works of Providence to mere natural causes, for, on reflection, he recalled that he had falsely attributed his recovery at Southampton to the ozone.)

Collapsing into hopeless, boundless self-incriminating despair, Cowper was filled with the 'sense of sin and the expectation of punishment'. He had uplifting conversations with his brother and his Evangelical cousin, Martin Madan. Eventually, ever more alienated from God, 'wild and incoherent', he was taken by John to the lunatic asylum at St Albans run by Dr Nathaniel Cotton, a medical doctor of Methodist leanings. Cowper recalls he went 'gladly'.

For eight months Cowper languished in Cotton's Collegium Insanorum under the most profound conviction of sin. He was a 'tophet of pollution', ever 'ungrateful'. Hourly, he expected 'fatal vengeance', the final destructive thunderbolt. He tried suicide again with a bare bodkin.

But at this point his brother John was able to offer reassurance. Might not this certainty of vengeance itself be a 'delusion', a facet of insanity? 'Oh, if this be a delusion,' William responded, 'then am I the happiest of men.' Once more, God showed His merciful providences. This time, humbled from foolish pride into the miseries of madness, Cowper heeded them. He had a divine vision of being pavilioned under a cupola of radiance, seeing 'glory all around'. Then, after attempting to convince a doubting Thomas of an asylum servant of the reality of special Providence, they experienced an exemplary thunderstorm in which a 'fiery hand clenching a bolt or arrow of lightning' appeared in the sky, hurling down lightning flashes to earth, but sparing them. One day, while he was flicking through the Bible – a book he had long neglected – Providence directed him to St Paul's Epistle to the Romans which spoke of his Saviour 'whom God has set forth to be a propitiation through faith in his blood, to declare his righteousness for the remission of sins that are past, through the forbearance of God'. The scales fell from his eyes. The text convinced him of Christ's atonement and forgiveness. Finally, in a dream, Cowper saw a radiant boy come dancing up to him.

Cumulatively these experiences worked a conversion and brought an epiphany. The burden of sin was lifted. Cowper felt redeemed by Christ. Thanks to his assurance of grace, he would be saved. His sanity returned. His madness had been a divine 'chastisement'; the madhouse, the 'instrument' of his 'reformation', became the scene of his 'second nativity'. Spiritual conversations with Dr Cotton (a man whom 'I love') restored him to a state in which he could face the world. Because he supplied spiritual solace and succour as well as medicine, some would say (Cowper confessed) that Cotton's behaviour was as crazy as his own.

After a year and a half inside, Cotton pronounced his patient 'cured', and Cowper was free to leave. Taking Cotton's own servant boy with him, he got lodgings in Huntingdon, to be near his brother who was a fellow of Bene't College – today's Corpus Christi College – in Cambridge. He grew friendly with an Evangelical family, the Rev. Morley Unwin and his wife

Mary. He began to board with them. On Morley's death, he remained on terms of intimate spiritual friendship with Mary. They moved together to Olney in 1767, partly to be near the Evangelical John Newton, who became their spiritual guide. Finding security in 'submission' after so much 'mutiny', Cowper was confident in the Lord: 'He has never left me, since he first found me, no, not for a moment. I know that the Everlasting Arm is underneath me, and the Eternal God is my refuge. O blessed state of a believing soul.' In the Unwin household ('a place of rest prepared for me by God's own hand'), Cowper wrote his Olney Hymns and penned his *Memoir* as an act of thanksgiving, recording his spiritual conversion.

Poor Cowper. God had a terrible fate in store. For someone who had thus felt, at long last, so rescued and secure, the precipitate loss of that sense of salvation by the early 1770s must have been doubly excruciating. We have few details of what precisely befell him. Cowper had busied himself in parish evangelizing; he seems to have found his part in these missionary activities somewhat phoney. A letter written in 1773 by Mary Unwin speaks of his fresh 'delusions' and 'temptations' (i.e. to suicide). Writing over ten years later, Cowper himself noted a dream in February 1773, 'before the recollection of which, all consolation vanishes'. In this, the terrible words were pronounced to him: *'actum est de te, periisti'* ('it is all over with you; you have perished'). Somehow, Cowper had come to think – first in a dream, but then as an *idée fixe* dominating his waking thoughts – that God had abandoned him, revealing a doom of predestined eternal punishment awaiting him at his death. Cowper was now no better than a prisoner in the condemned cell. He later dreamed that he was awaiting execution.

There is no sign that Cowper ever again shook off this conviction of irrevocable damnation. There were to be no further bouts of *therapeutic* madness, agencies for renewed conversions. At best Cowper endured long periods of suspended sentence, in which, breath bated, he successfully shielded himself from his terrors by cultivating a domesticity surrounded by civilized admirers such as Mary Unwin, Lady Hesketh, Lady Austen and, later in life, his fellow oversensitive man of letters, William Hayley. He gardened, tamed hares, and, above all, he wrote. But all these were no more than strategies of delay. And occasionally he spun dizzyingly down again into the depths of despair.

We catch just those merest snatches of the 'terrible malady' which he occasionally recorded. 'I can hope nothing – believe nothing – I am, and have long been, the most miserable of the human race,' he wrote. His melancholy becomes a 'companion for life'; there is no escaping: in a dream his doctor prescribes to him 'death as the only alternative to madness'. The blackness is quite 'insupportable'. Only constant employment, he confesses, can keep him from the depths of despair. Even his lighter verse may betray his condition. 'John Gilpin', beneath its infectiously jocular surface, is a tale of an innocent who becomes ever more conspicuously absurd and the target of derision. Never does Cowper entertain the slightest fantasy that madness confers on him great poetic powers. He wrote to keep madness away. For him, unlike his contemporaries Kit Smart and William Blake, madness and the muse were essentially at odds.

A downward spiral sets in from the late 1780s. His nights are the worst, for his dreams are full of terrors. He fears sleep. He becomes sleepless. But, sleepless, he cannot accomplish the writing which keeps his phantoms at bay during the day. So he begins to dose himself with opium and laudanum to induce sleep. But these drugs almost certainly in turn multiplied the horrors of his nightmares, as they did so alarmingly in Coleridge's case just a few years later.

For long stretches of the 1780s and 1790s, despair, dejection and despondency filled his waking moments. He had become convinced that 'it is not possible that He should save whom He has declared He will destroy'; whatever happens, 'I shall perish.' But the tone of his nightmares is all the worse, quite Bergmanesque. He writes in 1792 to his confidant, the schoolmaster Samuel Teedon:

> I have had a terrible night – such a one as I believe I may say God knows
> no man ever had. Dream'd that in a state of the most insupportable misery
> I look'd through the window of a strange room being all alone, and saw
> preparations making for my own execution. That was but about four days
> distant, and that then I was destined to suffer everlasting martyrdom in
> the fire, my body being prepared for the purpose and my dissolution made
> a thing impossible. Rose overwhelmed with infinite despair, and came
> down into the study execrating the day when I was born with inexpressible
> bitterness. And while I write this, I repeat those execrations, in my very
> soul persuaded that I shall perish miserably and as no man ever did. Every
> thing is, and for 20 years, has been, lawful to the Enemy against *me*.

The rest of that day, Cowper concluded, was quite 'unfit for description'.

What of course is so appalling about Cowper's sense of doom is the identity of the 'Enemy'. It is not Satan; it is God Himself. From his collapse in 1773, Cowper had convinced himself that, as a result of his committing the unforgivable sin, God had become an implacably vengeful foe. It appears that Cowper had believed that God had commanded him at that time to commit suicide. His failure to do so had proved an unforgivable, indelible disobedience – had turned, indeed, in Cowper's mind, into the true nature of the unpardonable sin upon which he had earlier reflected. His spiritual diary for 1795 – a year which found him as 'hopeless as ever' – tries to evaluate the appalling dilemma within which the Almighty had entrapped him. Cowper pleaded:

> What opportunities of Suicide had I, while there was Hope, except a most miserable moment, in 73? That moment lost, all that follow'd was as sure as necessity itself could make it. . . . Oh monstrous dispensation! I cannot bear the least part of what is coming upon me, yet am forced to meet it with my eyes open'd wide to see its approach, and destitute of all means to escape it.

The Creator had trapped him in a ghastly snare; 'it is I who have been the hunted hare,' for 'I perish as I do, that is, as none ever did, for non-performance of a task, which I know by after-experience to have been *naturally* impossible.' How could he 'have deserved so terrible a doom'? If judgement itself were just, that particular 'Judgement was infinitely disproportionate to Mercy'. The Creator would have shown Himself 'infinitely more merciful had he never made me at all'. For the deutero-Cowper, to be mad was simply to live in the unbearable tragedy which God had called the creation. 'I have been a poor Fly entangled in a thousand webs from the beginning.'

Cowper's blackness through the 1790s did not significantly differ from the mood he temporarily experienced during his collapse in 1763. In his earlier despair, he could cry out in his 'Lines Written During a Period of Insanity':

> Hatred and vengeance, my eternal portion,
> Scarce can endure delay of execution,
> Wait, with impatient readiness, to seize my
> > Soul in a moment.
>
> Damn'd below Judas: more abhorr'd than he was,
> Who for a few pence sold his holy Master.
> Twice betrayed Jesus me, the last delinquent,
> > Deems me the profanest.

An identical sense of isolation and of utter hopelessness unto death formed the message of his last poem, 'The Cast-Away', composed in 1799, only months before his death. It moves from the literal fate of a drowning seaman to his own, infinitely worse, spiritual condition:

> Obscurest night involved the sky
> Th'Atlantic billows roar'd
> When such a destined wretch as I
> Wash'd headlong from on board

101

Of friends, of hope, of all bereft,
His floating home for ever left. . . .

No voice divine the storm allay'd
No light propitious shone;
When, snatch'd from all effectual aid,
We perish'd, each alone;
But I beneath a rougher sea,
And whelm'd in deeper gulphs than he.

The anguish of isolation pervades almost all of Cowper's later thoughts; he is cast out, the castaway; he is alien and excluded; he is the blasted fig-tree. He is furthermore frail and frozen, incapable of action, perpetually imperilled in a dangerous world: the drowning mariner, the sinking ship in the storm, 'tempest-toss'd and wrecked'. Above all, he is the victim of gratuitous cruelty, rejected, deserted, disowned, disavowed, abandoned (in all senses of the word): the stricken deer left by the herd, sport of misfortune, everybody's prey.

Some recent scholars have analysed all this in terms of modern notions of personality disorder. For Patricia Spacks, Cowper oozes self-pity, and is a master manipulator of his inadequacy; he projects, she argues, a 'helpless passivity', forever seeking 'to avoid responsibility' for his actions, indeed engaging in a 'masochistic indulgence of fear'. He cherishes his isolation because that makes him special. His humility is inverted egoism, so much disguised pride, a manifestation of what Cowper himself calls the 'Monster Self'.

Such interpretations have their point – though they may also be seen as further cruelty, beyond the grave! But that point fades into insignificance when placed in context of Cowper's story of the God that failed. The most terrible form of religious madness occurs when the God one had worshipped plays one false.

6 · Mad Women

The opening page of what is effectively the very first autobiography in the English language presents an account of a woman going mad. 'When this creature was twenty years of age, or somewhat more,' wrote Margery Kempe – or rather dictated, since she, like most late medieval women, was illiterate – 'she was married to a worshipful burgess and was with child within a short time, as nature would have it.' She was sick during pregnancy and, after childbirth, puerperal insanity evidently set in. 'She despaired of her life [and] sent for her confessor,' for 'she was continually hindered by her enemy – the devil'. She believed she was damned. 'Because of the dread she had of damnation on the one hand, and [Satan's] sharp reproving of her on the other, this creature went out of her mind and was amazingly disturbed and tormented with spirits for half a year, eight weeks and odd days.'

We might assume that Margery Kempe's life set a pattern, and that a steady stream of mad women thereafter penned accounts of their tribulations. After all, we have been inundated this century with writing by disturbed and distracted women, some of it masquerading as fiction though essentially factual. Indeed, a 'special relationship' is highly visible in contemporary culture, establishing sets of affinities between mental and emotional disturbance, psychiatry and women. Many more women than men end up today under psychiatric care and in psychiatric institutions, or simply taking Valium. In turn, this may be because what is still an essentially patriarchal society places women under special strains, or at least uses psychiatry as a legitimating authority to bring the sex to heel (prison for men, the mental hospital for women, as is often said).

Certainly, ever since Charcot's and Freud's studies of hysterical women, it has paradoxically been the female unconscious and, by implication, the mystery of female sexuality which have been the inner sanctum of the psychiatric enterprise (the great question, thought Freud, was 'what do women want?'). In some sense, somatic diseases have become 'male', and mental

103

disorders 'female'. 'The female malady' is today the focus of attention in sexual and psycho-politics. The problems of being a woman in a man's world have led a disproportionate number of women to break down, and in turn have disproportionately preoccupied psychiatry.

Yet what is intriguing is how few self-portraits there are written by disturbed women during very long stretches of the past. Of course, women were never meant to speak for themselves. Differential rates of literacy and of the survival of evidence will count for something. But not for all. The period roughly speaking between the Reformation and the emergence of Romanticism – the epoch which saw the blossoming of autobiography as a genre – is as relatively lacking in writing by women recording or recalling their own journeys into the interior, as the last century and a half – the era of female emancipation – has been rich.

This is certainly not, of course, because during the early modern centuries women were pictures of mental health. Michael MacDonald's exemplary study of the casebooks of Richard Napier, the early-seventeenth-century Buckinghamshire doctor–parson, has shown that most of the clients attending him with what we would call mental problems – they called themselves 'distracted', 'disordered', 'melancholy' and so forth – were women. That is not surprising. They were bowed under by the weight of having to sustain multiple socio-economic functions – productive labour, running a household, raising a family. Moreover, the gynaecological problems of repeated dangerous childbirths eroded their health, both physical and mental. But practically all the writings by disturbed people which have come down to us from Napier's century are by men: those of James Carkesse, Goodwin Wharton, George Trosse, etc., and that whole crew of Puritan males who wrote within the tradition of the spiritual autobiography.

Another way of putting this is to point to the fact that for long the chief stereotypes of madness were quintessentially masculine. It is no accident that the twin symbols of insanity, the figures of Mania and Melancholia, straddling the portals to Bethlem were both male – indeed, were dubbed by Alexander Pope the 'Brainless Brothers'. Not surprisingly, Mania was thought of as a masculine disorder, personified in the ferocity of a brute. But the same was essentially true for traditional Melancholy as well. All the visual images of the melancholic festooning the title page of Burton's *Anatomy of Melancholy* (1621) – the superstitious religious melancholic, the hypochondriac, the melancholy lover, the misanthropic solitary or *penseroso* figure, and so forth – were pictured as men. Only with the coming of the age of sensibility from the mid-eighteenth century was disorder effectively 'feminized'.

In pre-Reformation times, what made female madness articulate was religion, or, more precisely, the specific forms through which medieval Christianity expressed itself. However patriarchal both medieval society and medieval Christendom were, special institutions and roles were set aside for women within the religious life and the Church – openings which were closed in later Protestant cultures. Above all, it was possible for some women to escape the routine cares of marriage and the dangers of motherhood by entering a cloister, where they might make their devotions to the service of spiritual replicas of the life they had escaped: the cults of God the Father and God the Son.

For the more zealous this could lead to highly intense and deeply spiritual experiences, sometimes soaring into mysticism. Christianity itself encouraged, while also insisting on setting strict limits to, ecstatic exercises such as mortification of the flesh and fasting. As Rudolph Bell has recently stressed in his *Holy Anorexia*, self-inflicted asceticism was occasionally carried to ambiguous extremes by holy women, who sometimes perhaps descended into a pathologically self-denying condition akin to today's *anorexia nervosa*. But it would serve no purpose to label the exercise of spiritual discipline as such a psychological disorder. For it was consonant with, indeed even an ideal of, the religious aspirations of the age, and it was regulated by the conscious control both of the individual ascetic and of ecclesiastical superiors. Mystical flights and contemplations were highly programmed activities.

It was against such a landscape dotted with holy women who had spiritually or physically renounced the world and devoted their lives to otherworldliness that the late-medieval Englishwoman, Margery Kempe, was able to make sense of her self, particularly in the aftermath of her madness. If what she got her scribe to write down for her in her *Life* (it is expressed in the third person) truly reflects what she felt and told people throughout her life (and there is no good reason to suspect it does not), she never sought to conceal that she had indeed been through an episode of madness in her early twenties. Strange experiences beset her later as well. Some of her actions, she admitted, were not those of 'reason'. She envisaged herself running around 'like a mad woman' or like 'a drunk woman'; she could think of herself 'without reason', living 'high above her bodily wits'. And she was kept acutely aware that her expressions of religious devotion – such as her incessant weeping, often for many hours at a time – were liable to be designated as crazy and believed to be caused either by the Devil or by a disease.

Margery never rejoiced in a celebration of madness as a positive, heaven-sent religious ecstasy. She was adamant that her chief bout of disturbance, after the birth of her first child, was a providential rap on the knuckles, brought upon her essentially because she was then a vainglorious, thoughtless and

105

proud young lady, vulnerable first to the temptations and then to the threats of the Devil. While mad, her conduct had been abominable; she had 'slandered' her husband and despaired of salvation. She did violence against herself and needed to be 'forcibly restrained both day and night'. She had forsaken God. By His infinite mercy, the Almighty had returned her to her 'right mind', rescued her from sin, and shown her His paths. Still she remained unregenerate, wedded to this world and its worldlings, and it took the business failure of the brewery she owned – her beer providentially all went flat – to humble her properly and teach her to turn from this wicked world to true holiness.

God's first warning had merely affected her head; the second penetrated her to the heart. Though subsequently leading a life which to many contemporaries appeared perverse and provocative, Margery Kempe did not present this way of life through the idiom of divine madness. On the contrary, she was insistent that her own conduct was regular and her faith orthodoxy itself. She had to be: she was living through an age when those who did not toe the religious line were readily accused of being heretical Lollards (proto-Protestants who proclaimed the sufficiency of the Bible and criticized the Church authorities for their corruption), and Lollards were often tried and sometimes burned.

Having undergone the twin crises of puerperal insanity and the failure of her business venture, Margery Kempe experienced a pressing desire to sever herself from all the ways of the world, convinced that, by contrast to conditions on earth, it was 'merry in heaven' (how did she know?, critics demanded). Breaking free involved some considerable wrench. She had been born around 1373, the daughter of a prosperous King's Lynn burgess (her father was successively mayor and MP of the town). She had a husband to whom she was lastingly, if unconventionally, attached, and by whom she had a growing family – she gave birth, all told, to fourteen children. She was in no position simply to renounce the world by entering into a nunnery: the authorities would never have permitted it.

As she was forcibly reminded time and again throughout the rest of her life, her attempts to follow what she saw as the divine signposts through life met enduring hostility. 'Woman, give up this life that you lead, and go and spin, and card wool, as other women do,' she was instructed by the worldlings and the authorities. Wherever she went there was such 'evil talk about her' that the cleric who took down her life story was even afraid of recriminations against himself.

Sickened by joys of the flesh, Margery began to campaign to free herself from bondage to the world. She fasted; she did bodily penance; she clad herself in a hairshirt. Above all in the midst of these mortifications, she strove to free herself from sexual slavery, knowing how the pleasures she and her husband had taken in carnal delights were offensive to God, and now finding them 'abominable' to herself. She told her husband she now loved God alone; His body alone was what she wanted, sacramentally, in a mystical marriage. She begged him to accept a pact of mutual chastity. He agreed in principle, but, echoing St Augustine, said not yet, and for long insisted upon having his will. Eventually they came to an agreement by which he signed away his conjugal rights in return for having Margery pay his debts.

Despite this apprentice mortification, she remained abysmally vainglorious. 'She thought that she loved God more than He loved her,' she was to recall. In that state, she was easy prey to the Devil's snares. He laid for her a trap of lechery. A man made advances to her. Flattered, she willingly surrendered, only at the last moment to be spurned by him. Mortified, she craved Christ's forgiveness; it was granted, and, in return, her Saviour promised her a life of wearing a hairshirt in her heart. As Christ had been persecuted, so should she be. Thereafter, tribulations were seen by Margery as secret signals of holiness. Life best made sense to her when battling with the moils and toils which constitute the bulk of her autobiography.

Her spiritual life began to blossom. She began seeing visions, and these were accompanied by the copious bouts of weeping which attended her to the end of her days. She started informally shriving penitents and acting as a mouthpiece for homely divine guidance. A 'miracle' secured her escape when a piece of masonry falling from a church struck her, but did not harm her. And, not least, Christ mercifully intervened to kill off her husband's sexual appetite for her. She told him she'd rather that he were dead than have to submit to his lusts, preferring to make herself 'freely available to God'. Her husband rebuked her: she was not a good wife. The general picture of their relationship given by the *Life* is, however, one of mutual understanding, support and charity.

Margery's increasingly conspicuous religious observances brought her public reproof. Her weeping bouts were despised, she was called 'false hypocrite', and her friends were advised to abandon her. Furthermore, she was accused of having the Devil in her and of being a 'false Lollard' ('and the people said, "Take her and burn her"'). But such trials merely enhanced her awareness of the divine indwelling. When she heard mention of Christ's Passion, she would swoon in ecstasy and experience divine music. The Lord called her His mother, His sister, His daughter, and she conversed – talking as in normal conversation, she insisted – with St Paul, St Peter and St Katherine.

Margery was initially perturbed. Were these voices and visions authentic? Or were they temptations of the Devil, or simply sensory delusions? Seeking guidance, she consulted Dame Julian of Norwich, the contemplative mystic. From her she received reassurance. These were not fantasies of her own devising but truly manifestations from God. Margery must persevere in her course of life: 'The more contempt, shame and reproof that you have in this world, the more is your merit in the sight of God.' Margery followed Dame Julian's words, which were reiterated by many sympathetic and 'honoured doctors of divinity, both religious men and others of secular habit'. Soon God was telling her that she would be the recipient of special revelations denied even to His own daughter Bridget, the Swedish mystic.

Reassured, Margery grew in confidence of her religious calling. Her holy circle grew, and she attained a reputation as a woman with a divine vocation. Her practical advice was sought by people anguished over the great decisions of life; she relayed to them God's answers. She acquired minor powers of prophecy. One day, she predicted a great storm. It came about. Many remained suspicious, and she continued to entertain great fears of 'delusions and deceptions by her spiritual enemies'. But God comforted her by saying that though he would load her with tribulations on earth, when in heaven she would be granted all her desires. At a later stage he told her that her earthly life would be the only purgatory she would ever be forced to undergo. Margery's conviction of divine love grew over the years. God informed her: 'to me you are a love unlike any other', and, later, 'you do not know how much I love you'. For her part, she wished that it had been God who had taken her virginity. Eventually, being now on 'homely terms with God', she had a 'wedding ring to Jesus Christ' made at divine command, with '*Jesus est Amor Meus*' inscribed on it. The love of God proved the shame of the world.

Eventually, she set off on pilgrimage for the Holy Land. This was, ironically, her one visit to Bethlehem. So joyful was she at seeing the holy sights that she nearly swooned and fell off her ass. And being so close to the scenes of Christ's Passion led her to weep and wail more than ever, and to 'wrestle with her body'. She was visited by a special vision of Christ's crucified body and was overwhelmed by an irresistible impulse to weep. She could not stop it; it was the 'gift of the Holy Ghost'. Her roaring and crying riled many of the other pilgrims. Some thought she was just ill-behaved, puffed up with 'pretence and hypocrisy', or physically sick, suffering from a form of epilepsy. Others accused her of drunkenness. Still others believed she had been possessed by an evil spirit.

It was a dilemma which continually faced her when her tears poured out her passion. On a later occasion, she records,

Many said there was never saint in heaven that cried as she did, and from that they concluded that she had a devil within her which caused that crying. And this they said openly, and much more evil talk. She took everything patiently for our Lord's love, for she knew very well that the Jews said much worse of His own person than people did of her, and therefore she took it the more meekly.

As she later put it, if it had been unavoidable that Christ's blood should flow, the least true believers should expect or want would be floods of their own lamentations. She asked God to grant her a 'well of tears', and to one who tetchily asked her 'Why do you weep so, woman?' she responded, 'Sir, you shall wish some day that you had wept as sorely as I.' What other behaviour could be so appropriate in this vale of tears? She knew her Psalter which assured her that 'They that sow in tears shall reap in joy.'

Apart from a further pilgrimage late in life to shrines in north Germany, Margery passed the rest of her days in England. She had undergone a formal religious ceremony binding herself and her husband in mutual chastity, and thereafter they lived apart. When her husband became old and senile, however, she returned to nurse him, against her own initial inclinations, but following God's advice. Meanwhile her religious reputation grew. She established good relations with numerous anchorites, contemplatives, scholars and other holy people. Many of these evidently read to her out of the corpus of mystical writings. Clearly, many ordinary Christians accepted her own special holiness, and were glad to have her weep for them.

Others were not so happy. Her fellow English pilgrims had found her a nuisance, with her continual wailing, her special dietary demands and her ceaseless moral and religious rebukes directed towards them. Sometimes they forced her to leave their party. Similar tribulations beset her in England. 'Evil talk' about her grew, and many said she had the Devil in her. Clerics and congregations deplored the way she constantly interrupted services and ceremonies by her weeping and wailing at the name of Jesus. A friar would not allow her to attend his sermons, claiming she was suffering from 'sickness'.

More seriously, she frequently ran the risk of imprisonment and ecclesiastical prosecution. Authorities both civil and religious naturally looked with considerable suspicion upon this wife and mother wandering around the country in the guise of a holy woman, berating people for their hypocrisy and ungodly ways, and sometimes urging wives to leave their husbands and follow God (God had informed her that many women, if only they could abandon their husbands, would love him the way she did). Her insistence upon wearing white linked her in the eyes of some with dubious flagellant groups, while others, including the Abbot of Leicester, accused her of being a 'false heretic', i.e. of involvement with Lollardy. 'She has the Devil in her,' she reported the 'clerics' as saying, 'for she speaks of the Gospel.' Under examination, however, her own faith proved triumphantly orthodox.

All the while, her love of God grew. She was privileged to overhear conversations about her between God the Father and the Son, and the Godhead informed her that he liked having someone such as her around to talk to. Her attention became fixed upon the 'manhood' of Christ, but it was the Godhead Himself who finally married her. The Father told her, 'I must be intimate with you and lie in your bed with you. ... take me to you as your wedded husband. ... Kiss my mouth, my head, and my feet as sweetly as you want.' The earlier sexual temptations which she had undergone were not, however, entirely a thing of the past, and in time she was visited by 'abominable visions', conjured up by the Devil, of being beset by threatening male genitals and being commanded to prostitute herself to them. Temporarily she felt forsaken by God, but recovered. At another point, she was overcome by a desire to kiss male lepers; her confessor advised her to stick to women.

How are we to assess Margery Kempe's life? One school of interpretation simply confirms the truth of her visions. Catholic writers such as Katherine Cholmeley have argued that because Margery's experiences conform so closely to those of other well-attested contemplatives and visionaries they must literally be true, and should be accepted at religious face value. Historically, such attempts to depict her as what we might idiomatically call a saint just beg all the questions, and prove hagiography not history.

The same applies, *mutatis mutandis*, to interpretations advanced by psychoanalytical sleuths, who (metaphorically speaking) seem bent on proving her a sinner. The truth about Margery Kempe, Trudy Drucker has argued, along these lines, is that she constituted a 'case of religious hysteria', occasionally overlaid with 'overtly psychotic' episodes. In a similar way Dr Anthony Ryle has diagnosed her as a case of 'hysterical personality organization with occasional "psychotic" episodes', during which she 'hallucinated about the sexuality of the males surrounding her'. She should best be seen, argues Drucker, as an 'unfortunate' who never recovered from puerperal fever, and who additionally suffered from other organic or hysterical conditions such as epilepsy and migraine. She indulged, moreover, in 'psychotic behavior', in particular a propensity to 'self-inflicted pain', which modern psychiatry associated with 'pathologic distortion of the sexual impulse'. Her hysteria was unconsciously designed to serve the 'protective function' of keeping her 'agonized and distorted sexuality' at bay; this was not always successful, however, concludes Drucker, and her 'disguised sexual fantasies and guilts' sometimes thrust their way to the surface.

Margery was thus a 'victim of hysteria', and some of its manifestations in her were 'repellent' and 'silly'. But this condition was not entirely her own fault, Drucker continues, because such hysteria is inevitable in ages when female sexuality is repressed. Nevertheless, hysteria afforded her many 'secondary gains', bestowing upon her 'unique attention' (she took a 'child-like pride in her attacks'). That is why Kempe 'resists any suggestion that her spells are of natural origin'. If she had accepted that view, she would have been demoted to being just 'another uninteresting sick woman'. The adult Margery should not simply be blamed for this vanity, however, for overall, behind her egoism, childhood events were responsible for her condition: 'probably the roots of her disease were buried deeply in childhood experiences thoroughly rejected by her adult recollection'. Alas, no talking cure was available to bring these to the surface and they remained 'past recall' and thus unrecorded.

Psychodynamic *post mortems* such as these seem trivial (for they amount to little more than affixing fancy labels on the unknown), gratuitously dogmatic (there is no reason in the absence of any shred of supportive evidence to attribute Margery's adult attitudes to childhood experiences), and, not least, harsh. They operate by identifying what are seen as psychological symptoms, and then turning them into moral verdicts which masquerade as medical diagnoses. When confronting abnormal experience, their blend of excusing and accusing isolates the individual and pays scant attention to the nexi of social, sexual and ideological pressures within which people's lives are led. It is an easy thing to speak authoritatively of Margery's 'distorted sexuality' (e.g. her wish to make her relationship with her husband chaste and to marry God); it is another to remember – as Drucker does not – that she bore her husband fourteen children, all but one apparently against her wishes. The absence of any substantial mention in her *Life* of her children surely indicates Margery's indifference to the motherhood which was thrust upon her. Likewise Drucker draws attention to Margery's anxieties about rape, suggesting that they are further symptoms of her hysterically distorted sexuality. She might have remembered that crossing Europe as a pilgrim can hardly have been a safe occupation for a woman. Phrases like 'distorted sexuality' and 'hysteria' are inevitably stigmatizing.

There is no master key to Margery's condition or way of reading her life (or her *Life*). She knew that many people thought her voices and visions – indeed, her whole course of life – signified madness, to be attributed to illness or the Devil. She pondered that dilemma deeply, and sought advice. But the path to which she aspired – a closer walk, a spiritual communion, marriage even with God – was a path legitimate within the beliefs of her times, though one of course exceptional and precarious. Margery wished, from early days, to free herself from a pattern of life (marriage, sex and childbirth) which had become associated by her with madness and the Devil's temptations. The numinal scenes into which she escaped of course replicated at a spiritual level the landmarks and values of the workaday world: marriage to God replaced marriage to her husband. But they did so in ways which to her were benign and which allowed her a substantial element of control over her own destiny, otherwise essentially denied to her sex.

Modern psychiatry dubs Margery Kempe as a hysteric. It postulates distorted sexuality as the cause of her hysteria, and it presumes that her neurosis had roots in childhood trauma. Margery never came under the care of medical doctors, but she was examined by the doctors of the Church, and the margin by which she escaped having heresy proceedings taken against her may not have been great. Over the next few centuries, tens of thousands of women all over Europe – and then in North America – likewise came to the attention of the ecclesiastical and civil authorities through being suspected of witchcraft.

In this book, I have chosen not to attempt to examine the 'text' of any witch. Partly this is because so far as I am aware no woman accused of being a witch freely and spontaneously wrote down an autobiographical testament of herself in which she interpreted her own condition principally as 'madness'. In the event of a witch-trial, a confession of 'madness' would not have served as an exoneration in the eyes of a court. On the contrary, it would have constituted further evidence of diabolical possession. For present purposes, moreover, practically everything we know about the minds of witches would in any case have to be treated as more than usually contaminated, since so much of it derives from the transcripts of court proceedings, when the constraints upon what could and should be said were overwhelming.

What it is crucial to emphasize, however, is how far these so-called witches came to be characterized as hysterics or, at a later stage, as neurotics. Many contemporary physicians such as the sixteenth-century German Johannes Wier and Edward Jordan in early-seventeenth-century England argued that such 'witches' were not indeed physically and literally possessed by the Devil but were rather suffering from the essentially organic disease hysteria, due ultimately to disorders of the womb and the reproductive system. They saw this diagnostic strategy as medically and morally enlightened, for if found merely sick, not satanic, the lady would not be for burning. And this 'hysterization' of the witches – blaming disease not the Devil – has found much favour amongst more recent scholars.

The psychiatrist Gregory Zilboorg devoted an entire book to celebrating the medical breakthrough involved in the 'discovery' that witches were not confederate with Satan but sick. Its sub-text was that this 'discovery' of the hysteria of witches had launched early psychiatry rather as Freud's later discovery of the origins of hysteria in infantile sexuality had launched modern dynamic psychiatry. And, using psycho-historical approaches deriving largely from Freud and Erikson, John Demos in his *Entertaining Satan* has more recently explored the hysterical element in the 'enactments' of new England witches in the seventeenth century along these lines. Demos hypothesizes that the 'narcissistic', exhibitionist behaviour of such witches betokens infant neglect. Overtly critical of these approaches, Thomas Szasz has remarked how the blanket use of diagnostic categories such as hysteria has allowed the stigma of witchcraft accusations to be carried forward to scapegoating patients within psychiatry today: modern psychiatry conducts its own witchhunts.

Early in his career, Sigmund Freud was bewitched by 'Dora' – his pseudonym for Ida Bauer – whose neurosis he wrote up in the inevitably entitled 'Fragment of an Analysis of a Case of Hysteria'. This eighteen-year-old patient presented that basket of symptoms with which Freud and all his fellow *fin de siècle* psycho-physicians were utterly familiar amongst their upper-middle-class female patients: nervous cough, general debility, migraine, *taedium vitae*, a disposition to flirt with suicide. Freud did not waste his time on a detailed examination for somatic disease; he had not the slightest hesitation in seeing her as a hysteric: she was 'unmistakably neurotic'.

She had been carried along to Freud against her will on the authority of her father. She had informed him that Herr K., a close family acquaintance, had sexually propositioned her. Herr K. reassured his friend that she had merely 'fancied' it all, and threw 'suspicion on the girl'. Her father in turn had brought her to Freud in hopes that he would make her 'see reason'. Dora knew very well – and Freud rapidly discovered – that her father needed to play along with Herr K.'s attempted seduction, because he was himself having an affair with Herr K.'s wife. Dora and Frau K. were thus objects of barter amongst the men. Dora was the price of silence.

The events in the story, as Freud elicited them from Dora, were quite simple. The Bauers and the K.s had become friendly. On one occasion in 1896, when she was fourteen, Herr K. had stage-managed an opportunity for trapping Dora alone in his locked office. Suddenly, without warning, he had kissed her. Dora had felt disgusted by the event. Contact between the families was kept up. Dora became intimate with Frau K. and helped nurse her children. In 1898 she had gone on a holiday with them. One day, while taking a lakeside walk with Herr K., he had made her a quite explicit sexual proposal. She had slapped his face and insisted she leave at once.

There has recently been a great proliferation of sophisticated analyses of Freud's analysis, and space precludes anything but the most superficial account here. But, to put it in the most simple terms, Freud concluded that Dora's revulsion from Herr K. was not to be taken at face value, that it was, indeed, hysterical. For Freud, it simply was not healthy for an adolescent girl, when kissed out of the blue by a close friend of her father, to feel disgust. 'This was surely just the situation to call up a distinct feeling of sexual excitement in a girl of fourteen who had never before been approached.' Dora's reaction was hence 'entirely and completely hysterical'. Properly understood, it signalled that her real and natural desire for the man had been overlaid by guilt and so forth.

At the lakeside, Herr K.'s modest proposal was 'neither tactless nor offensive'. Thus, Freud concluded, her current presentation of hysteria was symptomatic of the fact that she was unconsciously deeply in love with Herr K., but, driven by confused and unconscious motives of guilt, revenge and shame, was militantly repressing that urge from her consciousness. Freud believed that through a process whereby he could turn her unconscious longings for Herr K. into an acknowledged desire, her hysteria would depart. Hysteria was a self-inflicted wound, a form of self-blindness.

In the course of the analysis, Freud attempted to reveal to her how her imagined loathing for Herr K. was just a smokescreen, mere repression and resistance. Doubtless, her secret longing for Herr K. produced in her a deep ambivalence, since the nature of the Oedipus Complex meant that she must also sexually desire – indeed feel primary loyalty to – her father. That must explain why her recollection of Herr K.'s kissing her when she had been fourteen had stressed the *kiss*. Actually, Freud suggested to her, wasn't it the case that Herr K. had pressed his *erection* against her? In defence against desire, she had suppressed all memory of this, but had displaced it on to a kiss, registering nausea in her throat, instead of excitement in her vagina. This in turn, Freud was later to indicate, lay at the root of her nervous cough.

That cough played a key role in the thread of interpretations. It was Dora's way of identifying with her father (who himself was somewhat tubercular). It was also her means of reproaching him. For (Freud divined) Dora must have guessed that in his affair with Frau K. her father was being fellated. That Dora was aware of this was deduced by Freud from the following facts: (a) Dora could be persuaded to admit that she knew her father to be having an affair, but (b) she also believed him to be impotent, while (c) she was aware of the possibility of oral sex. (It never seems to have occurred to Freud, whose own sexual fantasies were phallocentric, that what was almost certainly going on between Herr Bauer and Frau K. was not fellatio but cunnilingus.) When Dora coughed, it was her way of accusing her father of having an affair. Above all, it was her own way of putting herself in Frau K.'s shoes. Through displacement, through her nervous cough, Dora was fellating her father. To corroborate all this, Freud quizzed her at length on her infantile thumb-sucking.

All these inquiries thus revealed that 'she was in love with her father'. Her inadmissible desire for him served for her as an invaluable protective screen for her inadmissible desire for Herr K. When confronted with this revelation, Dora denied it. Freud regretted that she would not go all the way with him in 'recognizing her own thoughts'.

Thus Freud explained to Dora why she resisted and rejected Herr K. Dora resisted and rejected Freud's explanation. That, Freud explained to her, merely confirmed its truth. For a 'patient', unlike a psychiatrist, necessarily lacked 'impartial judgement'. To an objective observer like himself, such denial really meant confirmation. Patients said 'No' in their consciousness. But, Freud explained, 'there is no such thing as an unconscious No'. In the unconscious lay a Yes; psychoanalysis would bring the unconscious Yes into the consciousness, for in reality 'in such a case, "No" signified the desired "Yes"'. Likewise, Freud assured her, when a patient, denying an interpretation, says 'I didn't think that,' the real meaning of the phrase is 'Yes, I was unconscious of that.' All this is, Freud assures his readers, an 'entirely trustworthy form of confirmation'. For nothing was to be taken at face value.

In particular, in dreams 'everything is turned into its opposite'. Thus 'give' means 'receive', and 'withhold' means 'reject'. In what Freud analysed as her 'first dream', Dora had imagined that a fire had broken out in the flat where her family was staying. They had to escape. Her mother delayed to collect her jewel case. Her father rebuked her, saying that he wasn't having his children's lives jeopardized by his wife's concern for her jewels.

Freud decoded the dream. Her mother's jewel case – as a result of necessary displacements introduced by the unconscious – stood for Dora's own genitalia. Her father's indifference to the jewel case really signified deep concern. Clearly, Dora had dreamed that her father was trying to protect her virginity. Why should she dream that? Because it served to defend her from her own guilty desire: 'what was suppressed was her love of Herr K.'. The dream was actually a disguised wish about her love for Herr K.

Moreover, the fire in the dream, following the tendency of the unconscious to deal in reversals, must really stand for water. Building on that, Freud was 'driven to the conclusion' that Dora had once been a bedwetter and an infant masturbator. This revelation about her masturbatory habits was in turn further proof of Dora's hysterical nature, and of her repressed 'sexual temptation'.

What is more, in the dream, she remembered having smelt smoke. Surely that must be associated with smoking. Dora knew that Freud was a smoker, and had he not often said to her 'there's no smoke without fire'? Obviously, Freud concluded triumphantly, the dream was really about himself: 'the idea had probably occurred to her one day during a session that she would like to have a kiss from me': 'everything fits together very satisfactorily', he concludes, in a tone which reminds one of Malvolio.

In his parodies such as *A Tale of a Tub*, Jonathan Swift perfectly personified the obsessional theorist, utterly self-deaf and lacking the slightest trace of self-irony, spewing forth an inspired farrago of pseudo-logical nonsense to convince his audience that up is down and black is white. It might seem that, through necessarily abbreviated summary, I have been reducing Freud's retrospective detection work on Dora to a Swiftian mad monologue. But at full-length, with all its paraphernalia of asides, self-vindications, digressions and parentheses, Freud precisely captures the authentic Swiftian tone. He even picks up Swift's trick whereby pseudo-confessions of ignorance are turned into a demonstration of omniscience. At one point, after a peculiarly dizzying sequence of free-associating argumentation, Freud momentarily confesses that all this might seem like a mountain of 'mistaken ingenuity'; but no! Further evidence and arguments serve to convince him of its truth: 'suspicion became a certainty'. 'No mortal can keep a secret,' he gloats.

The dénouement, of course, is well known. After she had listened to nearly three months of Freud's mistaken ingenuity, Dora quit, or, as Freud phrased it, 'deserted me'. For Freud, hers was typical of the acts of 'self-injury' which hysterics inflicted upon themselves, probably motivated by the 'jealousy' she felt towards other patients with whom she had to share his attention. In an act of spite and vengeance, she had rejected the first object of her desire, Herr K., foolishly repressing 'her love rather than surrendering'. Now, apparently driven by some neurotic compulsion to repeat, she had wreaked similar immature 'vengeance' on Freud. It was all 'an unmistakable act of vengeance on her part'. Hell hath no fury like an analyst scorn'd.

Freud reproached her for breaking off the analysis. He was magnanimously prepared to overlook her 'cruel and sadistic tendencies'; indeed, he was even 'willing to forgive her'. He could, of course, he explained to the listening world, have 'kept the girl under my treatment if I myself had played a part, if I had exaggerated the importance to me of her staying on and had shown a warm interest in her', and more of the same sad stuff. As Freud understood it, psychoanalysis was what hysterical women needed for their mental health just as regular doses of *penis normalis* was what they wanted for their sexual needs. Retrospectively brooding on why Dora had ended it, Freud concluded it was because 'I did not succeed in mastering the transference'. He meant the transference (as he saw it) of her emotions to himself. He never admitted any two-way transference. When she briefly returned some time later, Freud was glad to note she was 'remorseful'.

The unconscious works in wily ways. Freud advises us to disclaim dis-

claimers, to deny denials, to object to objections, to protest against protes-
tations, and to read reproaches against others as self-reproaches. 'It is a very
common thing', he assures us, 'for patients to recognize in other people a
connection, which, on account of their emotional resistances, they cannot
perceive in themselves.' It would be a bold interpreter who would claim
that in the case of Dora he applied any of his own maxims to his own interpretations, excuses or apologies. His reproaches directed against Dora remain
classics in the annals of victim-blaming, comparable to his treatment of Emma
Eckstein, discussed later. Freud always protected himself from seeing that
where there is transference, there too runs counter-transference.

But investigating the peculiarities of Freud's own fantasy world – what
did Freud really desire? – has not been the principal aim of this discussion.
It has been, rather, to pose the question of Dora. It is easy to see why she
might have been ill ('hysterical'), a pawn in the rotten game between her
father and his buddy. Her whole family nexus was a mess of troubles and
tensions. Her own father was cheating on his family; he had earlier brought
syphilis into the house. Everyone was traducing her. Herr K. called her
experiences mere fantasies. Her father colluded and took her to Freud to
make her 'see reason'. Freud then systematically explained to her that her
entire consciousness of reality was a tissue of self-delusions. Things were
the opposite of what they seemed to her. All men placed in positions of
trust in her life invalidated her, told her she was making everything up.
No wonder she was 'hysterical'.

Freud invested enormous efforts in trying to make Dora see that she was
in love with Herr K. Freud protests himself too much. He even suggested
Herr K. might have divorced his wife and married her. If she had surrendered
to Herr K. and a certain 'eventuality' had occurred, that would, after all,
have been 'the only solution'.

It is possible that Freud finally concluded that he had been simply barking
up the wrong tree all the while. In an appendix, added later, Freud, desperately trying to come to grips with his failure, explains that he'd been blind
to the fact that Dora had been in love all the time not with *Herr* K. but
with *Frau* K. (such lesbianism was just what you would expect from a
hysterical woman). Interestingly, radical feminists, seeing hysteria as an
engine of revolt and lesbianism as liberation, have been eager to seize upon
this particular fantasy as the true account of Dora's desires. Perhaps. Maybe
Dora was indeed emotionally entangled with Herr K., however, and was
perfectly well aware that she was. She may well have found Freud's gargantuan
expenditure of energy attempting to prove the obvious quite misplaced, so
much ado about nothing. At the conclusion of his triumphant analysis
of her second dream, all she could do was to turn to him and ask, 'Has

anything so very remarkable come out?'

The real point about Dora is how little she would collude in the psychoanalytical exploration of her troubles, in Freud's seduction of her unconscious. Freud fantasized he was verging on a breakthrough with her in the emancipatory project of psychoanalysis. But is it not better to see analysis's emotional rescue as the repressive liberator? Dora got out – quitting was the only form of falsification available to her – and, Freud noted, when she returned two years later she looked happier than at any time when she had been in analysis. In 1900, the tale which a hysterical woman would have told would have been profoundly shaped by the assumptions of her society, and its images of femininity. Thereafter, the stories which disturbed women have told have increasingly been mediated through the language of psychiatry.

In increasing numbers from the early nineteenth century, women – like men – came under psychiatric control by being locked away in lunatic asylums. It was widely suspected that such confinement was particularly liable to abuse in the case of women ('difficult' wives being sequestrated by their husbands, 'difficult' daughters by their parents, etc.). Thus Louisa Lowe, in her classic protest against wrongful confinement, *The Bastilles of England*, published in 1883, accused her clergyman husband of having had her certified as a lunatic essentially because she had taken up spiritualism. Lowe and other women made complaints about certain specific disadvantages experienced by female patients – e.g. they were often controlled by male attendants. All the same, the autobiographical writings of such women, like Janet Frame, against the iniquities of the asylum, suggest that the victim of asylum abuses was the *patient*, male or female, rather than specifically the woman.

It was, by contrast, the somewhat less disturbed woman living in society – the nervous case, the hysteric, the so-called 'neurasthenic' – who came under a distinctively penalizing psychiatric gaze. The cultural norms of eighteenth- and nineteenth-century society – patriarchal society – created a composite image of the lady, an ideology of 'femininity', which tight-laced women into being 'privileged inferiors'. Ladies were idealized, placed on a protective pedestal, as more delicate, more refined, more sensitive than men. Partly because of these cultural qualities, and partly because of their anatomical destiny, they were especially fit for the most exalted domestic duties of bringing up children, of being angels in the home and guardians of virtue. Yet this entailed in turn that women had to be 'protected' from the dangers, distractions and dissipations of the wider world – from public life and from intellectual over-exertion – in short, from the patriarchal public order for which men only were destined. Male medical opinion warned, sternly and ceaselessly, that the woman who trespassed beyond the domestic sphere would suffer psychiatric collapse.

Of course, many women found that the very reverse was true. The cabined, cribbed and confined milieu of the 'doll's house' itself became a madhouse of frustrations and thwarted energies, as Nora in Ibsen's play discovered. This was precisely the experience of Charlotte Perkins Gilman in late-nine-teenth-century America, young, ambitious, talented, but fretting in her mari-tal home. Overcome by depression, she sought help from Dr Weir Mitchell, probably the most distinguished East Coast office psychiatrist of the time. Mitchell had devised his own special schedule of treatment, the 'rest cure', precisely for neurotic female patients. This involved confinement in bed in his nursing home for a period of a month or more, complete abstinence from all activity, a course of massage and a fattening diet. Gilman underwent the treatment, and was sent home under instructions to pursue domesticity, not to write, and to curtail her reading.

She found it utterly ruinous. She turned autobiography into art. Her short story 'The Yellow Wallpaper' (1892) records the experiences of a woman like herself reduced to utter passivity, or compelled to regress to a baby-like condition (her room is called 'the nursery'), under the suffocating, cossetting regime of her physician–husband, who overprotects her into being a total invalid and subsequently into insanity.

In England, Virginia Woolf underwent a comparable experience. After her mother's early death, Woolf had suffered under the immense strain of having to serve as the focal point of the highly complicated and immensely demanding Stephen family. Her uneasy marriage with Leonard Woolf was somewhat a case of out of the frying pan, into the fire. Her mental health was sometimes precarious, and she suffered occasional breakdowns. She was induced to consult various society doctors. Some, like Sir George Savage, proved unsympathetic and dismissive towards what they diagnosed with distaste as hysteria. On Savage's advice, Woolf was persuaded to undergo a version of the 'rest cure' in Jean Thomas's rest-home in Twickenham. She was denied pen and paper, kept in a darkened room and fed up on cold rice pudding. Under such care, she became utterly depressed and demoralized.

Woolf was well aware of the dilemma. Society caged women in dolls' houses. Psychiatry promised keys to these cages – a healing therapy, the charisma of the individual doctor. But all these keys merely opened the doors on to new cages, subjecting women to further, subtler thraldoms. She read and reviewed Elizabeth Robins's novel *A Dark Lantern* (1905), the tale of a neuras-thenic woman who experiences a rest cure under a Dr Vincent [the name means conqueror]. He manhandles her; she falls in love with him; they marry; she is cured. The story confirmed what doctors such as Charcot had been saying all along, that what hysterical women really needed was to get laid. Woolf commented: *A Dark Lantern* 'explains how you fall in love with your doctor, if you have a rest cure'. The message, she commented, was 'brutal'.

Dora walked out on Freud. Since then, however, much writing by women recording their experiences of disturbance has involved variations on the theme of 'falling in love with your doctor'. Most spectacular was the love of Mary Barnes for Joseph Berke, forming a new 'holy family', which, as in the original one, produced a transcendental rather than a biological saviour: the gospel of sanctification through madness.

Mary Barnes's 'career' as 'patient' in the 1960s has significant affinities to the autobiographies just discussed. As with Margery Kempe, her madness led her to deep emotional involvement with Christianity. For Barnes, Catholicism and psychoanalysis offered equivalent and quite largely interchangeable symbolic languages of experience – good and bad mothers and children, sin, guilt, purgatory–expurgation, purification, and so forth. Like Dora, Mary was 'hysterical', although that was a term which the particular psychoanalytical group which treated her had discarded. But there is something novel about the madness of Mary Barnes: it comes to us (rather as in the fiction of Elizabeth Robins) as a love affair with psychiatry. Mary Barnes found redemption in psychiatry. As she put it, 'the five years at Kingsley Hall' where she underwent therapeutic rebirth under the guidance of Joseph Berke, Ronald Laing and their version of existential psychoanalysis, 'were all my years, for therein was held my past, my present and my future'. Furthermore, the very story she tells comes to us sandwiched within psychiatry, for her book is presented as a duet with alternating sections by Mary herself and by Berke. Predictably, as with Freud and Dora, the psychiatrist has the last word, quite dramatically imposing his own version on events. In the old days, 'burking' had a different meaning.

Dora didn't volunteer to be Freud's experimental material. She was pushed. By contrast, there was no stopping Mary Barnes once she determined to enlist as a Laingian living doll. Berke adds a disclaimer: Mary may have been the 'head guinea pig', but she wasn't simply 'acting out our fantasies for us'. She did, however, become their prime exhibit, often shown off to *Guardian* reporters rather like Charcot's starlet hysterics. And by the end of her five-year therapeutic novitiate, she has turned into the great proselyte for the analytical church militant, converting others to the gospel of salvation through psychosis with a missionary zeal which even the pros find embarrassing. Yet, as Elaine Showalter has rightly insisted, it is rather chilling to read Barnes's and Berke's accounts juxtaposed, since Barnes ends up utterly the child of psychiatry, hooked on a 'dialectics of liberation', which can be astonishingly deaf to her own perceptions as a woman, while being unabashed about imposing upon her its ancient Freudian dogmas about what a woman truly wants.

Mary Barnes's own story comes to us steeped in the language of psychiatry. She presents us with her life – she was born between the wars in the Home Counties – as seen retrospectively through the eyes of one who had been engrossed in psychiatry since her teens, making meaning of her past in the light of a powerful amalgam of Freud, Melanie Klein and 'object relations' theory. She especially embraces the Laingian notion that schizophrenia could be a rational way of coping with an irrational world, in particular the intolerable pressures and double binds imposed by the family upon its own 'scapegoat'. In Mary Barnes's eyes, her own psychiatric disorders stemmed from her infantile experiences with her family, above all her catastrophic and tragic relations with her mother. Mad people didn't blame their mothers, or families in general, in this way two or four centuries earlier. It is not that mothers had got worse, or children more vindictive; nor I would say is it that the master-key to mental disorder had at last been discovered. It is merely that psychiatry had moved on, and patients' perceptions with it.

For Mary Barnes, it could all be put in a nutshell: mother's breast had been dry. Her mother could not nourish; little Mary could not receive. Her mother wanted to love but could not give it; wanted to be loved, but could not accept it (no more from her husband than from her children: 'Mother never really let my father love her'). Little Mary grew up the same, in an utterly baffling scenario in which both giving and taking were all wrong, and endlessly caused emotional torment. But with Mary, to express wants was especially evil. Every desire she had was turned by her mother into a cause of guilt. To her, mother always said 'No'. Childbearing had been a pain. Now children were. Mary was always naughty or a nuisance. To want was to be bad. Her mother saw her as very bad and told her so. Mary was racked with guilt, and was made to accept that she was wicked.

Above all, desire was bad in a *girl*. Mary envied her younger brother Peter, for in the family eyes he was 'good'; it was proper for boys to make demands and have ambitions. Her brother throve at school and was encouraged. She was smothered and stifled. She hated her brother. She wanted to be a boy. She wanted to have her father. He tickled her in the bath. She liked that. Her mother told them off.

Her family was an emotional holocaust. But the lid had to be kept on. Everything happened behind a permanent veneer of being a perfect 'happy family', a paragon of petit-bourgeois respectability and sweet reason. Her brother, who had got into yoga and reading Freud, was (as she viewed it later) the first to have the guts to blow the gaff: he had a nervous breakdown.

It was then Mary who triggered the ghastly events which led to his being confined in a mental hospital and subjected to electro-convulsive therapy and insulin therapy. More cause for guilt: she later accepted that she herself had been responsible for 'seducing and castrating' Peter. 'The murder was mine.'

Mary became a nurse and converted to Roman Catholicism, 'bound to the body of Christ' and hoping to be his 'bride'. As a young woman she spent unhappy years of resentment, frustration, guilt and anger. She felt thwarted. She wanted a baby, but there seemed no escape from the 'denial of my body'. She too broke down, and was sent to a mental hospital. She liked the padded cell: a real 'womb' at last.

When she came out, she read leading psychiatrists and attended lectures on psychology. She tried convent life. A sympathetic prioress suggested psychoanalysis: 'I always feel that schizophrenics have got *something* "extra" to other people,' she informed Mary. (The prioress was called Mother Michael, an interesting mix of precisely what Mary wanted to be: both mother and boy.) She wrote to 'Freud's daughter', Anna, asking if she could go and live with her: no. She read Laing's *The Divided Self*; it was all about herself. 'I was in no doubt that Dr Laing understood about schizophrenics.' She contacted Laing. He agreed to see her.

She waits in his office. 'Over and over inside me I'm saying, Laing, Laing, Ronald David Laing, Doctor Laing.' 'I want analysis,' she tells him. At last she was expressing her desires. Laing responds: 'You need analysis twenty-four hours a day.' All is well. She leaves. At the station buffet, 'I drink warm milk.'

She passed a year of occasional consultations with Laing's colleague, Dr Aaron Esterson. She wanted to go mad, but not until 'Ronnie' could look after her properly. Laing found Mary a berth at Kingsley House, the community he had helped set up in the East End: 'I was saved.' There, under the close supervision above all of Joseph Berke, a young American doctor who had rebelled against orthodox psychiatry and become a convert after reading *The Divided Self*, Mary embarked upon the five-year descent into infantile regression and back again which she and the psychiatrists jointly agreed was her required therapy. She wanted to journey to a 'truer, mad state', to abandon her 'false self' for her 'true self'. She took to bed. She drank only through a baby's bottle. She wanted to be fed by a tube, in order fully to recapture the ultimate womb experience. Berke and Laing thought it would be 'interesting to see if any one could regress that far'. She shat and pissed over herself and played with her faeces (her 'babies'). She stopped using grown-up language. She screamed and shouted, bit and hit.

Above all, she got in touch with the violent anger she had been bottling up inside her all her life but which her overwhelming guilt had always barred her from expressing. It all came out (or rather 'IT', as she christened her rage). She had to learn for herself by trial and error that she could rage without being rejected. After this lengthy process of 'going down', eventually she began to 'come up'. Her divided self grew reunited; she ceased to feel an 'I' apart from her body. No longer was it bad to want or to have; she stopped her lifelong self-punishment. She began to feed herself. She expressed her anger through painting (great black breasts, painted in her own shit). She loved Joe. He was a 'safe breast'. In him 'I marry my father.'

She recovered. Her journey through psychosis reached shore. But she had become addicted to therapy. Everything she did or was involved in – every shopping expedition or meal – had to be seen as part of the treatment. This provoked Berke's anger: carrying it that far was 'absurd'. After all, no small part of the Laingians' self-image was that they weren't really professionals but people. Here was Mary insistently turning them back into doctors. Berke seems unaware, however, that in doing so she was deep down actually being *plus Laingian que les Laingians*. For she records: 'Joe reminded me that Ronnie says that life is therapy and therapy is life.' The words of Laing became the subtitles for the movie psycho-romance between his two epigoni.

Mary's desire to be doctored also put Berke in a bind. He often experienced her as exhaustingly demanding. On two occasions, he socked her on the nose. This therapeutic ploy endeared him to Mary ('I never loved Joe so much'). But it induced guilt in him, because biffing patients had not formed part of his regular training in medical ethics. He wished they could agree to think of him simply as a person, not a doctor. Then interpersonal violence could be legitimate, a way of working out anger. For Berke hints that he too had unconscious emotional problems akin to Mary's. It is an interesting reflection that in his contributions to the book he never explores his own motives and responses. Obviously, he reverts from being a person to being a scientific psychiatrist whenever he likes. Like Freud, Berke was quite anxious to resist the possibility of counter-transference. 'Mary continually attributed to me anger that was clearly hers,' writes the patient-puncher.

The truth is that Berke and his friends were unwilling or unable to interact with Mary on a footing of equality. They were in control. They gave the instructions to a Mary who craved the word of Ronnie (Berke himself calls him the 'guru'). Though obstreperous, she never questioned one jot or tittle of the broader therapeutic scenario. They told her what to think about her feelings. Thus she records that Joe explained to her on one occasion that 'going against Joe was really going against myself'. And it is worth noting here that Berke records that Aaron Esterson took to walking round Kingsley

Hall carrying a biography of Joe Stalin. Berke assures us it was a self-joke by the rather authoritarian Esterson: one wonders. Berke had little patience with regular therapeutic communities because, behind the pretence of a community general will, lay the diktat of the doctors; overall, they were no better than 'brain-washing'. He appears to have no perception that precisely that, albeit in a more sophisticated form, was what was perhaps going on at Kingsley Hall. Above all, the doctors seem to have had a view of Mary's condition which at a fundamental level did not tally with her own.

Mary's own story is one which burns with resentment at being first a girl and then a woman in a man's world. The world was her father's oyster (and would have been her brother's). As her self-denying mother saw things, it was wrong for a woman to attempt anything, because nothing is to be achieved. To want is to be bad. Its come-uppance is punishment: you'll pay for it. The woman's world is all deprivation and denial. So much so, that Mary sees that her only escape lies in rescue by heroes, and in the *Boy's Own Paper* adventure into the psychic interior (in her phrase, 'through madness to freedom'). Rather like Tarzan, 'Joe got me free.' 'Psychosis', says Berke, is the 'renewal of the inner self'.

To that degree, Mary was happy to allow the male doctors to speak for her. Like theirs, the analysis she developed of her own condition was fundamentally mother-blaming. Mothers imprison daughters within a cage of being dutiful, clean, chaste, docile and nice. Neither Mary nor Berke attributes any blame to Mr Barnes. The root of her problems was her mother. And the root of her mother's problems, she tells us, was *her* mother.

But on top of this, Berke is ready to leap in with the most stereotyped Freudian account of what really is the source of women's problems. What underlay Mary's psychosis? In a final chapter with the extraordinary title 'Untangling Mary's Knot', Berke gives the answer: the paradoxes of female sexuality. 'Mary Barnes was a hotbed of sexual desire and frustration.' She, however, 'did not know this'; indeed, she 'denied' her sexual desires. Above all, in fact, she erroneously thought that what she called 'IT' was her anger. It wasn't. 'IT' was, of course, her 'id', in other words, her 'sexual energies'. To be precise, 'IT' was the 'regurgitated remnant of undigested penises and vaginas'. That was her demon. She denied normal, mature, heterosexual genital sexuality. 'She even refused to allow a man to put his penis inside her.' Indeed, her desires to be a boy did not go away: 'she desperately wanted to be the penis'. If only her mistaken identity and her sexual frustration had been overcome, all might have been well. Liberationist psychiatry had no desire to free women from traditional gender-roles. Through psychiatry to freedom?

7 · From Fools to Outsiders

Every law has its outlaws, every territory its margins, all rule presupposes misrule and the unruly. Societies have instinctively been wise enough to know these facts of life and sometimes act on them. Whatever is strange and disruptive has been marginalized as monstrous, yet the theatre of life also allots walk-on parts for its misfits, madcaps and malevolents, even if only as those whom people love to hate. As Hans Mayer above all has stressed in his *Outsiders*, difference spells threat because it confers potency, and those whom society designates as outsiders are often kept in the wings, precisely because, at the right moment, their presence will be needed on stage.

Many people have been cast as outsiders: foreigners, Jews, blacks, homosexuals, witches, and so forth. Prominent amongst these, at least from medieval times onwards, was a certain type of madfolk: the fool. Harmless light-headed zanies, normal enough to communicate, abnormal enough to startle, offend and utter what no one else could, such 'fools' could win acceptance, even gain profession and privilege, in a society which would hardly listen to the mad as such. As Enid Welsford and Sandra Billington have shown, fooling was that kind of craziness which in the hands of the Court jester or the clown got a hearing, mingling sense and nonsense, raillery and buffoonery. The fool – indeed, comedy in general – challenged order, but it dissolved its own rebellion in laughter.

Jest-books, plays and paintings tell us much at one or more removes about such lords of misrule, temporarily licensed to wreak cultural havoc and spin the world upside down. Playing the fool became the ploy of a literary genre of 'praisers of folly' from Erasmus and Rabelais through Cervantes to Laurence Sterne and beyond. The device of the fictional Quixotic figure gave the author elbow room to play being an alien in his own land, offering a mix of wisdom, wit and lunacy impossible to unravel.

We are very familiar with literary fools – light-headed, bitter and sentimental – from Shakespeare to Beckett. We know little at first hand, however, about the authentic fools themselves. How many were just good pros, how many truly wits who had lost their wits? It is the unprofessional fools we know most about, men genuinely isolated enough to brood about their own marginality, yet able to cash in upon their own abnormality by railing in earnest. The serious fool is the mad outsider.

After the Aberdonian Alexander Cruden took the high road south in the early 1720s, he obtained a position as reader in French to the Duke of Sussex. Cruden had picked up fairly fluent written French while a student at Marischal College, one of the branches of the university in his hometown. But he had probably never heard the language spoken. The good Duke was therefore treated by Cruden to readings spelt out letter by letter as pronounced in English. Astonished at this palaver, he gave the young man his notice. Cruden, all his life a trying amalgam of meekness and pestering persistence, sent the Duke a battery of addresses, promising speedy perfection of his accent. He signed himself '*l'étranger*'.

It is no surprise that Cruden felt himself an outsider as a pious, upstanding Scottish Presbyterian recently arrived to make his fortune amidst that sinkhole of sin, Augustan London. Indeed he had already become something of an outsider back in his native Aberdeen, where his parents rated themselves high amongst the God-fearing Presbyterian burgess elite.

Cruden had probably been destined for the ministry. But shortly after leaving university he had become wildly infatuated with a young lady who not only proved indifferent to him, but seems herself to have been involved in an incestuous romance. When the details of this sordid scandal were made public, Cruden became unhinged, and in his deranged condition his parents had him locked up for some weeks in the city's tolbooth. On his recovery, everyone thought it wisest for him to go on his travels. His whole life was to prove a kind of spiritual exile. Although he despised many aspects of the London society in which he lived out his last fifty years, his desire for acceptance and recognition by it was deep – he was a great respecter of persons. Nevertheless exclusion and rejection dogged him to the end of his days.

Cruden settled down to earn his living in the metropolis as a proof-reader or corrector. He prided himself on making no mistakes. He opened a little bookshop, and by persistent applications got himself appointed bookseller to Queen Caroline. And it was to that Queen that he dedicated the composition which assures him literary immortality, his *Complete Concordance to the Bible*, a stupendous piece of accurate scholarship, apparently accomplished in just a year and published in 1737. (It made him, he noted in a nice phrase, a kind of 'apothecary to the parsons'.) Such gargantuan – one might say obsessional – single-handed labour in the service of true religion was characteristic of the man.

The book was hardly complete before love landed Cruden in trouble once again. He paid court to an affluent widow, Mrs Pain. She may have liked him as a person – Cruden showed touches of enthusiastic charm which people found endearing – but she had no desire for him as a husband, and made that clear (she was, in any case, probably already engaged to be remarried). Like Freud, Cruden never took no for an answer. He created scenes with the widow's friends, and at the chapel where they both worshipped began to make an exhibition of himself by singing the responses particularly loudly. Nobody slighted him with impunity. The outcome, however, was not as he intended. Friends of Mrs Pain arrived at his house, in particular one Wightman. On one occasion, blows were exchanged. Soon after, Cruden claims he was decoyed into a coach which whisked him off to a private lunatic asylum run by Mr Wright at Bethnal Green.

There Cruden spent nine weeks, from 23 March to 31 May 1738, confined against his will. In a pamphlet published the next year, *The London Citizen Exceedingly Injured*, Cruden made much of Wright's wrongful confinement and the barbarity of his treatment. He was bolted to his bedstead, and sometimes straitjacketed. He was bled and physicked. The madhouse staff were arrant ruffians. He was intimidated by the 'confederates' responsible for locking him away – they included the physician to Bethlem, Dr James Monro, whom Cruden vilified as a Jacobite and an adulterer. Unless he signed a paper indemnifying them, they threatened, he would be committed to Bethlem, which they and he evidently regarded as the ultimate deterrent.

Compared with later madhouses, however, Wright's seems to have been a bit ramshackle. Cruden's relatives came to visit him; the barber who arrived three times a week to dress his wig smuggled letters in and out; and not least, Cruden managed to keep a journal. Moreover, he was able to make a spectacular night-time escape over the madhouse wall after sawing his way through his bedleg with a table knife. Ever alert for the finger of Providence, Cruden identified himself with the Israelites escaping across the Red Sea from their Egyptian captivity, and began thinking of himself as a 'Joseph'.

Cruden celebrated his escape by prosecuting the 'conspirators' at the Court of Common Pleas, and suing for £10,000 damages to compensate for illegal confinement: he had been sane not mad (even Dr Monro, Cruden alleged, had said he was no lunatic but merely suffering from a 'fever upon the nerves'). The case was hopeless because Cruden's grasp of the law was no better than his spoken French. He claimed that the Act of Queen Anne 12 (1714) had rendered confinement of lunatics legal if and only if two justices had signed a warrant. The law stated no such thing, however. Rather, addressing itself only to vagrants, it had empowered justices to put pauper lunatics under confinement. The Act said nothing whatever about contractual arrangements for confinement with private asylum keepers.

Moreover, the fate of Cruden's action was finally sealed when the defendants obtained a letter from his father acknowledging that he had earlier been confined in Aberdeen as a lunatic. Cruden's case was dismissed. Cold comfort to him that the judge drolly advised him not to worry about being mad, since many eminent geniuses had been reckoned lunatics.

Cruden retired to nurse his wounds. Little is known of his precise activities for the next decade. But it is clear that he put increasing energies into a religiously inspired campaign to purify the morals of the nation. Such vices as swearing, profanity, drunkenness and, above all, Sabbath-breaking had been the targets of pressure groups campaigning for the reformation of manners from the close of the seventeenth century, and Cruden was certainly not alone in fulminating against the abominations of the modern Babylon. But, long identifying himself with Joseph, Cruden perhaps had a more elevated sense of his own mission than most. Increasingly he began to dub himself 'Alexander the Corrector' – a corrector no longer merely of proofs but of the nation's vices as well. Perhaps also he took action into his own hands more energetically than many, getting into fierce arguments with the ungodly.

Somehow – we have only Cruden's account – he found himself in the thick of a fracas in 1753, which resulted in his whacking a malefactor over the head with a shovel. His lodgings were then visited, a hubbub ensued, and out of the pandemonium Cruden once more found himself being whisked off, despite all his protests, to a madhouse, this time on the directions of his own sister, Mrs Isabella Wild (Cruden was plagued by names). Cruden was in Inskip's Chelsea madhouse for seventeen days. He experienced it as a terrible outrage (though even his own account gives evidence of quite mild treatment, with visits allowed from friends and provision for country rambles to Earl's Court). While inside, he made the acquaintance of one George King, whom he called King George: once more *nomen est omen*.

On his release, Cruden again sought what he called 'justice', though others clearly saw it as vengeance. He had insisted that by by way of 'atonement' and 'sanctification' directed to 'chastisement' and 'correction', his sister should agree to spend forty-eight hours in Newgate jail. When she refused, Cruden brought a legal action against her and three others. He fought his case on essentially the same faulty legal point as before, lost it once again, and poured out his grievances in a pamphlet entitled *The Adventures of Alexander the Corrector* (1753).

More troubles followed. Immediately on his release, Cruden had started to pay court to a woman he had never met, indeed was never to meet. Elizabeth Abney was the wealthy daughter of a former Lord Mayor of London. In his persona first as 'Alexander the Corrector' and later as 'Alexander the Conqueror', Cruden began to bombard her with love letters (he was to call them 'paper bullets'). He was, he assured her in letter after effusive letter, her 'physician', an 'extraordinary man'. She in her turn was 'God's gift' to him, his 'predestinated lady'. Her providential role would be to 'pave the way to Joseph's advancement and usefulness'.

So there could be no arguing: 'God's choice is the best choice.' 'Divine power', Cruden reassured her, 'would make him victorious and successful.' When she returned his letters unopened, the Corrector merely redoubled his 'campaign'. Issuing a 'declaration of war', he announced that he would 'reduce her to submission' by the 'rules of war', and laid siege to her Stoke Newington home. The figurative assimilation of love and war was of course as old as Homer; with Cruden – as a proof-reader, a most literal-minded and stubborn man – it is hard to be sure it was principally a metaphor.

Eventually, Cruden abandoned his campaign, but not before publishing in the third instalment of his *Adventures* a full account of how abysmally this ungrateful lady had treated him. His rebuffs in love, coupled with his experiences at law and in the madhouse, must have convinced him more than ever that he was living in flagitious times desperately in need of their 'corrector'. He grew ever more certain that he must be the 'instrument' of Providence, a 'Joseph', who, as in the Old Testament, had first been humiliated by God as a prelude to being made mighty: the lamb would be made a lion, greatness would be thrust upon him.

One of his co-religionists had prophesied that he would become both Lord Mayor of London and MP for the City. He now took action to fulfil his destiny. He nominated himself as a parliamentary candidate in 1754, but was prepared to accept victory only if elected unopposed (such was his pious hatred of divisive faction). His offer was not taken up. He also petitioned top people to pull strings to obtain for him the knighthood he deserved, and attended Court in order to grasp precisely how the ceremony was conducted. (On one occasion, Cruden, recently released from a madhouse, witnessed Laurence Sterne, who had recently put his wife in one, received by George III, soon destined for insanity himself.)

And above all he sought, by hobnobbing with people in high places and through yet another battery of pamphlets, to get himself a parliamentary appointment as Public Censor and official Corrector to the Morals of the Nation. Such promotion of righteousness seemed so rational. How could a professedly Christian nation lavish money on war and engage in profanities while neglecting the reform of morals? When these solicitations proved of no avail, Cruden took to the road. He presented his cause to Oxford and Cambridge Universities. He was politely received, for his name carried real respect as the author of the invaluable concordance. His enthusiasm was also palatable enough in small doses, even if, as a Mr Neville in Cambridge confessed, he was 'not quite in his right mind'. At Cambridge, becoming ever more Quixotic, he was 'knighted' in a ceremonial practical joke which may have been meant kindly or may have been cruel. Cruden himself elevated young ladies to the office of 'correctrix', and, on a later visit to Eton, appointed the schoolboys there his deputy correctors.

The older he got, the more Cruden quietened down. True, he mounted his own one-man campaign against the libertine John Wilkes, rushing round London with a wet sponge to wipe all the pro-Wilkite graffiti off the walls. But increasingly he gave himself over to practical good works. He helped prisoners, preaching sermons to them, but also obtaining bedding and provisions and securing commutation of sentences. When he died in 1770, he was appropriately on his knees at prayer.

Cruden commands an important place in the history of mad people's writings. For his is perhaps the earliest sustained campaign of protest in print by one who claimed always to have been fully in possession of his reason, up in arms against being labelled as insane by his family, neighbours and indeed his foolish times. Against all such people, Cruden sought to turn the tables. He was the one who was sane; and it was his persecutors, though backed by the sanctions of society at large, who were the true wrongheads. He was hurt when the judge condescendingly told him not to mind being mad. He responded by protesting that he was indeed in his senses, a 'meek man' but not a 'mad man'. Neither did he leap to play the part of divinely inspired religious madman. The notion of being a 'holy fool' held no allure. The prophets, he insisted, had always been taken by the world as mad. They were not. They were the Lord's anointed.

It had, of course, been a literary and theological ploy in earlier centuries for the truly wise man to wear caps and bells, the asses' ears of folly, thereby making a travesty of the rationalized hypocrisies of the worldly wise. Such was the device used by Erasmus jingling his bells in his *Praise of Folly* (1509). The belief in the wisdom of fools, passed down through the tradition of the Court jester, was still going strong in Cruden's youth. When Ned Ward presented Bedlam in his journalistic *London Spy* (1710), one of his favourite crazy types was the lunatic who argued that there was more sense in the madhouse than in the world, more justice, truth and liberty in Bedlam than in Britain. One of his mad characters syllogizes how the truly sensible man will prefer to live in Bedlam than out in the world, because only in the madhouse does a man have an absolute privilege of free speech and free action. In Cruden's own day, the jest or euphemism was kept up which christened madhouses 'academies' (Bedlam was known as 'Imperial College'), housing their 'scholars', under the supervision of 'tutors'. There was (in jest at least) wisdom in folly.

But there is not the slightest sign that Cruden saw the mask of madness as integral to his higher mission. This was perhaps at bottom for prudential reasons. In Erasmus' time, or in the heyday of the Court jester, the lunatic might well be a prized object of attention in the world, given the run of the stage to mouth his gibes. But by Cruden's day the fate of the lunatic was increasingly confinement. Private asylums, such as those to which Cruden was sent at Bethnal Green and Chelsea, were springing up, above all around London. Public asylums, funded by charity, were growing too. Bethlem itself had taken mad people since the fifteenth century; St Luke's joined Bethlem as a major London public asylum from the mid-eighteenth century. Cruden feared being sent to either of these public Bastilles more than he dreaded the private asylums which actually housed him (where he knew that money bought privileges).

The traditional wisdom up to Cruden's day had been that lunatics should be confined only if dangerous to themselves or to others. Lunacy itself was not a sufficient ground for incarceration. But this policy was gradually being eroded. The in-laws of the poet Kit Smart had him confined in the 1760s. Smart was undoubtedly a rum fellow; but even if a lunatic, he was clearly harmless. Samuel Johnson protested againt Smart's confinement. True, Smart had insisted that passers-by in the street should get down on their knees and pray with him, but 'I'd as lief pray with Kit Smart as with any man'. True, Smart was dirty and indifferent to 'clean linen', but, confessed Johnson, 'I have no passion for it.' Johnson himself – a man who confessed to having been 'mad all my life, at least not sober' – was perturbed about his own precarious balance of mind, and worried lest, if he gave way to his obsessions, he might himself be certified. It is little wonder then that, against such a backdrop, Cruden should have valiantly protested his sanity. For he must have felt that the 'harmless lunatic' – which is clearly what many people took him for – was now at risk. In any case, as is so graphically shown by the speed with which he was himself removed to the madhouse whenever his own zeal got the better of him, the boundary-line between what people might accept as the harmless, and sequester as the dangerous, lunatic was not one in which to put one's trust.

Cruden's *cris de coeur* deserve attention and respect. They stand at the headwaters of a long and honourable tradition of protest against arbitrary confinement and the evils of asylums. But they must not simply be assimilated into that tradition. For much that later inmates in the Victorian age and beyond complained about was not a bugbear to Cruden or to his age. He was not subjected to the routine drills which demoralized later patients, not put to mindless work, not indiscriminately mixed with all manner of other lunatics, not put into uniform, not deprived of pen and ink. He was not the victim of dangerous, experimental medical treatments (he received only rather standard purgings and bleedings). Above all, he was never confined for long spells – the longest period was only nine weeks.

All the same, however benign the motives of those who had him confined, Cruden's *exposé* gives not the slightest indication that Wright's Bethnal Green asylum or Inskip's Chelsea asylum could possibly have been therapeutically beneficial. Their methods were arbitrary. Nothing was explained to him. Aggressive acts, such as removing his belongings, were inflicted upon him. He was subjected to threats (indeed, removal to Bedlam was itself used as a threat). Cruden personally protested against these evils; not on behalf of better forms of therapy (believing himself to be sound of mind, what need of that?), but in the name of the liberties of a free-born Briton and a citizen of London, indignant against what would later be called the 'English Bastilles'.

Most Scots who came south in the eighteenth century assimilated themselves into polite metropolitan culture as fast as they possibly could. Cruden never did, always remaining rather estranged, on the margins. Was that due to some fundamental streak of his nature? What is clear is that his religious commitments permitted him to make sense of his own enduring experience of being an outsider. Indeed, his faith positively gloried in it, reverberating with its images of the prophet without honour in his own country, of being a Joseph amidst the Egyptian captivity. When the world is Babylon, exclusion from it is an honour.

Cruden felt confidence in the uses of adversity because of his unshakeable providentialism. He unswervingly saw his entire life as a saga of special divine providences. He admitted, of course, that to dull spirits there was little but unfathomable 'mystery in Providence'; the operations of its 'wheels' were 'secret and wonderful'; Providence enshrined a 'mystery' that 'reason' alone could not reach. Personally, however, Cruden felt utterly privy to Providence: how could a true believer doubt the evident signposts? The proof-reader had proofs aplenty in his 'visions, revelations or impressions' (he was not quite sure what to call them). Fellow Christians too had received prophecies that he would be 'great at court' and would become a 'great man'. And God Himself had set down Joseph in the Bible as plain as a pikestaff as the 'emblem' of himself:

Joseph the son of Jacob was called a Dreamer, hated by his brethren, let down into the pit, sold to the Midianites, and by them sold to Potiphar an officer of Pharaoh, and was afterwards falsely accused by Potiphar's wife and cast into prison. And Alexander the son of William was falsely accused of insanity by some unthinking persons, who little expected that he who behaved with the mildness and meekness of a Moses, could upon proper occasions act with the undaunted courage and resolution of an Alexander. . . . Alexander is of opinion that Divine Providence purposes to make him Corrector of the People.

So everything fitted. Evidently, the Corrector was a 'great favourite of Providence' and 'Providence always appears for the Corrector'. The Corrector for his part humbly 'accepts' his providential destiny, knowing that whenever it worked his 'humiliation', such abasement was merely preparatory for his 'exaltation'. For many contemporary Christians, the problems of lapsarian man living under Providence could prove so perplexing as to bring on madness – one sometimes resolved, as in the case of George Trosse, or ultimately insoluble, as with William Cowper. For Cruden, however, the rationality of Providence was crystal clear. He never had a doubt, never 'made a mistake', and never, of course, had a crisis of faith. He kept his pristine alien vision intact.

That is why his pamphlets make such fascinating reading. For they present us with a hall of mirrors where all is consistently and utterly reversed. The world thinks Cruden is mad; it is wrong. It is the Corrector who is actually correct. It is the world that is incorrigible. Not just generally, in its insane pursuit of carnal lusts and all those other sins of the flesh requiring 'correction'. But specifically. Cruden identified himself as the victim of a succession of 'plots', stirred by 'conspirators' such as his 'furious' and 'unaccountable' landlady and Wightman, who could have had no possible grudge against him. There were worse still. On the one hand, his 'light-headed' sister, Isabella Wild, whom Cruden punningly dubs a 'wild woman' and a 'hussy'. And then the mad madhouse-keepers, such as the adulterer and Jacobite James Monro, and the owner of the Chelsea madhouse, Inskip, who, given the opportunity, given the reward, would have been glad to incarcerate the President of the Royal College of Physicians like a 'Tom o' Bedlam' – though, of course, Cruden adds, that would have been no foolish thing, for the College itself was truly 'mad'. The Corrector needs none of these physicians. Rather the nation needs him as its physician.

In other words, it would be quite wrong to think of Cruden as a man revealing to the world that 'madness' was just a chimera or a socially imposed stigma. Madness and reason were real and polar opposites. But society was upside down. From his outsider's position he could see that the world, like Swift's broomstick, was standing on its head. Cruden sought to turn the tables. He wanted the persecutors prosecuted. He wanted that sister to be confined who had confined him (though he would do it out of love whereas she had put him away out of raving hatred). It was a corrupt society which had given him no reward for his invaluable *Concordance*. Instead, he would ban from the bookshops the works of atheists and infidels such as Bolingbroke which were scandals to the morals of the nation.

Cruden stands at the crossroads in the tradition of the mad outsider, the man who was *solus contra omnes*. From the Middle Ages onwards, some sort of licence had been extended to the outsider on the margins. The wild man, the melancholy *penseroso*, the hermit, the vagabond, the pilgrim – all had threaded their way in and out of the civilized world. A figure such as Jaques in Shakespeare's *As You Like It* was allowed to rail at his fellows, precisely because dramatic convention had it that in the end he would resign his rights over society and retire into the solitude of the forest. What is more, the Jaques, or indeed the Quixote, was a figure of fun. The mocker had to allow himself to be mocked.

There is much of this type in Cruden (though how consciously it is hard to say). He is the perfect fool, an embodiment of the egoist crazed with writing, one who, knowing that the real is the written, scribbles a pamphlet about himself at every opportunity, and so turns his own self into a character in his own delusional dramaturgics. Cruden *becomes* the Corrector in a sort of mock-heroic epic where his life fulfils fiction. Surely his increasingly monstrous egoism was spiced with a pinch of – indeed, an enjoyment of – self-parody. It is hard to see how people would have put up with his officious self-importance unless it had been tempered by a capacity to play to the gallery and see that the joke was on himself. And some of his activities – above all his involvement with prisoners – signal a greater capacity to sympathize with other outcasts, an ability to put himself into their shoes.

Yet there is also an unnerving blinkered egoism to Cruden, one of course absolutely bolstered by his fundamentalist Protestantism, and translating itself into an earnest celebration of the lone stranger: *l'étranger*. There may be a self-caricaturing smile when he talks of the 'wars' in his 'adventures in love' or about his 'battles' in the courts. But he is in deadly earnest about his 'injuries', as he is when he tells us that he is scribbling his pamphlets in order to 'vindicate' himself – presumably against the 'vindictive'. The whirligigs of time would have their revenges. Cruden is for ever correcting the world: 'do as you would be done by'. But he has the true loner's incapacity to see himself as others see him. The reason why his persecutor Wightman is such an appalling man, Cruden informs us, is that he is a 'busybody': 'it is no inconsiderable Part of Social Duty to manage our Conversation with such Caution and Prudence, that it does not become mischievous and intolerable to others', he prates, unaware that he is the chief of offenders. In one of his early publications, he compares his own 'adventures' to those of Robinson Crusoe. It is a very telling likeness. Crusoe is the humourless Protestant solipsist, imagining his own world entirely from within himself. In many ways, Cruden is the father of the tradition of the crazy outsider who seeks to remake the world anew from within.

To jump from Cruden to Nietzsche seems at first sight like a suicide leap from the ridiculous to the sublime. Imagine Nietzsche's disgust at being linked with the epitome of those petty-bourgeois philistine God-fearers who spent their lives resenting *Übermenschen*; indeed, Cruden would have made him sick. But the succession is not so bizarre. Each in his own way felt profoundly alien from the society in which he felt a living exile (Nietzsche demanded something stronger: 'Europe will need to discover a new Siberia where it can exile the originator of these experiments in valuation'). Both castigated their fellow men for being decadent, debauched, degenerate. Both clowned around and played the buffoon – in Cruden's case perhaps guilelessly, in Nietzsche's with irony piled upon irony – as a medium for expressing, while also shielding themselves from, what inevitably gets called megalomania. Nietzsche of course could profess to be a simple man, destined to be appallingly misunderstood. As he wrote in *Ecce Homo*,

> I have a terrible fear that one day I will be pronounced *holy*; . . . I do not want to be a holy man; sooner even a buffoon. – Perhaps I am a buffoon.

Cruden turned himself into Alexander the Corrector, Alexander the Great. Nietzsche called himself a *Doppelgänger*, loved Don Quixote, thought his role might be to 'entertain follies', assumed the mantle of Antichrist, and, when he was going out of his mind, came to sign himself 'Nietzsche Caesar'.

Thus Cruden and Nietzsche represent two centuries of aliens. While God was alive, the outsider was bound to be His prophet. Once God was dead, he could become Antichrist.

With Nietzsche's insanity, it is possible to date quite exactly the crossing of that bourn from which that traveller never returned. From the autumn of 1888, he cut loose, shed the normal social inhibitions, and his delusions of grandeur increased. With boundless euphoria, he described himself as 'the foremost mind of the period', and signed a letter to his sister, 'Your brother, now *quite a great person*'. As he was writing *Ecce Homo* he grew ever more solipsistic, more grandiloquent: 'I am not a man, I am dynamite.' And his behaviour too took on an explosively bizarre quality. By the close of November in that year, he can reflect upon himself:

I play so many stupid tricks with myself and privately do such inspired clowning that sometimes I go about the streets *grinning* – there is no other word for it – half an hour on end.

By Christmas Day, he is prophesying, 'In two months, I shall be the foremost name on earth.' But events stepped in. On 3 January 1889, while walking the streets of Turin, he saw a horse being whipped by a cab-driver. He flung his arms round the animal's neck, collapsed and fell unconscious. Taken back to his lodgings by friends, he was now utterly in the grip of the Dionysian demons which had been gradually taking possession of his mind. He shouted, thumped the piano and gestured obscenely. He wrote professions of love to Cosima Wagner and threatening letters to the King of Italy. He would sometimes sign himself 'The Crucified'.

Nietzsche was taken to a Basel clinic and then on to Jena, where he was admitted to Dr Binswanger's psychiatric asylum. He had suffered mild paralyses and was highly excitable and occasionally violent, though always pleased to see friends. Generally harmless and sometimes quite well – was Nietzsche's insanity just another piece of clowning, yet one more mask? Visitors wondered. But his right-side paralysis, behavioural peculiarities and incoherence of mind gradually worsened.

In March 1890, he was released from the asylum, and went to live with his mother in Jena. There, the once neglected man became a living legend as the crazy prophet. But his condition steadily deteriorated. By 1894 he recognized hardly anyone except his mother and sister and lay prostrate on the sofa all day, his apathy punctuated only by occasional roaring and shouting. The family moved to Weimar (Nietzsche's vile sister, already cashing in on the Nietzsche industry, wanted him to be apotheosized in death in Goethe's hometown). In August 1900, he caught a fever and died, just short of his fifty-sixth birthday.

No end of attempts have been made to reach a diagnosis of the cause of Nietzsche's insanity, but none has been convincing. Freud thought 'some sexual abnormality' was involved, and his psychoanalytic colleague Federn believed Nietzsche had displayed 'the symptoms of a severe neurosis', adding, 'one could wish that many poets, founders of religions, and other men of stature had submitted to therapy; then they might have accomplished great things'. Nietzsche's contemporary, the neuropsychiatrist Paul Möbius – it was he who designated Schumann schizoid – identified him as one of that tide of geniuses-cum-degenerates then flooding Central Europe. For all Nietzsche's own hatred of the decadents, he had proved one himself after all. Möbius thought his nervous condition had been inherited. Nietzsche's father Ludwig had died in 1849, suffering from 'cerebral inflammation', and an autopsy revealed a softening of the brain. Möbius assumed that Nietzsche had suffered from the same condition. There is, however, no positive evidence in favour of this view (though Nietzsche himself, reflecting upon his father's fate, had certainly agonized over his own possible descent into incapacity). Yet there is no convincing proof either for the much touted theory that Nietzsche's growing paralysis was the long-term aftermath of a syphilitic infection picked up from prostitutes, though Nietzsche himself seems to have given this view currency.

To understand Nietzsche's calamity properly, we must in any case step back from a narrow concentration on (non-existent or inconclusive) clinical data. It is not implausible in his case to suggest a largely psychogenic impetus for his descent into insanity. For over the years, and especially from the mid-1880s, Nietzsche's isolation, his habitual, unremitting, self-lacerating autobiographical bent, and particularly his absorption in his own health as a barometer of identity all contributed to put him under intense mental strain. Though he generously acknowledged his debts to Schopenhauer, to Wagner, indeed to Socrates, his mind grew more self-preoccupied, his thoughts grander and more frenzied, his loneliness more acute and terrifying. If we can call him clinically insane from 3 January 1889, he had been preparing the masks of madness well in advance.

Yet it would be utterly mistaken to identify Nietzsche too closely with those many eminent nineteenth-century intellectuals, writers, artists and Bohemians who were more than half in love with bearing the arms of sickness – mental and physical – seen as the escutcheon of genius. Being ill, being degenerate, being in decay (decadent) was an essential act of aggression, of nay-saying, for so many writers – Flaubert, Baudelaire, the brothers Goncourt and so forth – in their revolt against normal, balanced, pussyfooting philistine mediocrity. Their pains set them apart. Self-defining lepers, they wanted their own sickness to show and to shock, they wanted to be revolting. Then they could blame their own morbid condition upon the pestilential age in which they were forced to languish, with its deadly viruses of primness and tiny-minded respectability, while at the same time they could experience their own agonies as proofs of the consuming fires, the dark demons, of their genius, their suffering as a mark of superior febrile sensibility.

In his self-appointed role as arch-critic ('corrector') to his age, Nietzsche loved to scorn all this as so much self-deceiving posturing poseurship, as intellectual bad faith. For Nietzsche, it was not only Christians and mean-minded moralists who were the enemies; so were the sick of soul and the sick of body as well. Degenerate intellectuals were *symptoms* of the sick society, not principally – despite what they thought – its scourges, surgeons or saviours. Truly to stand apart, to be an authentic outsider, exile or Antichrist, it was necessary to be a crusader for health, to offer health to the world, even at the cost of having one's own destroyed. (There was no virtue in weakness, but weakness might be the price of virtue.)

In thus espousing the cause of 'fitness', however, Nietzsche of course had no neo-Darwinian, proto-Nazi metaphysical mumbo-jumbo in mind. The quests for the healthy soul and the healthy body – above all, the union of the two in wholeness – became for him a campaign uniting his own personal medical history indissolubly with his mission as the *doctor* of his age, its *malleus maleficarum*. Arguably, Nietzsche's concern became obsessional, a sort of hypochondria reversed, threatening the very values it aimed so passionately to protect.

Nietzsche was a chronic sufferer. From the 1860s onwards his letters recite a crescendo of sickness. His eyes pain him appallingly: 'to use my eyes is impossible', he writes in 1876. He is troubled by migraine after migraine, which reduce him to acute agonies. He finds it impossible to sleep. His stomach is utterly disordered, he cannot eat, he vomits, he cannot keep medicines down, an ulcer is suspected. 'Everything is kaput,' he tells his friend Overbeck in 1883, 'my stomach so much so that it even refuses the sedatives – in consequence of which I have sleepless, terribly tormented nights.' Plagued by unremitting ill-health, he resigned his chair of classical philology at Basel University in 1879, and spent the next decade wandering around Europe, moving from doctor to doctor, from health spa to the mountains, taking the waters, trying bathing and repeated changes of air, all in a quest for health, all to no avail. Yet often his call was for 'Doctor Death'.

At times Nietzsche blamed his ill-health on that *Pseudokultur* of the age which so drastically nauseated him. Being ill was in that sense a healthy reaction to a diseased society. And we may guess that his own stance as the embattled prophet, always at odds with his contemporaries, striving for total honesty with himself, 'truth at any price', reduced him to unstable morbid sensitiveness, which found outlet in hypochondriacal forms. But the main expression of these preoccupations lay in his constant denunciations of that sick self-deluding society which he felt was suffocating and poisoning him. Civilization was exhausted, enfeebled; youth had grown pale and spectre-thin, and had died. Lacking stamina, contemporaries had lapsed into conformist torpor, pusillanimous paralysis, and spineless mediocrity. The omnipresence of doctors, of so much medication, proved the point. People could no longer survive without physical irritants, stimulants and narcotics for the mind – drugs, alcohol, tobacco, religion. Desiccated and divided, contemporary man was for ever self-consciously blathering about himself, cut off from the instinctual well-springs of assured vitality. Thinking had paralysed action; as minds and bodies became severed from each other, the wisdom of the body was lost, and healthy simplicity yielded to sickly self-absorption. Contrast the healthy Greeks of old, Nietzsche never tired of hectoring his age. They were the exemplary free spirits, whole, fit in mind and body. 'They understood how to *live*.'

Combining its hygiene of the mind and gymnastics of the body, the Greek ideal was the kind of health Nietzsche celebrated. He doubted whether society at large could any longer achieve it. Yet he certainly had a driving will to health for himself. After all, he recognized that his own *illnesses* were 'holistic': 'people like us never suffer just physically – it is all deeply entwined with spiritual crises'. So why shouldn't holistic *health* be possible too?

Indeed, his own wretched ill-health might oddly be a hopeful sign. Seeing that true health in these twilight times was no longer a purely intrinsic gift from the gods, might it not be the trophy of a successful struggle against sickness, of self-conquest? As he argued in the Postscript to *Nietzsche Contra Wagner*,

> As far as my own sickness is concerned, am I not infinitely more indebted to it than to my health? It is to my sickness that I owe a *higher* health. . . .

He saw such a potentiality for health embodied in his role as a Promethean doctor, as surgeon-general to his age, fighting his own disease by fighting society's. Identification with health, with life, with energy increasingly set him apart, and confirmed his own messianic sense of himself as the moralistic immoralist. At the same time, it surely drove him further down the path that led from estrangement to insanity. The unbearable loneliness of being was something he himself had recognized as a threat as early as his *Human, All Too Human* (1879):

> what I always needed most of all for my own cure and self-restoration,
> was the conviction of *not* being so alone, not *seeing* so alone – an enchanting
> suspicion of some kinship and likeness in glance and desire, a moment
> of relaxation in the assurance of friendship. . . .

Nietzsche thus felt condemned to live out a self-punishing destiny of being 'doctor and patient in the same person'. The implied duality in the face of the struggle for unity created profound tensions which took their tragic toll.

If Nietzsche became ever more grandiloquent, less inhibited, during the course of 1888, does that mean that his last writings, the *Twilight of the Idols*, *The Anti-Christ* and *Ecce Homo*, were manifestations – manifestos even – of madness? Was the autobiographical *Ecce Homo*, completed only days before his final collapse, Nietzsche's diary of a madman? Of course, the answer is no. By their shockingly raw rhetoric of paradox, their egoism which mocks (or, even, which destroys with a hammer) the phoney selfless modesty of the classic spiritual autobiography, they manifest a masterly irony which bespeaks utter control.

But we may put the question of the 'insanity' of Nietzsche's later writings in a more plausible form: does he *masquerade* as mad, does he, ever the supreme showman, assume the mask of madness (perhaps like Swift or Blake) through which to speak his painful truths? The answer again is no. Though Nietzsche loved 'simplicity', his works are not tales told by idiots.

Neither are they, of course, hymns to pure reason. Nietzsche is the avowed foe of false and footling rationalism. Idealism and ideology shatter before his hammer and it is indeed twilight-time for all the idols. While Nietzsche appreciates the acidly critical strand of French philosophy, the rationalism of the Reich is detested as nothing but a sort of mental catarrh, Scotch mist; and the system-building itch of the scholars, of the *poseurs* and *penseurs* is itself diagnosed as a mode of decadence. All theorizing which corrodes the instinctual is mendacious and sick. But Nietzsche precisely denounces such 'idealism' against the yardstick of healthy reason, for its own 'fundamental irrationality'.

For idealism is a defence, a big lie, which while pretending to self-know-ledge creates only cowardly self-deception. And emancipation from these idols is the road not to some divine insanity but to reason itself. As Nietzsche argues in *Ecce Homo*, the pettiness of petty-bourgeois minds made him sick. 'It was only sickness that brought me to reason.'

In other words, Nietzsche does not set up madness to topple reason. For just as he commands that we should strive beyond good and evil, so too in his Zarathustran persona he points beyond the sterile, abstract antithesis of reason and unreason. Reason, interpreted as the Cartesian cogito, ceases to be the ultimate touchstone of the sane. True sanity lies in whatever confers the bloom of life – power, vitality, health – whatever nourishes the self and the soul's greatness. Inspiration, ecstasy and affirmation are all, *amor fati* the watchword. Mere reason's infatuation with Being is superseded by life's pursuit of Becoming.

Nietzsche pursues an essentially Greek holism. Unlike Cruden and Freud, who claim to be new Alexanders, he is, he tells us, a 'counter-Alexander' who will restore Greekness by retying the Gordian knot. Within his philoso-phy, there lies no room for the Cartesian dualism which postulated an indepen-dent ontology of thinking. There is thus no meaning for 'psychiatry', except as another stigma of decadence. Moreover, within his post-Christian morality, there is of course no detached soul. All there is is what is alive, and life is a unity. If Nietzsche the Dionysian thus partakes of fire and frenzy, that is not 'madness', precisely because it expresses organized energy, rather than the self at war.

Nietzsche opens *Ecce Homo* by asking of himself: 'who am I?' He concludes by triumphantly addressing the decadent 'crucified': 'have I been understood?'

For Nietzsche, madness presents a kind of defeat, the resentful having their revenge, envious of his championship of health in a sick world. The life – and, indeed, the madness – of Antonin Artaud in many ways re-ran Nietzsche's tragedy half a century later. Both led lives in the possession of a burning, painful genius, which proved literally the dissolution of the self even as it was the creation of truth and art. In Artaud's case this found expression through theatre and painting as well as by those forms of utterance he shared with Nietzsche, poetry and prophecy.

Both felt a passionate loathing for the mass civilization of nobodies who threatened them and by whom they would never be understood. For Nietzsche, that society was bloated, sclerotic and sick unto death. For Artaud, living in the century of world war, it was not primarily diseased but destructive; and in turn it needed to be destroyed. Artaud ceaselessly hurled his thunder in every way he knew against all that was conventional and traditional, life-denying and dead. Like the Dadaists and Surrealists with whom he associated, Artaud, following Nietzsche, expelled himself from society in a twin motion of being rejected and rejecting, being cast out and casting himself out. He would be an outsider, a rebel. As Anaïs Nin remarked of him in 1933, 'he wanted a revolution, he wanted a catastrophe, a disaster that would put an end to his intolerable life'.

Repudiating the conventional channels for expressing themselves before the public, both Nietzsche and Artaud followed the vocation of the fool: they wore masks, they developed alternative selves. Nietzsche became Zarathustra and the past-master of irony. Artaud literally turned mask-wearer as actor and theatre-master, seeking, in a way which the analyst of *The Birth of Tragedy* would have appreciated, to use drama to strip bare the stagey conventionalities of bourgeois life and art. Both men were thus triumphant embodiments of paradox.

But for Nietzsche, madness itself had no part to play in this enactment of 'why I am destiny'. The reverse was true for Artaud. From quite early in his career, madness and a cultivated otherness were doubles. Madness was the only proof of identity, of integrity, for the true human, the true artist, forced to sojourn in a society of surpassing evil. Who is the authentic madman?, he asks in his study of Van Gogh (the man, as Artaud phrases it, 'suicided by society'):

It is a man who has preferred to go mad in the socially accepted sense rather than give up a certain higher ideal of human honour.

That is how society has organized the strangulation in lunatic asylums of all those it wants to be rid of or protect itself from, because they have refused to be accomplices in certain supremely dirty acts. Because a madman is also a man to whom society does not want to listen. So it wants to prevent him from telling intolerable truths.

Artaud followed the Romantic vocation of living out life as a work of art. But true art was madness. Madness therefore was a mantle which he adopted from his youth onwards, of which he never divested himself.

His health – and it makes little sense in his case to attempt to separate 'physical' from 'mental' – was precarious from infancy. Born in Marseilles in 1896, he suffered a severe bout of meningitis as a child which may well have left a legacy of lasting head pains. He grew up sensitive, solitary, literary. Illness and withdrawal led to a spell at a sanitarium around 1915 where, to counter the pitiless headaches, he turned to opium as a painkiller, thus initiating a habit carried with him for the rest of his life. A brief spell in the army was ended by a medical discharge, and the years between 1916 and 1920 were spent moving from clinic to clinic, where he gave himself over to intense and tormented broodings which found some outlet in a rather mystical Roman Catholicism and in poetry.

In 1920 his life changed when he became a patient of Dr Eduard Toulouse, a progressive Parisian psychiatrist, and lived with the doctor and his wife. Toulouse had poetic and literary leanings, and through him Artaud became part of the literary *avant garde*, having his first poems published and winning his first parts as an actor. He enthusiastically embraced and over the years extended the philosophy of theatre developed by Charles Dullin in his *théâtre de l'atelier*. Discarding the established conception of drama as 'plays', mere entertainment, dependent upon the literary device of words and the 'illusion' of 'realism', Artaud came to see it as an enactment of spontaneous being, of improvisation. Actors had a unique capacity for recovering the great subterranean life forces from which the fripperies and defences of civilization had insulated modern man. Movement, mime, gesture, ritual, music, light and sound – all these, rather than authorial prosings, were pure expression. Just as for Nietzsche, actors had to *be* rather than think or declaim.

These convictions became the energizing vision behind the embryonic 'theatre of cruelty' which Artaud was to launch in 1927 through his own ill-fated Théâtre Alfred Jarry. In a very Nietzschean way, Artaud's cruelty aimed to be a cleansing and purifying force, stripping away rationalization and artifice and putting mankind back in touch with the primordial life-forces of the self and the cosmos.

Artaud further developed his theory of theatre as primal event during the 1930s. He was profoundly affected by watching a Balinese troupe achieve a dramatic unification of inner impulse and physical expression, through dance, incantation, mime and magic. Artaud looked to theatre as the great agency of destruction, purgation and rebirth. His *Le Théâtre et la peste* (1933) offered drama as a scourge: like a true plague, theatre would destroy the unhealthy and renew life's vigour. He would plague the bourgeoisie with theatre.

'I suffer from a frightful disease of the mind': from the 1920s onwards Artaud was consumed by pain in a relentless cycle of illness. 'My frightful destiny', he wrote in 1923, 'has for a long time put me *beyond human reason*, outside life.' He pictured himself in the lineage of Poe and de Nerval, Rimbaud and Lautréamont, a *poète maudit* whose voice could be expressed only at the price of untold suffering and isolation. He was a reincarnation of Rimbaud's '*JE est un Autre*'. In his poetry, he came to terms with this demon by experiencing himself as a nightmarish, terrifying emptiness. His consciousness was anguished nothingness, but out of the void there would body forth creation. The artist embraced anarchy, was the uncreated creator (he began to fantasize that he had had no parents); his excruciating agonies were the birth pangs of art.

In the public sphere he reconciled himself to this abyss of maddening pain and his civil war of the feelings by espousing first Dadaism and then Surrealism. Both raised the bloody standard of shock, revolt and rejection. Dadaism's repudiation of Cartesian logic, of the Gutenberg cage of syntax, chimed with Artaud's lifelong distrust of mere verbiage and his quest for pristine and pure utterance. Surrealism's mockery of the irrationality of *homo rationalis* struck further chords.

But he soon felt uneasy with the slick pseudo-Sadeanism of the Surrealists whose own toying with the unconscious proved just another ritual of rationalism. And above all he could not abide the increasingly close ties André Breton and others tried to forge between Surrealism and Communism. As for Nietzsche, so for Artaud, the artist had to be above politics, outside society: beyond. All else was but a betrayal of art. Poetry soared beyond propaganda.

Yet Nietzsche had his Greeks. And Artaud for his part sought living analogues for the searing passions which inflamed his mind. His inner pilgrimage took geographical form. He went in quest of illumination amongst the primitives. In 1936 he sailed for Mexico and journeyed into the interior to commune with the Tarahumara Indians. Amongst them, he believed he had found

143

what he was looking for ('seething forces which pressurize the blood') – a people in touch with the sun and the skies and the soil, at one not just with the elements but with their own inner feelings. An art of enchantment. For Artaud, as for D.H. Lawrence, here was an organic culture rooted in the organs – not least a people whose very mythology squared with his own convictions. For Tarahumara religion was essentially androgynous. They saw male and female, mind and body, spirit and flesh as united. They seemed to suffer none of the Western war of the soul against the body which had made Artaud so tortured about his own sexual urgings.

Feeling restored, Artaud returned to Europe, and attempted to get married to the daughter of a Belgian businessman. The engagement was called off in uproar, however, because he would not divest himself of his refusal to conform. Once more needing to restore his contact with the truly primitive, he sailed for Ireland. Hearing the voice of Christ each day bombarding his head, his behaviour grew more agitated. He sought asylum at a Jesuit monastery. The holy fathers turned him over to the police. The police put him on a boat back to France. Following some kind of violent incident on the ship, Artaud was straitjacketed on disembarkation and confined in a lunatic asylum in December 1937. His head was shaven. He remained locked away for nearly nine years, a literal alien at last.

At Rodez Asylum Artaud gradually became more composed. He changed his persona, abandoning the patronymic Artaud and adopting his mother's maiden name, Nalpas. He recovered his fervent Christianity and, encouraged by the superintendent, Dr Ferdière, a man of literary sympathies, began once more to write poetry. Ferdière grew convinced that Artaud's muse needed the psychiatric stimulus of a dose of insulin treatment and electroconvulsive therapy. But after undergoing these in 1944, Artaud regarded himself as nothing but a wreck. His memory was gone, his feelings were numb. He was dead. In 1946, he was released, and went to stay in Paris at Dr Delmas' clinic at Ivry.

His was now the madness of rage. In his last years pain was turned to a ferocity of hitherto unprecedented intensity. Artaud threw over his Christianity (repudiating the 'horrible little bewitcher from Judaea') and waged total Nietzschean war against the crucifying society. He had long felt plagued and persecuted by amorphous forces from beyond which he called black magic or sorcery. Now he felt more possessed than ever. The ECT was merely the most physical manifestation of his persecutors' oppression. As he saw it after his ECT treatment,

The mind, the brain, the consciousness and also above all the body of Antonin Artaud are paralysed, held, garrotted by methods amongst which electric shock is a mechanical application and prussic acid or potassium cyanide or insulin a botanical or physiological transposition.

Psychiatry was pure persecution, a final solution for the insane:

Lunatic asylums are consciously and premeditatedly receptacles of black magic.

His last word on art and madness came in his book on Van Gogh published in the next year. There, that mad artist appears, not as a 'degenerate' as the psychiatrists had so often called him, but as the true hero of humanity, a man of illumination, blessed or cursed with a 'superior lucidity' which enabled him 'to see farther, infinitely and more dangerously further than the immediate and apparent reality of facts'. Van Gogh had been hounded to death by his psychiatrist, Dr Gachet, for he was too dangerous to be allowed to live. Society drove him to suicide. By a nice irony, *Van Gogh suicidé de la société* was awarded the Prix Sainte-Beuve just before Artaud's death in 1948.

For Artaud, the rest was nonsense. His last poems (*Le Retour d'Artaud, le Momo*) liberated themselves in what the psychiatrists would have called glossolalia:

> o dedi
> a dada orzoura
> o dou zoura
> a dad skizi
>
> o kaya
> o kaya pontoura
> o ponoura
> a pena
> poni

Was he understood?

8 · Daniel Schreber:
Madness, Sex and the Family

In October 1893, the chief judge to the Dresden court of appeal, Daniel Schreber, suffered some sort of nervous collapse. This was not the first time – he had experienced something similar just over a decade earlier. He came under the supervision of the doctor who had treated him on the previous occasion, Dr Paul Emil Flechsig, who ran the university psychiatric clinic in Leipzig.

Flechsig was not a surprising choice of physician. Like Schreber, he was an eminent and well-respected member of the professional *haute bourgeoisie* in Saxony. Judge Schreber and his wife Pauline felt gratitude towards him for Schreber's recovery from the earlier bout of hypochondriacal depression – indeed, Frau Schreber so 'worshipped' Flechsig that she kept a photograph of the physician on her desk. What is crucial, however, according to Sigmund Freud's reconstruction of the case eighteen years later, is that Schreber's unconscious wishes had induced him to fall ill in 1893, specifically in order that he might be in Flechsig's hands: for Schreber had, Freud believed, profound sexual longings for the neuro-anatomist.

What would have happened in 1893 if, instead of entering the Leipzig psychiatric clinic, Schreber had been put on the first train to Vienna and given an appointment with Freud? That, of course, was hardly a likely eventuality. Though in his late thirties, Freud had hardly made any kind of a name for himself. His first major publication, the *Studies in Hysteria*, co-authored with Josef Breuer, had only just come out. Who could have known in 1893 that Freud was in fact to psychoanalyse Schreber – not on the couch but off the printed page – eighteen years later in 1911, when, in reality, Schreber was dying in Sonnenstein Asylum?

It is very difficult to say – to continue this fantasy – whether, if Schreber had arrived at Berggasse 19, Freud would have found analysing him a feasible proposition. As a general rule, Freud believed that the process of free association which constituted the 'talking cure' was viable in cases of neurosis, but that psychotic cases were too locked in to their own delusional worlds to make intellectual and emotional contact. Certainly in retrospect Freud had no doubt that Schreber's condition was serious enough to require the label 'psychosis'. In his published study, Freud called Schreber a 'case of paranoia (*dementia paranoides*)', and others who treated him saw him as suffering from *dementia praecox*, or in the fashionable new language of the day, as 'schizophrenic'. Freud quite explicitly argued that the defence-systems of paranoiacs were typically so watertight as to render analysis fruitless. This view has been echoed in a recent review of Schreber's case by Dr Austin McCawley, who, reflecting how he might have treated Schreber, states that if the judge had started talking to him about his delusions he would have tried to 'look out of the window and think about how to change the subject'. For McCawley the treatment of choice would have been a good dose of electro-convulsive therapy.

So Freud may not have got anywhere (and, as we shall see later, Schreber for his part would have found it hard to loll on the couch). But supposing the clinical alchemy had been right, the Freud of 1911 felt pretty sure what would have taken place: a fierce and hostile transference from Schreber to the analyst, excited by Schreber's homosexual longings for Dr Flechsig, which themselves were sublimations of his libidinous feelings towards his (dead) brother and his (dead) father.

For Freud saw Schreber as a *locus classicus* of a startling connection he claimed to have discovered: he was paranoid and the root cause of paranoia was homosexuality. Since in Schreber's case, these erotic longings were absolutely repressed, Freud would have encountered them – initially at least – in reversed form: Schreber would have claimed that he was being persecuted by Freud. How would the Freud of 1893 have responded? At that stage, of course, Freud had no inkling of transference, still less of counter-transference. Nevertheless, he would surely have been highly sensitized to the ambiguities of such desire, since by then he was becoming intimately involved with his fellow doctor, Wilhelm Fliess, a relationship which confronted him face to face with his own homosexual tendencies. Whether the homoerotic charge would have flowed, in whatever refracted form, from Schreber to Freud and back again, naturally depends upon whether Freud's subsequent diagnosis of Schreber was along the right lines.

Popular myth has it that it was Freud who, after a century of 'Victorian' prudery, made it possible for people to talk about sex frankly and to plot the connections between sexual problems and wider neurotic disturbances. At least in a superficial sense, however, that was not so. A glance at Schreber's own *Memoirs* gives startling indication of the sort of sexual fantasies and perversions which could be discussed openly in print in Wilhelmine Germany. Homosexuality – its identification, classification and aetiology – was elaborately explored in the sexual psychopathologies of Richard Krafft-Ebing, Havelock Ellis and other prominent *fin de siècle* contributors to clinical medicine and socio-cultural theory. Sexual abnormalities were very widely blamed for being at the root of psychological disorders long before Freud – witness how from the 1870s Charcot and his Parisian colleagues saw the female reproductive system, and its projections in the female mind, as the root of hysteria. In other words, Freud did not so much put an end to a conspiracy of silence about sex as make a very special type of contribution to an already widespread debate about exactly how sexuality played a role in mental and emotional disturbance. His distinctive claim was that adult neuroses were typically the legacy of infantile sexual conflict (the Oedipal syndrome), which resulted in repressed sexual desire swept under the carpet in the unconscious.

Given this general climate, it should be no surprise that Judge Schreber's *Memoirs*, in tune with the *Zeitgeist*, should be so preoccupied with questions of his own sexual identity – or, indeed, should be so frank in dealing with them. Once again, as has appeared so often in this book, the mind of the patient and the mind of the psychiatrist are both speaking the same language, even if they are often at cross-purposes. Indeed patient and practitioner dissolve into one, in that Schreber published his *Memoirs* with the quite express hope that they should be received as his contribution to the science of abnormal mental states. There is perhaps a characteristic touch of grandiosity about Schreber's self-image as both guinea pig and experimenter, but it also helps remind us that at precisely this time Freud too was suffering a psychoneurosis and was conducting an 'analysis' of it. Since Schreber, mad people have often thought they have been making contributions to the advancement of psychiatry.

Both Freud's self-analysis and Schreber's *Memoirs* were to become, in their different ways, foundation documents of a new psychiatry. On their publication, the *Memoirs* were welcomed by the psychiatric community as offering invaluable new insights into schizophrenic states (it must have been a relief at long last to have a sufferer's-eye account which did not simply denounce the evils of asylums). Freud himself used the *Memoirs* to exemplify his own interpretation of paranoia and, ever since, lively debate has continued about how to situate Schreber's experiences within the psychiatric understanding of persecution feelings.

Schreber, it is widely admitted, has become the most famous patient in the history of psychiatry, precisely because his own concerns so felicitously mesh with the language and assumptions of the new discipline. Twentieth-century psychiatry has drawn remarkably little on the published writings of most mad people of earlier centuries, yet it has always felt at home in discussing Schreber – or, at least, as has been pointed out, those elements of Schreber as were passed down to us by the Freudian canon.

How then did Schreber himself understand his condition? Schreber believed that his first breakdown in 1884, when he was forty-two, had been due to 'mental overstrain' brought on by his candidature for the Reichstag. (Schreber did not mention in his *Memoirs* that he had been heavily defeated in the poll and mocked in the newspapers – presumably highly wounding experiences.) The disorder had presented itself in 'certain hypochondriacal ideas', and had led to the desire to die and to two suicide attempts, but had not involved any broader delusional system. Schreber spent nearly six months in Flechsig's clinic, where he recovered.

The next decade proved a successful period in the life of Schreber and his wife, 'rich ... in outward honours' though blighted by their continuing childlessness (Frau Schreber suffered six spontaneous miscarriages). In June 1893, Schreber was appointed Senatspräsident, that is, presiding judge to the Dresden court of appeal. It was a plum promotion, particularly for one so relatively young. Perhaps it was also ominous, as Daniel's elder brother, Gustav Daniel, had committed suicide sixteen years earlier in 1877, after his appointment to a comparably onerous office. The memory presumably weighed on Schreber's mind.

By October of that year, he was beginning to be overwrought and was having nightmares of his former condition. He later remembered a further strange dream. It contained 'the idea that it really must be rather pleasant to be a woman succumbing to intercourse. The idea was so foreign to my whole nature that I may say I would have rejected it with indignation if fully awake.' Schreber's health deteriorated quickly once he actually assumed office. He became profoundly insomniac and eventually attempted suicide. By early November he was back once more in Flechsig's clinic.

For three months Schreber languished there, depressed, unable to sleep and preoccupied with morbid thoughts about death. He was perhaps kept on a reasonably even keel by his wife's daily visits. In February 1894, however, she took a short holiday, which precipitated a crisis. What precisely happened is unknown, except that one night Schreber experienced 'a quite unusual number of pollutions (perhaps half a dozen)'. On his wife's return Schreber felt too ashamed of his state to see her. A long period of deep isolation ensued.

It was now, for the first time, that Schreber began to be assailed by the supernatural. He saw man as a dualistic creature, made up of a body and a soul, the latter being entirely contained in the nerves. God was wholly composed of nerves, and communication between God and humans was possible through the medium of nervous rays which God emitted. Nerves were pathways of power, and whoever could control, concentrate or disseminate nervous impulses naturally enjoyed sway. Into that category fell nerve doctors such as Flechsig. Schreber believed he was suffering from nervous disease. Not surprisingly, therefore, he saw himself as particularly liable to Flechsig's control. (There is an obvious parallel in James Tilley Matthews' notions of Mesmeric influence.)

Schreber came to suspect that Flechsig harboured 'secret designs against him' via 'influences on my nervous system emanating from your nervous system'. For one thing, he believed the doctor might be using his control of divine rays in order to perform 'scientific experiments' upon him, possibly of a mind-reading kind. He heard Flechsig's voice when he was not present. Worse, he conceived the abominable idea that action was being taken by Flechsig to 'unman' him. This meant that his 'soul' would be handed over to Flechsig, and his body too ('transformed into a female body') would be 'left to [Flechsig] for sexual misuse and simply "forsaken" and left to rot'. In some way Flechsig had inveigled God into joining this plot.

Within the strategy of writing the *Memoirs*, Schreber obviously had very ambivalent feelings about imputing wicked designs to Flechsig: after all, the *Memoirs* were composed by him as an earnest of his own sanity, and wild accusations and doctor-blaming would have been unseemly. Certainly Schreber's account is rather confused about whether he thought that Flechsig (and, for that matter, God) wished to destroy him or, on the other hand, to attempt a cure (Schreber hints at hypnotherapeutic treatment, using 'rays', carried out by the superintendent).

Nevertheless, the judge grew convinced that Flechsig had a most terrible fate in store for him: soul murder. Soul murder was a notion familiar from folklore which enjoyed wide cultural currency in the Romantic era in such works as Byron's *Manfred*. What it meant to him Schreber never precisely clarifies. But broadly it was a sort of vampirism; it entailed the captivation of the will, and the possession of the spirit of another, in order to prolong and promote one's own existence. Schreber advances a rather obscure account of how, over the generations, the Flechsig family had long been plotting soul murder against the Schrebers, above all to bring about the extinction of their line. Schreber himself was the last surviving male of this family, and by then was likely to remain childless.

In June 1894, for reasons that are not clear, Schreber was removed from Flechsig's clinic. He was soon transferred to the Sonnenstein Asylum, under the medical direction of Dr Weber. He was to remain there for almost nine years. Very gradually, his feelings of being threatened by Flechsig's designs diminished. He wrote that Flechsig's soul had 'progressively lost its intelligence so that now hardly a trace of awareness of its own identity remains'. Replacing Flechsig, his main assailant becomes God (at one point Schreber actually refers to 'God Flechsig'). Schreber presents himself as being the chief battleground of a war in heaven, fought over the fate of his own person. His own supercharged nervous condition thereby became a threat to the stability of the macrocosm.

For in some ways God was continuing Flechsig's plan of 'unmanning', with a view to allowing Schreber's 'body to be prostituted like that of a female harlot'. As part of that transformation, Schreber gradually felt – initially with gross indignation – his very body becoming more feminine, increasingly filled with 'nerves of voluptuousness (female nerves)'. Yet, paradoxically, that transformation made his body highly, indeed dangerously, attractive to his oppressors, to God's rays. God simultaneously desired, yet feared, Schreber's enfeminization, or, we might say, Schreber felt himself oppressed simultaneously with another's hate and love.

In order to put a halt to Schreber's dangerously attractive feminine 'soul voluptuousness', God began to direct punitive 'miracles against my person'. These consisted of a series of invasive actions ('interferences') which tormented Schreber, depriving him of peace and sleep. Echoing James Tilley Matthews' fate, excruciatingly painful bodily curses were rained down upon him, such as 'the so-called purification of the abdomen', 'the compression of the chest miracle', the 'cursed creation of a false feeling', the 'coccyx miracle' and so forth. His ears, inner or outer, were never permitted to be free from a 'nonsensical twaddle of voices', his brain was picked, his mind was constantly being read and rebuked, his thoughts repeated after themselves with a sinister echo, and there was no let-up of voices of instruction, issuing him commands such as 'Do not think about certain parts of your body,' or 'A job started must be finished.' Voices would keep telling him to correct his posture.

He was furthermore assailed by 'little men', standing around his head, interfering with his person and subjecting him to thought compulsions. Overall, he was never permitted to be 'master of my own head', and this ceaseless torture felt to the judge like an 'infringement of the freedom of human thinking, or more correctly thinking nothing'. Thus a protracted war set in between otherworldly powers and Schreber, in which he saw himself as cursedly attractive and vulnerable through being highly desirable to God, yet also flailed by Him for threatening His divine existence.

Meanwhile, Schreber continued to become 'unmanned'. He thought his penis was disappearing, and that he was growing breasts. For long his very being as a man fought against this degradation, being ashamed to hear voices taunting him with sayings like 'fancy a person who was a Senatspräsident allowing himself to be f-----'. Yet very gradually he came to embrace his fate and to associate femininity, with its 'soul voluptuousness', with a much higher and more privileged mission.

151

For Schreber had become convinced that he was the sole surviving human being. In part this belief arose from his own direct empirical observations. No one else was in his cell. He hardly saw a soul; he received no visits; nobody was visible from out of his cell window. But these personal experiences made wider sense to him within the Christian eschatology of the imminent ending of the world, and in the context of scientific ideas with which he was familiar, which spoke of cosmological and geological catastrophes periodically extinguishing life from the planet. Every so often, life was wiped out, in preparation for the earth's reseeding. Schreber convinced himself that he would be the instrument for such a renewal of mankind, through divine impregnation, a new virgin birth.

In this situation, Schreber began to get a clearer sense of divine mission. As he saw it, it had become his divine duty patiently to submit to his fate. Earlier, he had violently rejected his enfeminization, doing physical battle with the 'rough attendants' in an attempt to prove to himself and to them his own macho virility. Now he increasingly believed that by absolute stillness he would be able to attain a nobler end, to absorb and thereby overcome the hostile rays which were creating war in heaven. Thereby he would prepare himself for his coming out as a woman.

True, his earlier conviction that the 'world had perished' and that he was the 'last real human being left' was in time undermined. Figures and forms which he had taken to be mere shadows and shades he eventually accepted as *bona fide* fellow humans. Even so, his transformation into a woman proceeded apace, and at last he became so enchanted by his new gender that he paraded himself before a mirror sporting a low-cut vest, ribbons and costume jewellery: 'I have wholeheartedly inscribed the cultivation of femininity on my banner.'

Schreber's mental stability improved, and he basked unabashed in his feminine voluptuousness, to which he felt entitled 'as a small compensation for the excesses of suffering and privation' he had suffered in the asylum for many years. In 1900 he petitioned for his release from legal tutelage, whereby the juridical management of his affairs had been taken out of his hands by reason of insanity. He was still, he admitted, suffering from nerves, but he was not insane, not mentally ill. The fact that he was writing, and intended to publish, his *Memoirs* was evidence, he argued, of his command of reason, for he had no doubt they would form 'an important source of information about the structure of an entirely new religious system'.

Schreber's petition was opposed by Dr Weber on the grounds that he was still suffering from gross paranoid delusions and had no insight whatsoever into that fact. The court found for Weber. Two years later, by which time Schreber had occasionally been out on parole and had comported himself well, he pressed his case once more. This time Weber offered little opposition (though he did cite Schreber's desire to publish his scandalous *Memoirs* as proof of lasting moral insanity), and it was granted. Not long afterwards Schreber left Sonnenstein, about the same time as his *Memoirs* were published. He lived with his mother. When in 1907 she died and his wife had a stroke, it proved necessary to have him readmitted to Sonnenstein, where he died in 1911, just before Freud's analysis of the case appeared.

How are Schreber's experiences to be interpreted? As he himself saw it, he had twice fallen nervously sick through overwork. On the second occasion, the extraordinary intensity of his sufferings resulted from a plot against him hatched by his doctors and backed by the heavens. This he had managed to overcome by making destiny his choice, and accepting his new-sprouted femininity. Schreber was somewhat unsure *why* all that had happened. Ultimately, however, he believed in an order of divine justice; all events were regulated by the Order of the World, a sort of overriding cosmic rationality to which even God Himself was subject.

Certainly, he protested, he did not intend his *Memoirs* to be read as a *J'accuse* (indeed, his ability to rise above mere vitriol, he contended, was one of the signs of mental health which the court should take into account). Overall, he regarded his sufferings as stigmata of divine favour. He was the medium of some sort of new religious dawn, an agent of the redemption of mankind. While not fully understanding the meaning of all his experiences, 'one thing I am certain of, namely that I have come infinitely closer to the truth than human beings who have not received divine revelation'.

Schreber's attempt to give meaning to his experiences in terms of religious destiny was discounted of course by medical opinion. Dr Weber in particular straightforwardly dismissed Schreber's divine visions as downright delusions, the product of 'schizophrenia'. At this dismissal, Schreber became indignant. If all claims to experience supernatural agency were automatically to be invalid, *eo ipso*, as hallucinations, then Christianity itself must be treated as a delusion. If all who thought that they were in contact with transcendental beings were to suffer his own fate, then every medium or spiritualist was in jeopardy of the straitjacket. The doctrines of the doctors precisely exemplified the degenerate materialism which was sapping the true religion and culture of Teutonic civilization. He would not deny that he had suffered – indeed, was still suffering – from a 'morbidly excited nervous system', yet why should that not be a favourable seedbed for receiving real messages from beyond? By contrast, many 'a person with sound nerves is mentally blind'.

Clearly none of Schreber's physicians accepted him as an authentic visionary, or saw his delusions as meaningful. They did not interpret them, but merely identified them as symptoms of psychosis. Nor did they even feel called upon to attempt an aetiology. For them it was enough that he was mentally sick. It was thus with Freud in 1911 that the first major attempt was made to explain the hidden secrets of Schreber's delusions. To Freud, Schreber was of course paranoid. In particular, his enveloping persecution fantasies revealed deeply repressed homosexual urges now at last finding perplexed expression. Overall, 'the exciting cause' of Schreber's psychosis was 'a feminine (passive homosexual) wishful fantasy', which constituted 'the basis of Schreber's illness'. In other words, what brought the psychotic condition into being was resistance to an unacceptable desire.

The core of Freud's account of the case attempted to lay bare Schreber's censored homosexual desires. These had been brought to the surface and released by his contact with Flechsig. Freud aimed to show how Schreber's conscious mind had been forced to transform these dark and scandalous desires into feelings which he could handle more safely, producing his psychosis in the process. For Schreber's consciousness naturally could not admit that he desired Flechsig. The price of this denial was his psychosis.

How then did Schreber – indeed, any paranoid person – protect himself from his illicit desires? To mask his real feelings, the truthful proposition 'I love him' had to be transformed, initially into 'I hate him'. As Freud puts it, there is a 'simple formula' in such cases: 'The person who is now hated and feared for being a persecutor, was at one time loved and honoured.' But it was also equally unacceptable for the very respectable Schreber to confess to motiveless and spiteful hatred against his healer. Hence Schreber's straightforward putative formulation 'I hate him' had to be masked in the more acceptable form, 'He hates me'. From there it was but a stage to the further rationalizing, 'HE PERSECUTES ME'. Therein lay the real meaning of Schreber's notion that Flechsig aimed to emasculate him. Paranoiacs inhabit a looking-glass world in which symptom-formation thus proceeds by reversal, projection and denial.

Freud argued that Schreber's inadmissible homosexual longings for his psychiatric doctor should further be seen in the light of the psychoanalytical doctrine of transference. The real object of Schreber's desire was not Flechsig at all, but doubtless his own dead elder brother and his dead father. Freud notes in passing that Schreber *père* was in fact an eminent physician, hence a very understandable object of adulation: 'The patient was reminded of his brother or father by the figure of the doctor.' Of course, Schreber could no more admit 'his longing for his father and his brother' than he could his sexual desire for Flechsig. Once again, a more acceptable expression of illicit desires had to be found. As the object of his love and engine of his persecution, Schreber's father was transformed into God and also the sun. Freud sees Schreber's stance towards God as a tell-tale Oedipal one of 'mutinous insubordination and reverent submission'.

How had these inadmissible homosexual desires led to Schreber's saviour-like delusions of grandeur? Freud explained at length that paranoiacs such as Schreber suffered from a 'fixation at the stage of narcissism'; 'the length of the step back from sublimated homosexuality to narcissism is a measure of the amount of regression characteristic of paranoiacs'. In other words, as Schreber regressed in his psychosis, as he became more catatonic, his fixated infantile narcissism expressed itself in withdrawing of libidinous energy from everyone else, and in his new delight in auto-eroticism. Narcissism ('I love nobody') implied megalomania, hence Schreber's dreams of grandeur fantasizing his unique role in the destiny of the cosmos. Drawing upon ideas worked out jointly with Wilhelm Fliess, Freud also suggested that Schreber, who at the time of his second illness had reached the magic age of fifty-one, was in the throes of the male climacteric (the female cycle was governed by the number twenty-eight; the male by the number twenty-three; add them together and you got fifty-one).

Freud's reading of Schreber's text is intriguing. On the one hand, it hardly addresses itself at all to many of the central experiences constituting the vast bulk of the *Memoirs*. Freud has peculiarly little to say about Schreber's tale of turning into a woman destined to give birth to a new race. As has very commonly been pointed out, Freud's own unremittingly phallocentric viewpoint gave pride of place to explanations deriving from the presence or absence of the penis, as solutions to the Oedipal struggles of childhood. He never seriously considered the possibility that the arrow of envy might primarily be directed not from the female to the male, but, in the other direction, might be a boy's envy of the woman's capacity to have babies. Freud can perceive Schreber's enfeminization only in negative terms, as loss ('emasculation'). He has no theoretical framework within which he could see Schreber's mutation as a consummation or a true enhancement.

This may be put in another form. Schreber speaks of being 'unmanned'. Freud unhesitatingly identifies his experience of being unmanned as castration – i.e. pure loss – and interprets that experience wholly in terms of Schreber's putative desire to be sodomized by Flechsig and (by derivation) by his brother and his father. Freud thus axiomatically transliterates Schreber's feminine fantasies into male-directed homosexual desires. Of course, Freudian theory possesses good *a priori* grounds for the claim that Schreber must have had such anterior homosexual desires for the brother and the father. But there is no independent evidence that Schreber's own libidinal desires were that way inclined – except in so far as, following Freud's system of linguistic translation, his denials give the game away. Why, in any case, should we automatically call Schreber's fantasy about being transformed into a woman 'homosexual'? Schreber has his own perfectly intelligible reasons for wishing to be a fertile woman – so that in view of his wife's failure to give birth he can perpetuate the Schreber dynasty – which cannot simply be waved aside.

The same caveat must apply to Freud's discussion of Schreber's castration fear in relation to the 'father complex'. We lack any shred of direct evidence of Schreber's childhood attitudes towards his father, or even his memories of them. (The fact that chapter 3 of his *Memoirs*, which dealt with his family, was suppressed as unfit for publication, is obviously suggestive, but it cannot be decisive of anything.) In these circumstances, Schreber's alleged infantile castration fears must remain matters of supposition, reinforced only within the universalist claims of Freud's Oedipal theories. For airing all these again Freud offers a characteristic exculpation: 'I must disclaim all responsibility for the monotony of the solutions provided by psychoanalysis.'

What *is* directly demonstrable, however, though it was a fact not known to Freud, is that Schreber quite explicitly feared that Flechsig would castrate him, for his hospital notes record that fear. But such a fear was not paranoid; rather it was well grounded in reality. For the neuro-anatomist Flechsig made therapeutic use of castration at his clinic. It is hard to imagine that Schreber, an unusually well-informed man, did not know this. It is gratuitous to invoke suppositious repressed childhood experiences to explain fears well grounded in imminent threats.

Above all, it is surely inadequate to regard Schreber's sexual thoughts exclusively in terms of castration. For the *Memoirs* are not just about being 'emasculated'. They positively embrace being enfeminized. A very large section of the *Memoirs* – one almost totally ignored by Freud and all subsequent psychoanalytic commentators – records Schreber's growing pleasure in his transformation into a woman. This made perfectly good sense both in cosmic terms and in respect of a deeply experienced crisis in his own personal life. Schreber was profoundly distressed that he was the last of his own line. Because of the soul-murdering activities of the Flechsigs, his stock seemed doomed to extinction. He also believed that he might be the only surviving human. Devastating pandemics of plague and other diseases were, he thought, sweeping over mankind. The sun's powers were waning; the earth seemed in the throes of an appalling ecological disaster.

There were of course other semblances of people around. Schreber called them 'fleetingly improvised men'. In some sense they really were just that: shade-like beings who flashed in and out of Schreber's cell-bound life – servants, attendants, doctors – who passed quickly in and out of his consciousness, hardly breaking his isolation. For he was, as he emphasized, 'always alone'. Of course, this may simply be said to be symptomatic of his catatonic phase as a schizophrenic. But what Schreber felt was a terrifying and perplexing isolation, he wrapped up in a story about being the last survivor and so a divine instrument.

We may call these disaster fantasies symptoms of megalomania. But is that very illuminating? Surely it is better to see how Schreber was essentially inserting his own life-story into the deepest anxieties of late-nineteenth-century culture. For many reputable thinkers, moralists and scientists, *fin de siècle* looked for all the world perilously like *fin du monde*. The death of the sun and the end of time formed one of the gravest anxieties of the contemporary sciences of cosmology, astronomy, geology and so forth. Palaeontology showed the wrecks of many previous worlds, the extinct greatly outnumbering the survivors. Geology revealed the grand catastrophes which had repeatedly wrecked the globe. Thermodynamics was predicting a heat-death of the universe. Everything was run down, entropic. These threats of cosmic disaster were deeply imprinted on Schreber's mind, for page after page of his *Memoirs* – pages always passed over in silence by all the interpreters – record his deep familiarity with the scientific chiliasm of nineteenth-century scientists from Cuvier to the post-Darwinians.

Moreover, cosmic crisis seemed to Schreber – as to many of his contemporaries – to be mirrored in civic catastrophe. Like many doctors and psychiatrists of his era, Schreber was terrified by the spectre of social degeneration, the death of the city, the collapse of civilization. Classical culture, the Protestant religion and the social hierarchy were the bastions of civilization for 'God's chosen people', the Teutons. But everywhere Schreber (like his father before him) saw it subverted by its enemies. Roman Catholics and the Jews were the enemies within; the Slavic peoples constituted a barbaric threat from beyond. The masses were on the march.

Life itself was threatened. How might it be regenerated? Schreber's *Memoirs* teem with solutions, with his speculations about the life force, about the source and nature of creation – ideas patently based upon a layman's impressive familiarity with recent scientific publications.

He was of course absolutely *au fait* with the gamut of theories of divine creation advanced not just by Christian theologians (the Virgin Birth, Resurrection, etc.), but also within other faiths – he was deeply attracted to Persian religion. He pondered the logistics of creation *ex nihilo*, explored the transmigration of souls and was intrigued by spontaneous generation. In its vulgar materialist mode, that notion was clearly invalid, but he was attracted by the idea of spontaneous production by miracle. When flies and wasps suddenly impinged upon his field of vision, Schreber liked to see them as proofs of sudden, spontaneous creations.

But Schreber was also well disposed towards evolutionary doctrines of the regeneration of life out of death, and was fascinated by the thought that scientific truth in these matters might lie encoded time out of mind in myth and folklore, in the tales of Noah, Deucalion and so forth. If all around lay the shroud of death, how could life stir again?

Obviously in these speculations Schreber saw his own plight reflected. He might be the instrument whereby the future could be secured through a regeneration of life. For this to occur, male must turn female and become a parthenogenic life-reproducing force. Schreber deeply pondered these matters of life, death and generation. Does it make sense to reduce all these preoccupations to castration anxieties initially induced by desire for the father?

None of the psychoanalytic accounts of Schreber's *Memoirs* pays heed to these ideas, this recension of ontogeny and phylogeny, which occupy at least a sixth of Schreber's entire text. Of course, granted their own pet concerns, this is perfectly proper. For their business is not with Schreber's conscious mind, his 'rationalizations', his engagement with the *Zeitgeist*. They home in on what can be unearthed about his unconscious, and how it supplies the materials for an archaeology of his Oedipal struggles, which in its turn explains the orientation of his psychosis.

The psychoanalytic enterprise of retrospectively analysing Schreber – and how extensive it has been! – has thus consisted of attempts to place his case within the wider framework of psychodynamic theory. Where exactly should this paranoia be classed with respect to the borders between neurosis and psychosis? Should Schreber's paranoia, with its overtly destructive elements, be seen as primary? Or should the masochistic dimensions be foregrounded? Is Schreber to be understood principally with respect to his infantile relations to his father, as Freud saw it? Or should attention be paid to his responses to his mother as well? Thus Freud interpreted the sun in Schreber's *Memoirs* as a symbol for the father, but other psychiatrists – in particular the mother-and-son team of Macalpine and Hunter – have contended that it stands for the mother. These are the psychiatrist's main concerns.

It is not the business of this chapter to adjudicate between these interpretations (still less to psychoanalyse them). They are legion, they conflict with each other and they continue to proliferate – witness this extract from a summary offered by Philip Kitay in 1963 of a symposium which debated some of the rival interpretations:

> The classic Freudian interpretation of paranoia and of the Schreber case was viewed as giving initially insufficient recognition to the importance of hostile destructive drives. . . . Rivalry between Schreber and his father

for his mother's affection, and probably also between Schreber and his brother, consistent with Freud's later views on paranoia (1922, 1923) was seen as an important factor in the development of his illness. Both Carr and Nydes considered the study of the interrelationships between hostility and homosexuality crucial for an understanding of paranoia. Carr took note of the hypothesis that the anal–sadistic component in homosexual love was the source of the threat to the paranoid patient, whereas Nydes postulated that homosexuality was defensive against both parricidal wishes and the danger of retaliatory destruction of the patient. . . . Specific factors in the etiology and course of Schreber's illness emphasized by individual speakers included the following: failure to overcome fear of ego-loss entailed in intimacy (White), infantile omnipotence aroused by success in receiving appointment to the position of Senatspräsident (Nydes), surrender of power-seeking in order to obtain love (Nydes), and multiple cross-identification and confusions in identifications (Niederland). [and so forth]

There may be a touch of truth in any of these stories. What is clear is that the explanatory model underpinning them all is that Schreber's (or indeed Everyman's) problems can be adequately understood exclusively by reference to his inner psychological development, his own disturbed emotional and intellectual processes, the struggles between his wishes and his fears, between drives and inhibitions, and so forth. Freud began this process by labelling Schreber paranoid, i.e. suffering from delusions of persecution, and linked this to Schreber's supposed homosexual longings inferred from Schreber's expressed feelings of persecution by Flechsig. The locus of the illness is seen in the projections of the patient, which are interpreted as a flight from reality.

But what if Schreber said he was being persecuted, not as a result of a smokescreen fantasy, arising from not being able to own up to loving a man, but because he really was being persecuted? And what if his psychosis arose not from an attempt to shield himself from the object of his desire but from the terrors of being systematically mistreated? What if his crisis lay in masking not love but hatred? The only ground for ruling such explanations out of court would be to say that Schreber was mad, therefore his perceptions can only be deluded symptoms. But this strategy is circular and nakedly victim-blaming.

Morton Schatzman has eloquently argued the case against the Freudian party-line. For Schatzman, Schreber should be seen not as paranoid but primarily as persecuted. He had been systematically abused by his father as a child. He had been rendered inhibited in such a way that, as a dutiful, loving, conformist son, he viewed his father not as the bully he was but as a paragon of goodness and rectitude. He had been brainwashed so that he could not confront his persecution head-on. Any protest had been pre-empted and silenced. His subsequent psychosis represented a series of direct and literal transformations of his experience of actual persecution, but also created a highly distorted framework within which to give vent to them.

What lends Schatzman's interpretation general plausibility is that it looks at Schreber's stories as the product not solely of his own personal projections but also of his experience of what was dinned into him by others. Schatzman quite reasonably assumes that much that registered and took root in his young mind was not fantasy but propaganda, i.e. the receipt of messages from outside, from his parents, above all from his father.

What lends weight to this view is that Schreber's father was one of the most enduringly influential paediatricians in the German-speaking world, and a would-be founder of an Institute of Orthopaedics. Although we have no chapter-and-verse evidence about Schreber's own upbringing, we do possess some eighteen books and pamphlets written by Dr Schreber on the principles and practice of child-rearing. These place overwhelming emphasis upon the values of duty, discipline, control and 'unconditional obedience': thus educated, children would avoid 'unhealthy sensitivity, hypochondria, hysteria and fantasies'. Dr Schreber's books moreover tell us that his techniques had been successfully tried out first on his own children. What is particularly revealing is that although Freud was thoroughly familiar with Dr Schreber's paediatric principles, he saw no relevant connection between them and his son's psychosis. Freud came to believe that girls' reports of infantile sexual assault were hysterical fictions. Presumably in the same way he thought that any account that Schreber *fils* might have offered of pedagogical persecution would be paranoid.

Schatzman convincingly argues that much of Schreber's persecution experience is beyond reasonable doubt a veiled memory of his own upbringing under his father's thumb. At the specific level, there are numerous close analogues between techniques which Dr Schreber urges fathers and educators to deploy on children and the tortures Schreber recorded during his psychosis. For, obsessed by fears of orthopaedic imbalance, physical weakness and deformity, Dr Schreber had devised a battery of physical harnesses and contraptions in which to confine children from two to twenty, designed to impede improper movement and to correct posture. Many of these seem explicitly reflected in Schreber's later experiences.

For example, Judge Schreber said that he suffered in the asylum from endless assault against the muscles of his eyes and eyelids. This appears to echo the advice offered by Dr Schreber in *The Systematically Planned Sharpen-*

ing of the Sense Organs (1859) for training children in eye movements and concentration. Judge Schreber then records the extremely painful 'coccyx · miracle', whose foul design was to make both sitting down and standing up impossible ('when I was lying down, one wanted to chase me off the bed', and when 'I was walking one attempted to force me to lie down'). This seems directly to reflect his father's crusade against the bad postures children habitually got into when sitting, slouching, resting, etc., and his requirement that parents should vigilantly instruct their children to change posture: 'as soon as they lean back . . . or bend their backs [the doctor argued] the time has come to exchange at least for a few minutes the seated position for the absolutely still', and so forth.

Similarly, Schreber records suffering during his psychosis the horrifying 'compression of the chest miracle. . . . It consisted in the whole chest wall being compressed, so that the state of oppression caused by the lack of breath was transmitted to my whole body.' This was a reliving of the experience of being encased in his father's *Schrebersche Geradhalter* (Schreber's Straight-holder), a bar fixed in front of a table at which the child was writing, whose effect would be to press heavily upon the chest of any miscreant infant who dared to round his shoulders and lean forward.

The worst of all the 'miracles' Judge Schreber suffered was the 'head-compressing machine', a vice which, by turning a screw, clamped and elongated the head. Once again this directly reflected another piece of his father's paediatric technology, the *Kopfhalter* (headholder), a strap fastened to the head, chin and clothes, designed to tug at the hair if the head was not held straight.

These and many other technological analogues – embryonic straitjackets – show how Schreber's persecution experiences in middle age reproduced quite literal engines of control to which he had been forced to submit when young. Through the experience of his body pains, his hypochondria, Schreber was trapped in the contraptions of his childhood.

But Schatzman further shows that the persecution of the young Schreber was even more comprehensive. During his psychosis, Schreber felt totally under external direction, utterly taken over and possessed. For long periods he was beset by noises issuing him with a babel of peremptory commands. Everything he said, did or thought was overheard, played back, scrutinized, screened. His head was literally opened up to the rays and nerves oppressing it from outside. This was Schreber's way of reliving his childhood as conducted by his father as a system of planned, unremitting tutorial surveillance.

One of the torturing miracles Schreber suffered consisted of being surrounded with pictures and writings about himself, replaying and offering a commentary upon his own turpitude. This was a recall of his childhood experience of having his actions and state of mind endlessly corrected by his parents. In particular, it mirrored another of Dr Schreber's wheezes, putting a moral blackboard on the child's bedroom wall, listing all his recent crimes and punishments.

At the most concrete level, even the language of Schreber's psychosis reflected the actual language dinned into him by his father. For Schreber believed himself to be assailed and penetrated by 'rays' (*Strahlen*). Now his father had written that the 'rays' of God's love, and of course of parental love, should permeate and penetrate the family: 'a childlike mind is completely penetrated by love'.

Here lay a subtler stratum of oppression. Schreber *père* taught a doctrine of plenitude of parental power, to be assimilated by the child under the guise of 'self-control' and 'freedom'. Spite, anger and self-will had to be overcome. Absolute obedience was required. The good child had internalized obedience to the parental will. Mature discipline, in Dr Schreber's moral book, was self-discipline, was perfect freedom.

The young Schreber indeed became good and obedient. He utterly internalized the law, the name, of the father: 'few people [he noted] have been brought up according to such strict moral principles as I'. This moral hegemony still governed his feelings during his psychosis. For he certainly felt unable to escape being beset by God's rays and the miracles they wrought against him. He was surrounded by them, not because he desired to be (as is the thrust of Freud's scenario of unconscious and repressed homosexual desire), but because that was for him the condition of his own childhood, never being left alone to his own devices.

Yet nowhere does Schreber unambiguously blame his persecutors. The *Memoirs* are unusual as a 'paranoid' text in not cursing those who incessantly and maliciously harm him. Mad people's writings commonly curse the doctor of the asylum. By contrast Schreber goes out of his way to be fair to Flechsig, to argue that Flechsig's evil designs against him were not the work of the real flesh-and-blood physician but rather the deeds of his 'tested spirit', i.e. a disembodied, displaced Flechsig, a sort of alter ego. Many mad people's rants – witness Cowper's for instance – curse God. But Schreber's actually exonerate Him. God persecuted him, but it was not His fault. For God Himself was not all-powerful; He was drawn into conspiracies by the attraction of the rays.

It is as though it is a world of persecution without an identifiable persecutor. And this is so (Schatzman plausibly argues) because Schreber's father had browbeaten his son into accepting that authority was always right. His mind's eye had been trained to be blind to his oppressors (or at least to transform those who did him harm into surrogate 'little men'). And Schreber had been

162

too well trained by his father to be able to rebel through an aggressive psychosis. Instead his crisis took a much more submissive form. Schreber eventually overcame the persecuting miracles by absorbing them all and emerging as a new whole. He opted out of male struggle and became a woman.

There is much that surely commands assent in Schatzman's account, not least because he probes the actual dynamics of the family – so far as they can be reconstructed – in which Schreber learned good from bad, and to which his every thought and action was laid bare. Surely it makes more sense to see infants as acted upon as well as acting, to see them responding to information, to invasion from without, than simply to saddle them with all the responsibility for the Oedipus Complex. After all, what historian would simply blame the poor for their own penury, or slaves for their own chains? More particularly, Schatzman is willing to place this micropolitics of the family in its wider context, distinctively German, indeed Bismarckian. It is not too tendentious to regard Dr Schreber's preoccupation with disciplined physical culture as a seedbed of Nazi obedience. After all, in the 1930s, Alfons Ritter, a pro-Nazi author, paid lavish tribute to Dr Schreber's winning ways with children. Or, put another way, the younger Schreber was incapacitated by and in later life confusedly rebelled against that very system which (according to Wilhelm Reich) fathered the psychopathology of Nazism through its sexual puritanism and rigidity towards the body.

More generally, Schatzman is right to see the Freudian account of Schreber's 'paranoia' as an implicit form of victimizing the victim, a subtle mode of siding with the authorities. Schatzman detects Freud doing the same in the case of Little Hans, the little boy whose fear of horses was interpreted by Freud as a castration fear within the Oedipus Complex. For Freud judged Hans's behaviour as disturbed rather than regarding that of his parents – friends and followers of Freud who told Hans that if he misbehaved his penis would be cut off – as disturbing. The same, as I argued in chapter 6, may be said for Freud's browbeating of Dora.

All the same, Schatzman himself curiously perpetuates the blind spot of the neo-Freudian interpretations, in choosing to say next to nothing about Schreber's lavish fantasies about being a woman. Within the continuing canon of Freudian interpretations, father–son conflicts seem to rule out any positive appreciation of the feminine. Obviously we may see Schatzman's radicalism as rebellious son to the orthodox Freudian father.

More broadly still, all such interpretations, canonical Freudian or revisionist Freudian, miss the point. For they are trapped within a mistaken notion that true explanations of present disturbances lie in the events of the past. They share a psychogenetic approach which presumes that, because the child is father of the man, the key to a person's present behaviour lies in his childhood, lies quite specifically within a narrow band of childhood years (for Freud, the Oedipal period). It becomes axiomatic that the events of those years, swept under the carpet into the unconscious, turn into a kind of time-bomb.

One attempt to break free of this dogmatically historicist approach – one all too often bogged down in theoretical sterility – lies in the use made by the literary critic Barry Chabot of techniques of textual interpretation to highlight the preoccupations of the *Memoirs*. Chabot rightly sees that behind the literal and mechanical decoding exercises that can be attempted upon this text (what do 'Flechsig', or the 'sun', or 'God' really stand for?) certain structural patterns recur. One of these is a preoccupation with the dialectic of dependence and independence. Schreber represents himself as essentially impotent and as beset by stronger forces. But, rather as in Greek mythology, there is no single omnipotent force dominating the heavens, nor even a simple clash between God and Satan, good and evil. Even God's powers are not almighty; His understanding of human action is imperfect; indeed (says Schreber) He cannot learn from experience.

The rays of God assail; but God Himself, obeying a kind of inverse square law, loses His strength the more He extends Himself; and so, even when extending His influence, prudence warns Him to withdraw. Yet God must entangle with, indeed enter, Schreber in order to regenerate the world. But, for that to be effected, Schreber must himself succumb to another contradiction, and become a fully voluptuous woman. Yet the accomplishment of that transformation is perennially frustrated by the tormenting miracles. However, Schreber, though persecuted, is himself able to overcome these, through absorption, through soaking up punishment.

Chabot is perceptive in bringing out the ambiguities which bedevil these struggles. They represent the confusions as to agency and authority experienced by a man whose cosmos is in disarray. They show the strivings towards order of a man of the law, a judge, for whom individual will or muscle power should be merely contingent by contrast to the ultimate fitnesses of law, order, justice. True autonomy is a goal that can be achieved only within the framework of a harmonious universe: 'There must be an equalizing justice.' Despite all his trials and tribulations, Schreber insists, 'I emerge albeit not without bitter sufferings and deprivation victorious, because the order of the world is on my side.'

Yet Chabot's reading remains rather abstract, imprisoned in the text. What neither he nor any other commentator has much considered are Schreber's actual experiences in the asylum. After three depressed months inside, he suffered some sort of acute breakdown as soon as his wife was absent on holiday, as soon as contact with the outside world ceased. Whatever the nature of his collapse, he thereafter felt too ashamed of his condition to see her. For at least the next five years, he lived a day-to-day life of extraordinary isolation, spending days on end in his own room, punctuated only occasionally by more or less solitary walks and recreation. Accounts of asylum life commonly depict a lively sub-culture of fellow lunatics and attendants. John Perceval's *Narrative* is deeply preoccupied with disorientation and reorientation towards patients and doctors alike. Clifford Beers explicitly tells us that he snatched back his reason from unreason as a result of a relationship with another patient. And so forth. But the impression overwhelmingly given by Schreber is one of utterly desolating isolation. There is no depiction of any close contact with patient, attendant or doctor.

To say this is not to blame anyone. After all, Schreber's clinical records show how difficult he was, bellowing, irritable and self-absorbed – though it is worth noting that none of Schreber's doctors seems to have had the slightest notion that relating to his 'delusions', or even engaging with him closely, offered therapeutic hope. And of course it may simply be right to say that he was submerged in the kind of schizophrenic condition which would necessarily cut him off from all human contact. But there is grave danger here of jumping to conclusions. Freud says that Schreber had 'withdrawn from the people in his environment and from the outside world generally'. It is less obvious that he was 'withdrawn' than that he had been 'withdrawn'.

Above all, it is important to remember that Schreber's own most painful and poignant memories of his early years in the asylum were of torture in the here and now. He believed he was brutally treated by the attendants. He experienced mystifying and arbitrary interference from the doctors, and feared they would castrate him. On one occasion, he claims, he was unceremoniously and without warning or explanation removed by main force from his rooms and dumped in a dark padded cell without a word. For two and a half years, he had to sleep in a padded cell reserved for maniacs. No reason had been offered to him for this treatment. We do not know what objectively happened. We do know that Schreber experienced his treatment as utterly alienating and desolating.

His bereft feelings involved grief at his abandonment by his nearest ones (when his wife came and visited him in Sonnenstein, he was – like Schumann – surprised; he had thought she was dead). And they spelt out endless loneliness, the soul-deadening, soul-murdering tedium of one without company, deprived of books, pen and paper, of anything to occupy his mind: *sans* everything. He took to counting numbers to save his mind. Under those circumstances what else could Schreber do but go mad? 'Only he who knows the full measure of my sufferings in past years can understand that such thoughts were bound to arise in me.'

We have had extensive theories from the psychiatrists about the aetiology of Schreber's malady, back in his infancy, back in his unconscious. We would do well to remember that the occasion of so many of his 'delusions' may have been in the present, all those years of solitary confinement, in which thoughts preyed so terribly on his mind.

9 · John Perceval: Madness Confined

The previous chapter has suggested that two of the preoccupations of the autobiographies of the insane in the eighteenth and nineteenth centuries were, on the one hand, religious doubts and delusions, and, on the other, the torments of profound family tensions. Both bared elemental and contradictory emotions, and it is not surprising that they often were intertwined. Increasingly in the nineteenth century these perturbations are joined by a third: the trauma of being confined in a madhouse as a lunatic. The turmoils of making sense of lunacy were intensified by the terrors of coping with life in the asylum.

Before the eighteenth century only a small proportion of these people judged odd in the head were confined in madhouses. Till then, *ad hoc* provision had been much more common. People so crazy as to be a menace to their fellows or utterly incapable of looking after themselves were taken care of by their family, or by charity, or by their parish. Occasionally they might be locked away in a jail or house of correction. Systematic confinement of lunatics instigated by the state developed in France from the mid-seventeenth century as part of the 'great confinement' of troublemakers launched by Louis XIV's absolutism.

No precise parallel to this act of state occurred in Britain, and the biggest growth sector for the confinement of lunatics before the nineteenth century lay within the market economy, where a 'trade in lunacy' grew up, centred upon the private madhouse. Such institutions might be run by doctors or laymen. Some were big, others small; some mainly catered for paupers, others for the rich; some charged low fees, others high. What coloured them all was their essentially private nature. They were secluded and secret, and their owners were absolute. Not until 1774 were any legal safeguards enacted to protect patients held within them.

Unsurprisingly, private madhouses were widely accused of shady practices, above all the iniquitous confinement of sane people. Daniel Defoe amongst others alleged that such madhouses were tailor-made for husbands who wished to put away their wives so as to be able to enjoy their mistresses in peace, for parents wishing to deliver short, sharp shocks to recalcitrant daughters, and so forth. There was undoubtedly truth in such allegations.

It is not surprising then that so many of the earliest autobiographical writings of English 'mad people' raise a howl of protest against the private asylum and its abuses. Two works by obscure authors date from around the time of the earliest legislation, apparent testimony to the need for it, but also to the fact that its supposed 'safeguards' were proving inoperable. Both authors claim to have been perfectly sane, although their self-vindications must leave that question open.

Samuel Bruckshaw was a merchant from Stamford who in 1770 had a series of brushes with local officials. Bruckshaw believed that he was being cheated out of titles to property and that a conspiracy had been formed against him. His enemies, he records, then had him forcibly carried off by two surgeons, who drove him to Ashton-under-Lyne in Lancashire where he was confined in Wilson's private asylum. He was kept there for some nine months under what he claimed were brutal conditions: he was housed in an attic without a fire, abused by the attendants, poorly fed and denied exercise – overall, he described himself as 'kept prisoner'. No pretence to treatment was offered; the loutish keepers simply ensured that he remained secured. Most of his letters were intercepted, though ultimately he was released through the good offices of his brother.

Bruckshaw vindicated himself in two pamphlets, *The Case, Petition and Address of Samuel Bruckshaw, who suffered a most severe imprisonment for very nearly a whole year* (1774), and *One More Proof of the Iniquitous Abuse of Private Madhouses*, published in the same year. The aim behind the pamphlets was to angle for financial restitution. But interpreting them poses deep problems. For Bruckshaw presents himself as an innocent lamb, led to the slaughter by diabolical conspiracies hatched by his fellow citizens. Yet his tone is, to say the least, fractious, suspicious and litigious. And though he claims his complete and constant sanity, he records that while confined in the asylum he had heard disembodied voices.

Slightly later, William Belcher offers a different though equally puzzling experience. Belcher had been locked up in a private asylum in Hackney between 1778 and 1795, when he was released partly on the word of Dr Thomas Monro, physician to Bethlem. Belcher claims he had been judged insane by a jury which had never even seen him, and that he was then kept in filth and squalor, force-fed and taunted while under lock and key. His wrongful confinement had been directed towards the seizure of his estates.

The thrust of Belcher's argument, contained in his *Address to Humanity: Containing a Letter to Dr Thomas Monro, A Receipt to Make a Lunatic and*

Seize his Estate; and a Sketch of a True Smiling Hyena (1796), is that he had certainly been sane when first confined. It is less clear whether he believed he still was when he was released and wrote his pamphlet. For in his view, the inevitable tendency – perhaps even the very function – of madhouses is to drive the sane crazy. As he put it, 'the trade of lunacy' is 'an approved receipt to make a lunatic'. It is revealing perhaps that a later work, *Intellectual Electricity* (1798), forms an extraordinary parody of the metaphysics and science of his period, at times elevated and earnest, at others mock-serious, sprinkled with occasional footnotes confessing his own utter and understandable confusion about what he is writing.

Institutional confinement itself was sometimes the focus of autobiographical outrage. But very often getting his bearings on the madhouse was utterly bound up with orientating himself to experiences of undergoing religious trial and family misfortune. The persecution which many underwent in their heads through diabolical assault found physical extension and incarnation in the systematic torture regime of the asylum; the mad-doctor himself became a devil. Furthermore, precisely because the asylum itself laid pretensions to be a home, a mad*house*, endowed with its own surrogate family – while of course it simultaneously separated the confined from his true family – the writer inevitably became absorbed with the need to juggle the double images of 'home' in his own mind. The Holy Family, the biological family and the therapeutic family all jostle against each other in many a madman's memoirs.

In 1812, when John Perceval was nine, his father, Spencer Perceval, the Tory Prime Minister of the day, was assassinated as he stepped inside the House of Commons. The government did not stay to inquire very deeply into the state of mind of the assassin, a businessman named Bellingham. A few days later, he was tried and hanged. Within two years, John's widowed mother remarried. Her new husband was a military man, Lieutenant-Colonel Sir Henry Carr, and she became Lady Carr. Spencer Perceval's twelve children were provided for by a parliamentary grant of £50,000, and they seemed to grow up like any other rich early-nineteenth-century gentry family. The father's extreme Evangelical and rabidly anti-Catholic religious convictions (even sympathetic sources called him a bigot) were imbibed by his children, notably by the eldest son, Spencer, and by John, who was the fifth son.

John attended Harrow, where he was a contemporary of Lord Shaftesbury, before joining the army as an officer. He saw no action, but did a tour of service in Portugal. A strict, earnest and even grave young man, he found the cocktail of violence, dissipation and indolence which characterized the soldier's life uncongenial, and his religious convictions became out of step with his gentlemanly ethos over the propriety of the profession of arms.

169

He quit the army, and in 1830 matriculated at Oxford University.

There he found peace and was relieved to make the acquaintance of fellow students who could match him both in social rank and in Evangelical ardour. 'Conflicts of mind' about his dutifulness, the sincerity of his faith and his divine 'election' had already troubled him for several years, leading him to subject himself to an arduous programme of prayer, watchings and fasting. But now he achieved a new serenity, particularly after he began to experience divine visions and voices, apparently in answer to his prayers for divine guidance. His hesitancies about their authenticity were overcome when he found they were indeed 'pictures of what *came to pass in reality*'.

To such a man, the strange events then taking place at Row, near Glasgow, naturally held a great fascination. There the minister and members of his congregation were not merely experiencing visions and voices. They were specifically speaking in tongues, apparently under the immediate direction of the Holy Ghost. Perceval travelled to Scotland to see for himself, suspended between enthusiasm, suspiciousness and curiosity, between an elitist scepticism towards this peasant pentecostalism and a passionate hope that the manifestations might indeed be authentic, that he too might be converted, and thereby receive that absolute assurance of salvation which had hitherto eluded him.

His experiences while at Row left Perceval appallingly torn. Did the Holy Ghost really speak through the mouths of these Scottish nobodies, employing an unintelligible tongue which sounded utter gibberish to some but which Perceval thought resembled Greek and possessed a rare lyrical melody? Or were these mouthpieces nothing but deceived or deceiving? Perceval felt an almost uncontrollable urge to scoff at what he suspected was a 'damnable delusion', and confessed to his profound dread of making a fool of himself. But his longing to be filled with the Spirit, and thus to be sure he was one of the chosen, was even stronger. Soon he too was singing out in tongues: 'the voice was given me, but I was not the master of it; I was but the instrument'. Yet his tormented suspicions that it was not a 'miraculous blessing' but all a 'delusion' did not abate, though he castigated himself mightily for being 'ungrateful'.

Perplexed and harassed, he moved to stay with friends in Dublin, where his torment about the genuineness of the spiritual experiences transformed itself into a veritable cacophony of competing voices in his head: an 'inward cross-examination'. Many urged him to further, supreme tests of faith, others upbraided and accused him of duplicity, hypocrisy and bad faith. An encounter with a prostitute – he went with her to warn her of the 'dangers' of her condition – left him with syphilis, further cause for guilt and the source of severe physical pain. Convinced of his own ineradicable sinfulness, he was soon experiencing damnation; the flames of hell – the symptoms of syphilis – were 'consuming my mortal body'. Delirium ensued and in this state of prostrating physical and spiritual torture, his friends placed him under medical care in December 1830. Strapped immobilized to a bed for a fortnight, he turned raving and delusional, racked by his 'utter worthlessness', and consumed by 'hopelessness and ingratitude', until his brother arrived and removed him to Dr Edward Long Fox's lunatic asylum at Brislington near Bristol in January 1832. There he remained for seventeen months.

For a long while, Perceval did not recognize that he was in an asylum; he thought the house was the residence of a friend of his father's. Neither did he grasp that he was, or was believed to be, lunatic, thinking instead that he had been lodged there to pray for the inmates. Eventually he understood that his family and the doctor had diagnosed him to be insane. Quite when he himself came to regard himself as mad is not clear. During most of the time Perceval spent at Brislington, he was in the grip of dreadful delusions, assailed by 'the incomprehensible commands, injunctions, insinuations, threats, taunts, insults, sarcasms and pathetic appeals of the voices round me'. He was above all bewildered, disordered and confused. In a mystifying way, the Three Persons of the Trinity, the asylum superintendent and his servants, and his own father and mother, brothers and sisters, all became superimposed upon each other, their identities changing, dissolving and merging into one.

Moreover, voices in his head urged him to self-destructive acts to prove his Christian 'sincerity' – above all, to suffocate himself in bed on his pillow and to hurl himself headlong out of the privy. The failure of his attempts to fulfil these impossible divine commands further deepened his sense of guilt and ignominy. After some months, however, Perceval came to feel less under the empire of these otherworldly commands. He grew better able to resist them. As he saw it, his erstwhile superstitious enslavement slowly gave way to a healthier doubt.

As he later recalled, Perceval, who by then had acknowledged himself to be mad, gradually found his reason returning. He demanded his freedom from the asylum, either to return to his family or to be looked after in private care. For his experience of Brislington was entirely negative – indeed he had thought of the asylum as being under satanic supervision, a kind of materialization of the spiritual oppressions he endured in his head. The asylum was inquisitorial, inhumane, degrading. Instead, however, of being granted the freedom for which he begged his family, Perceval was merely transferred to a different asylum, Ticehurst House in Sussex, possibly the most lavish private madhouse in the country, run by Dr Charles Newington. Ticehurst proved scarcely better than Brislington. Here too he found himself being brutally manhandled by lower-class attendants he looked on as 'hinds' and 'clowns'; and his resentment of his betrayal by his own family had grown more acute. Being now more stable and rational, he was, however, better able to cope with his troubles, and after ten months in Ticehurst he was finally released in 1834.

Surprisingly little is known of the remaining forty-two years of his life (he did not die until 1876), though he was affluent enough to lead the life of a leisured gentleman. He married within a year of leaving the asylum and had four children: a good indication that it was confidently believed that his insanity was not constitutional and that the balance of mind had enduringly returned. In the 1840s he devoted some of his energies to the Alleged Lunatics' Friend Society, a pressure group aiming to protect the interests of the improperly confined. Differences which arose between him and other founder members – not least, over his continued religious zeal – perhaps suggest that he remained a difficult person, but there is no evidence of any relapse into mental disturbance.

Perceval's chief claim to fame is that he wrote down his memories of his derangement and confinement. These were published in two volumes in 1838 and 1840 as *A Narrative of the Treatment Experienced by a Gentleman During a State of Mental Derangement*. Its subtitle spelt out its twin avowed aims. It was *Designed to Explain the Causes and the Nature of Insanity, and to Expose the Injudicious Conduct Pursued Towards Many Unfortunate Sufferers Under That Calamity*. The work also, of course, served many other more surreptitious purposes for Perceval. It was his vehicle of revenge against Dr Fox, Dr Newington and the psychiatric confraternity, and also against members of his family, especially his eldest brother, Spencer, and, more obliquely, his mother.

It was also his own spiritual autobiography, rectifying his relationship with God, with the nation and indeed with himself. Unlike many lunacy reformers such as Alexander Cruden, Richard Paternoster or Louise Lowe, but centrally in the tradition of the religious *apologia*, Perceval confessed that he had indeed been truly insane – a religious insanity compounded of sin and satanic temptation. But now he had recovered his reason. Overall, the experience of insanity had been a divine trial, which he had successfully negotiated. Madness had proved a literally salutary experience.

What did being mad mean for Perceval? We cannot be confident precisely what was going through his mind during the period of his derangement and confinement, for he kept no diary at the time, and his book was presumably written several years after the event. Thus his account is bound to be coloured by hindsight. Above all it is shaped as the record of a former voyager into the unknown who has at last found his way, and can look back and plot the course he had taken. The *Narrative* – purportedly the work of a man now sane – still perhaps bears with it a whiff of delusion.

All the same, it may indeed be quite an accurate register of Perceval's consciousness during his mad bout. For in it Perceval prints lengthy extracts from family correspondence written during his confinement, whose tone and content match his retrospective account. Moreover the *Narrative* is indeed largely narrative. Though distanced from the events by perhaps five years, Perceval forbears from presenting the reader with a series of loaded retrospective interpretations of the meanings of those events which had been devastatingly bewildering to him in 1832 or 1833. On the contrary, his book conveys his enduring puzzlement about the trials he had undergone, their causes and the precise status of his visions. He records his dreams, but rarely interprets them for us, or imprisons them within a framework of unfolding sequential meanings. He tells us in a revealing footnote that 'I fear the death of my poor father was at the root of all my misfortunes ... [but] I do not YET understand his loss.' The candour warrants a certain confidence that Perceval's mind in 1838 did not think wholly differently from the way it had in 1832.

It would be tempting, and surely illuminating, to offer retrospective diagnosis of Perceval's condition, using his *Narrative*, from the viewpoints of modern theories. To some extent this has already been done. Gregory Bateson recently published an abridged edition of Perceval's writings under the subtitle *A Patient's Account of His Psychosis*, and the editor confidently speaks of the state of 'schizophrenia' which Perceval underwent, triggered (thinks Bateson) by the 'double binds' his family situation constantly created for him.

But Perceval's own family background also seems particularly tailor-made for Freudian analysis: a father murdered while his son was but a child; a mother who quickly remarried, but who clearly remained the overwhelming focus for her unmarried son's love and loyalties, even when a thirty-year-old; a son who still saw his father's ghost everywhere, who tried out the profession of his military stepfather, but abandoned it to return to the religion of his real father. The Oedipal – indeed quite specifically Hamletian – echoes are strong, though they are not present to Perceval's own consciousness. He does admit, however, to a delusion that he was not the son of his 'reputed' parents, but that his father had adopted him from a Bristol woman called Robinson, knowing that 'I was ordained to be a herald of the second coming of the Lord, from my conception.'

The Freudian might also suggest that we have here a case of that dialectic between paranoia and homosexuality which Freud outlined in the case of Daniel Schreber. Perceval perhaps affords us some positive evidence of unconscious homosexual urges. He recalls a dream set in Portugal in which

173

he had robbed a monastery, assassinated a vicar and in the company of monks had become the 'enjoyer of their unnatural lusts'. Of this dream he himself offers no interpretation. He openly admired the male form and frequently wrestled with young men in the asylum. Perceval's text may inadvertently reveal such desires, but there is no sign that he was conscious of any. Full of confessions, excuses, self-vindications and rationalizations, and saturated with a sense of guilt, menace and punishment, the *Narrative* affords abundant evidence of a raging world of unconscious desire beyond the conscious candour of his own professions of innocence.

In a parallel way, a follower of the developmental psychiatry of Erik Erikson might well choose to highlight the 'identity crisis' undergone by 'young man Perceval'. To have an assassinated Prime Minister for one's father must have been a hard act to follow. Furthermore, Perceval clearly found it difficult being a younger son, and a little reading between the lines of the *Narrative* suggests that his junior and subordinate position in the family was one which won him plenty of 'rebukes', 'mockery' and 'humiliation' for 'disobedience' and 'cruelty'. He reached almost his thirties without a life of his own firmly established. His army career had proved abortive, unlike that of his younger brother; at this belated stage he was just beginning to become a student; he was undecided about taking holy orders; and, as he himself ruefully pointed out, as yet he had no wife. Yet great things had surely been expected of him, and he himself speaks freely about long entertaining hopes that he was a 'prophet of the Lord'. His insane fantasies are eloquent about his own importance. He strode around the asylum grounds shouting 'I am the lost hope of a noble family. . . . I AM the redeemed of the redeemed of the Lord.' On one occasion he felt sure that his dead father and a dead sister had providentially interceded for him, and that his friends and relations had 'defended me from the violence of the mob at the sacrifice of their own lives'.

Of course, the twist in the tail of these fantasies of self-importance is self-punitive: it is on *his* account that other patients in the asylum are stricken with madness, that ships sink with the loss of all hands, that the cholera has come to plague England in 1832. No one else is so evil, so guilty, so deserving of punishment as he. In a phrase which echoes William Cowper's fears, he alone is to be 'eternally damned'. But the authorial voice of the *Narrative* also conveys the impression of a man impressed with a sense of mission and gifts, one with a powerful, if highly vulnerable, conviction of his own social and personal superiority, yet one still terrifyingly unsure of the precise directions of his destiny. Perceval's acutest feeling in 1832–4 was one of vertiginous disorientation, and his instinct was to look back to his family, for blame, pardon and guidance.

To pursue these and other parallel psychodynamic approaches would be rewarding. But it is equally illuminating to probe what the loss of his reason consciously meant for Perceval. What did he think was the nature of his insanity? What had occasioned his descent? How and why had he recovered? How had he been treated? How well grounded were society's attitudes towards insanity? I shall explore these issues below. My account will draw centrally upon ideas which are quite explicit in Perceval's account, contextualized against the explicit beliefs and values of his times.

For Perceval, insanity was, first and foremost, loss of reason, or reason overwhelmed by imagination. In making this ascription, Perceval was clearly drawing on a dominant mode of conceiving of sanity and madness in the mainstream traditions of philosophy and medicine. Just how aware he was – in 1832 or in 1838 – of specific writings about insanity remains unclear. His text shows him to be a man of some reading, familiar for example with Berkeley's philosophy: he tells us that Berkeley's immaterialism corroborated his belief in spirits. Yet it is noteworthy for its total absence of reference to psychiatric works.

Perceval shows no inclination to attribute his condition to bodily disease as the fundamental cause. Admittedly he argues that some of his 'experiences' – his physical sensations of hellfire, for example – which he initially regarded as spiritual were, on reflection, rather the product of 'nervous excitement', brought on by 'bodily pain', presumably his syphilis. He also surmises that his strange views of other patients while at Brislington were due to some defect of his eye, and that fading impressions on the retina could offer a physiological explanation of certain other visions. Nevertheless, practically speaking, his insanity was the descent of his consciousness into profound chaos.

Perceval appears to believe in the literal reality of the Devil, and he regarded diabolical temptations as contributing to his mental confusions. But, unlike men such as George Trosse who had earlier undergone comparable spiritual crises, he does not regard his disorder as a case of diabolical possession. Consequently, he does not seek exorcism or its equivalents. Clergymen would admittedly be fitter men to handle the mad than surgeons and physicians; but, he explains, this is principally a matter of social rank. The Anglican clergy are gentlemen, and would treat sufferers man to man as their peers. The same cannot be said for mere doctors.

It may not have amounted to possession, but at the highest level Perceval viewed his loss of reason as a religious process: 'my mind was deranged by overstudy on religion'. Transcendentally speaking, it was a divine trial, providentially permitted or directed. He was duly familiar with Deuteronomy 28:28. 'The Lord shall smite thee with madness, and blindness, and astonishment of heart.' Though Perceval finally became sceptical about the reality of most of his 'voices' and 'visions', scornfully dismissing them as delusions, he continued to regard these 'delusions' as themselves implanted by God for His higher ends. Writing in 1838, Perceval does not find the notion of mysterious, indeed baffling, providential pathways inherently implausible. In that sense one of his aims was to vindicate 'the reasonableness, if I may so call it, of my lunacy'. Such a spiritual pilgrim's progress was, as he perceived, central to, not a crazy aberration from, a creed which proclaimed the primacy of the spirit, the immateriality of the soul and the free providential actions of the Holy Ghost.

What had indisputably caused the 'ruin of his mind' back in the early 1830s, however, was the appalling problem facing a pious Protestant of how to know religious truth, how to winnow it from 'false zeal', hypocrisy, vanity and pride, or sheer error. How could a believer truly know whether his own faith was lively and vivifying, truly assay the mettle of his own heart? And how was he to plot the will of God, in so far as it might be manifested through particular providences, through signs and callings, through dreams and witness? How could he be sure of salvation? The path was perilous. On the one hand lay the sins of vanity and presumption; on the other, the evils of disobedience and diffidence.

It was all very well for the easy-going Latitudinarian middle-of-the-road Anglicanism, which had arisen from the latter part of the seventeenth century, had been expressed in Locke's faith in the *Reasonableness of Christianity* and had turned into the 'Broad Church', to discount these fears as overprecise. It was all very well for medicine to regard such preoccupations as morbid manifestations of the disorder known as 'religious melancholy'. But serious-minded Evangelicals could not so readily shrug off the problems of saving faith and direct divine action. Nineteenth-century Christians of Perceval's generation – he was, after all, in Oxford at precisely the moment when the Oxford Movement crisis was brewing – struggled mightily to strike a true path between blind faith, or superstition, on the one hand, and corrosive doubt on the other. And many of them – some, like Hurrell Froude and John Henry Newman, at Oxford at the same time as Perceval – were to be pitched into profound crises, agonies and depressions as a result of their seeming inability to resolve these problems. Here, as in many other respects, Perceval's experiences were essentially of the same kind as those of his age, only more acute, more personal.

In his *Narrative*, Perceval contended that he had fallen into insanity because his mind had grown oppressed with these intractable religious dilemmas. He knew he required a saving faith. He was unsure whether he possessed it. He relentlessly scoured his soul. He hoped that visions and voices would be pointers towards proof. But might they prove no more than 'false zeal'?

He never could be sure whether his own experiences were delusions, brought on by his own will to believe; and so his doubts scourged him further.

And what was worse, the voices ringing in his 'head of fire' issued him with a multiplicity of commands, utterly contradicting each other. Many of them smacked of blasphemy. For instance, he would be instructed to kill himself in the flesh – for instance, by suffocating himself on his pillow – so that, through sacrifice, he might then be resurrected as a purely spiritual being. He tried, night after night, failed, and felt all the more anguished, remorseful and disobedient, a child of ingratitude. 'I groaned and struggled, and loathed and hated and abhorred my own soul.' His voices thus engendered in him 'a degrading and self-loathing sense of moral turpitude from accusations of crimes I had never committed'. Yet not to believe, not to respond to such voices, was surely to lack faith, and to make a 'mockery' of the spiritual world itself. It also meant denying tenets fundamental to his witness as an Evangelical: a belief in the radical sinfulness of man, in the wiles and temptations of the Tempter, and in the inescapability of spiritual dilemmas in this fallen world of duplicity and hypocrisy.

The primary occasion of Perceval's loss of reason was thus his utter inability to align his own daily life to the cacophony of spiritual commands filling his head. As a consequence, he came to regard himself as a doomed, damned and unspeakably afflicted wretch. Unlike some, Perceval found he could not simply once and for all take a successful leap of faith; nor could he live contentedly with doubt (as might those the Victorians liked to call 'honest doubters'). Indeed, Perceval did not begin to recover his sanity until he finally managed to fortify himself against the besieging spirit world, and accept that to live in a state of doubt – following Donne's injunction to 'doubt wisely' – was not necessarily 'sinful'.

It would seem natural to us nowadays to 'read' the pandemonium of voices in Perceval's head in the light of his family experiences. After all, his father had been a vocal Evangelical, soaked in the prophetic writings of the Scriptures. John Perceval grew up in a household in which a great premium must have been put upon religious self-examination, as a prelude to cast-iron righteousness. And, more generally, we would nowadays surmise that Perceval's voices echo the commands and prohibitions, the demands and denials, the promises and threats, which he had heard from his parents and elder siblings. As Ford K. Brown has documented, contemporary memoirs and novels record for us the high-tension moral training of the early-nineteenth-century Evangelical family, dinning righteousness into the ears of children. Be good. That is nasty. Do what is right. Show gratitude. Do as I say. Do what you're told (though, all too often, children were told all sorts of contradictory things). Father or mother knows best. God punishes wicked children. Such idioms of blame, guilt, obedience and punishment leap out from every page of Perceval's text. His confusions towards his spiritual voices surely repeat his ambiguities towards the authorities of his youth. He should be obedient; but which authority should he obey? Moreover, sometimes those who commanded seemed themselves to be tainted with hypocrisy, though it was inadmissible to entertain such a thought. Such difficulties over authorities must have been all the greater given that, from the time John was nine, his father had literally been translated into a spiritual voice, interpreted to him via his mother or his elder brothers, or even by his stepfather. How many times was little John told: Your father would have wanted . . .?

How far, however, did Perceval himself see connections between his religious crisis and his problems with his family? There is no simple answer. Perceval certainly found the faith of certain members of his family – in particular, his eldest brother, Spencer – so much humbug, oozing professions of love and faith, but in reality canting hypocrisy, a mere 'mask of Christianity'. John spoke of the religious assurance felt by such as his brother as 'delusion': 'the worthless are putting themselves forward continually as God's truest servants'.

In time, he regarded such duplicity as the watermark of his entire family – something akin to the sanctimonious masking of selfishness and indifference which leaps out from the pages of Samuel Butler's *The Way of All Flesh*. His was a family which made fulsome and unctuous professions of love, piety, concern, care, which indeed elevated the sanctity of the family itself. But it did so in ways which created in mad John Perceval insupportable emotional tensions and conflicts of loyalties. He was always being told, in letters sent to him in the asylum, how much his family cared and how he ought reciprocally to be grateful. Yet he was never grateful enough, and so was always being rebuked. Moreover, the role of the family as the provider of love automatically gave it the right of command over him. When he was thirty, his mother was still addressing him as 'my dear child', and reproving him for the pain his anguished letters were causing her. When visiting him at Fox's asylum, Spencer would address him 'as if speaking to a child'.

Furthermore, the reality of the matter, as experienced by Perceval, was that these expressions of loving care were at bottom pure poppycock. For, once he fell mad, what he received was not their love but their neglect. His eldest brother conveyed him to Brislington, dumped him there, and did not explain what was happening; he did not even say goodbye. Above all, there was no attempt to empathize. Spencer failed (as John saw it) to say to himself: 'There is something strange here; I will try to understand it.' Subsequently, the family kept contact with him to a minimum. They argued, presumably in good faith, that Drs Fox and Newington advised that close communication between lunatics and their families was apt to over-excite.

Perceval was adamant that one of the main reasons why his insanity grew both severe and protracted arose from his abandonment by his own family. He loved his family 'almost with a romantic attachment'. But their neglect of him convinced him he was the victim of family hypocrisy: 'to have been so loved, or so duped by the appearance of my family's love, and to be so abandoned'. It was a betrayal which echoed earlier experiences. After all, he tells us, his one-time hero, the Duke of Wellington, had betrayed Protestantism – the faith of his father – by introducing Catholic Emancipation, and countenancing parliamentary reform was further treason. John's accusations in print in his *Narrative* against 'the sin' of his brother Spencer and his mother are quite extraordinarily bitter and vitriolic, the spleen of a man unable to go beyond a feeling of having been betrayed. Yet he still believed that, at root, though he could little understand how, it must have been his own fault: 'I accused myself.'

There is no sign, however, that Perceval actually attributed his insanity to his infant or childhood experiences with his family, and to what Bateson would call the 'double binds' in which it knotted him up. In this view he would have been at one with the mainstream of opinion of his day, lay and psychiatric. Doctors recognized of course how family problems and tensions frequently triggered insanity or depression: a bullying, drunkard husband, for example, or the death of a spouse. But Perceval's contemporaries did not regard disturbance as a product of infants' inability to cope with the competing and bewildering emotional demands imposed upon them by their parents, still less of infantile desires. Asylum records indicate that, in cases of adolescents and young adults confined by their parents, the root problem was invariably seen to be some moral delinquency, disobedience and rebellion on the part of the youngster.

Perceval did, however, explicitly link family and religion in one rather elaborate and intriguing way. At Brislington Asylum he naturally made the acquaintance of Dr Fox the proprietor, his sons and the crew of servants and attendants. He also associated with his fellow patients. He felt driven to superimpose the identities of members of his family upon these people. Thus he would identify a particularly pretty maid, called Louise, with one of his own sisters; he would see the hated son of Dr Fox as his eldest brother. On occasion he would regard Dr Fox himself as his father ('I called him my father'). Sometimes, however, one or other of two aged attendants was his father. One of them, called Honesty, would 'put me to bed ... kiss my forehead, saying God bless you'. At other times, he would see his father in certain of the lunatics themselves.

At an earlier stage, he had had a vision of 'my father bending over me weeping ... [he had a] long flowing white beard': Perceval clearly saw his father as one of the prophets whose writings he had so religiously studied. Now his spirits told him that a particular servant was his father, 'raised from the dead, in order, if possible, to assist in saving my soul'. He would believe that the attendant Marshall's wife, or the housekeeper, was his mother. Indeed, at first, when he saw his family's faces in the asylum staff, his voices told him that so greatly had his own misconduct impoverished his family that they had all been reduced to drudging at the asylum (more blame). Yet when he *failed* to recognize his family in the asylum his spirits accused him of still more ingratitude.

At the same time, this cast of players also assumed the identities of the Godhead Himself or the Three Persons of the Trinity. The man whose real name as a servant was sometimes Zachary Gibbs and sometimes Samuel Hobbs was renamed by Perceval Herminet Herbert, and identified with Jesus (Samuel Hobbs = S.H. = *Salvator Hominum*). Perceval thought this man had once been one of his mother's servants. Marshall was renamed by Perceval Herminet Herbert Scott. He was given a spiritual attribute: Sincerity. Perceval understood him to be one of his father's servants. The servant Poole was renamed Herminet Herbert the Simple, and assumed the form of God Almighty; another became the Holy Ghost, or Kill-All; a lunatic, called Waldony, was the Lord Jehovah, or Benevolence.

Through these complex moves, the Holy Family, Perceval's own natural family and the surrogate family of what Dr Fox saw as a family asylum meshed into a single system – albeit one which was shifting and baffling – in Perceval's mind. Perceval himself called them all 'manifestations of the Trinity'.

What did this system of 'triple or quadruple persons' mean to Perceval? It certainly perplexed him bitterly (it confuses us too!). It signified for him that he was deluded, that he was suffering from mental aberration. At a later stage, as I shall indicate, Perceval was able to make some sense out of his babel confusion of names and tongues. But he was never led to speculate how his own religious crisis might be emblematic of his family troubles.

Perceval believed that religious terror had brought on his insanity, and that the behaviour of his family had exacerbated it. But the real cause of the appalling severity and prolongation of his condition was the medico-psychiatric treatment he had received. Perceval unambiguously condemned as intrinsically counter-productive the very philosophy of placing mad people in lunatic asylums. It set the lunatic amongst 'strangers' precisely when he needed to be with his fellows in familiar surroundings. It estranged him from his family. It put him in the charge of an unknown doctor, rather

than those members of the caring professions he knew well, his regular physician or his clergyman. It set him in the midst of fellow lunatics, who, if
truly mad, must surely be those people least capable of sustaining the mind
of one who had just been crushed under a terrible blow. Precisely at the
moment when a person needed his morale to be boosted, he was thrown
into a situation that must 'degrade him in his own estimation'.

But not only was the whole idea of institutional confinement misconceived.
The specific living conditions inside the asylum must inevitably hinder the
recovery of a mad person. The mad were sentenced to lose their privacy,
precisely when they felt too ashamed to face company. Almost inevitably,
herded together in dayrooms, they would be subjected to a regime of enforced
idleness, precisely when they needed occupation and stimulus for their minds.
The dayrooms had hardly any books, few amusements, no employment. This
merely ensured that new delusions took root. Patients were routinely confined,
in bed, in their own rooms or in straitjackets and other forms of mechanical
restraint. This was all utterly counter-productive. For, as Perceval recounted
from his own experience, confinement provoked the spirit of resistance and
encouraged disobedience. How could supposedly sane people not understand
the stupidity of these arrangements?

Tie an active limbed, active minded, actively imagining young man in
bed, hand and foot for a fortnight, drench him with medicines, slops,
clysters; when reduced to the extreme of nervous debility, and his
derangement is successfully confirmed, manacle him down for twenty-four
hours in the cabin of a ship; then for a whole year shut him up from
six A.M. to eight P.M. regardless of his former habits, in a room full of
strangers, ranting, noisy, quarrelsome, revolting, madmen; give him no
tonic medicines, no peculiar treatment or attention, leave him to a
nondescript domestic, now brushing his clothes, sweeping the floors,
serving at table, now his companion out of doors, now his bed-room
companion; now throwing him on the floor, kneeling on him, striking
him under all these distressing and perplexing circumstances; debar him
from all conversation with his superiors, all communication with his
friends, all insight into their motives, every impression of sane and well-
behaved society! Surprise him on all occasions, never leave harassing him
night or day, or at meals; whether you bleed him to death, or cut his
hair, show the same utter contempt for his will or inclination; do all in
your power to crush every germ of self-respect that may yet remain or
rise up in his bosom; manacle him as you would a felon; expose him
to ridicule, and give him no opportunity of retirement or self-reflection;
and what are you to expect? And whose agents are you; those of God

181

or of Satan? And what good can you reasonably dare to expect? And whose profit is really intended?

In other words, the great evil of asylum life was that its regime was tailored not to the needs of the patients, but entirely to the convenience of the proprietor and his staff. The wants and will of the insane counted for nothing. No one had put himself in the mad person's shoes. As Perceval stressed, when he entered the asylum he was suffering from the delusion that his own will counted for nothing, that he was possessed by forces beyond his control. In this respect, the asylum turned the dreadful delusion into reality. For one was never treated as a human being, with a mind of one's own. One was handled as anything but a man: as a child, as a deaf-mute, as an animal, or as 'a piece of furniture, an image of wood, incapable of desire as well as of judgement'.

> Men acted as though my body, soul, and spirit were fairly given up to
> their control, to work their mischief and folly upon. My silence, I suppose,
> gave consent. I mean, that I was never told, such and such things we
> are going to do; we think it advisable to administer such and such
> medicine, in this or that manner; I was never asked, Do you want any
> thing? do you wish for, prefer any thing? have you any objection to this
> or to that?

Overall, Perceval 'was no longer a free agent, but under the control of beings superiorly enlightened.' In short, he 'was brutalized'.

Programmatically the asylum – how like his family! – insisted upon treating the patient as a child. The notion of an analogy between infants and mad people had become orthodoxy over the previous century. Ever since John Locke had argued that the essence of insanity lay in mental error, pinpointing the similarity between intellectual delusion and the learning errors of children had been an attractive strategy, by virtue of its optimistic potential; a mad person might recover, rather as a child would gradually learn to think properly. Pioneers of more humane ways of treating the mad, such as the Tukes at the York Retreat, had prominently blazoned forth the notion that proper care of lunatics was akin to good child care.

Perceval's own feelings about such identifications with the child were quite complex, not least because he positively subscribed to the scriptural view that in children lay wisdom: 'a child or a fool may speak wisdom'. Indeed, he begged his own readers to 'bring the ears of children'. He was prepared to admit that in his insane state he had been reduced to 'childish imbecility'. But he deeply resented the way in which the therapeutic system adopted by Dr Fox infantilized mad people, as if they had no will of their own and no understanding at all: 'steps were taken, but the reasons never shown to me'. It perpetuated rather than dispelled confusion. For, Perceval insisted, 'amidst all my lunatic childishness and simplicity, I was a grown-up man'. It was moreover demeaning and degrading. Not least, as Perceval suggested, such authoritarian condescension was no way to treat children.

No end of further disgraces and abuses were built into the very fabric of the asylum. The sparse and rough food reminded him of his Old Harrovian schooldays. Washing and lavatory facilities were disgusting, possessing neither cleanliness nor privacy. Patients who dirtied themselves were not attended to. Even the medical care itself became associated with 'punishment and degradation'. He would be manhandled into cold shower baths even in the depths of winter, and that as part of a soothing therapy! Whatever the philosophy behind them, their effect in actuality was to provoke excitement, disgust, resentment and vengefulness. Perceval would often resist. He would then be beaten by the servants. His spirits told him that such 'crucifixion' was merited.

Above all, asylum servants would inevitably be violent ruffians ('I would be bound to say that the greatest part of the violence that occurs in lunatic asylums is to be attributed to the conduct of those who are dealing with the disease'). They were disrespectful, rude and entirely lacking in true deference. They showed 'gross want of respect to situation, rank, character or profession'. Patients of superior rank such as himself were, of course, honour-bound to display 'gallant resentment' to this 'mockery, insult and oppression', but such displays of English spirit were taken in turn 'as the signs of mania'. Such conflicts merely further exacerbated insanity, for violence towards the genteel must be calculated further to confound their sense of themselves, to make them feel like 'slaves'. The 'ignorant empiric and his tools' could thus only be looked upon as 'persecutors'.

Overall, the asylum amounted to a system of 'oppression' which Perceval likened to boiling lobsters alive. Its 'tyranny' made a mockery of the very name of 'asylum'. It was run by people 'who pretend their cure, but who are, in reality, their tormentors and destroyers'. The system was built upon and bolstered by a tissue of lies and double-talk. Terms like 'wholesome restraint' were used to describe what was in reality naked 'ill-treatment'. Perceval was euphemistically described as a 'nervous patient', but all his treatment was clearly designed to multiply his nervousness. The thoroughgoing contradictions between its professions and its real nature, its systematic 'duplicity', meant that it was the asylum which was truly insane. At last the confusion of names ended: 'I can no longer ... call Dr F—'s house by any other name than that it deserves, *madhouse*, for to call that, or any like that, an *asylum*, is cruel mockery and revolting duplicity!'

In this respect, Perceval found Dr Fox's 'conduct' especially 'insane'. Fox was a 'quondam Quaker' – though now an Anglican convert, and so doubly 'treacherous' as an egregious social climber. Following what Perceval called the 'burlesque doctrines of that sect', Fox defended the 'familiarity' shown by the servants on the grounds of the biblical spiritual equality of man. Had not Jesus made us all equal?, Renard reminded Perceval.

To Perceval, as to any early-nineteenth-century Tory, this was all stuff and nonsense, and yet further religious hypocrisy ('I never saw Mr Hobbs sitting at Dr F—'s dinner table'). It was also a crazy and destructive denial of the rationality of the social hierarchy outside, a fantastic conceit that one might cure the anarchy of disordered minds by locating them within a wider anarchy. The frequency with which Perceval insists, throughout his *Narrative*, upon his own distinguished rank as an English gentleman, and condemns its systematic denial in the asylum, indicates how, amidst the quicksands of his insanity, his social standing gave him some residual roots of stability. He might be mad, but, though mad, he still knew he was a gentleman. Stable personal order was evidently inseparable from the maintenance of a stable socio-political order. Indeed, in a way echoing the macrocosm–microcosm ideas of an earlier day, Perceval explicitly associated his own derangement with contemporary revolutions in the outside world. As a millennialist, he believed he was living through an age when the 'end was at hand' – Catholic Emancipation was its sign, the cholera epidemic probably its instrument. Moreover, treacherous parliamentary reform was being passed ('the government then acted the part of madmen, if not worse'), to the accompaniment of riot and threats of revolution. At Brislington, he could even see the flames of Bristol burning under the hand of the incendiary mob, and he was exposed to the subversive *sotto voce* comments of the asylum servants, talking 'in an insolent radical manner of the gentry'. The very order of the asylum itself thus lacked the characteristics of rational society. It was subversive of reason, the negation of civilization. Like many confined lunatics before him, such as Alexander Cruden, Perceval saw his standing as a freeborn British gentleman as his only ultimate protection against madhouse oppression.

The asylum did not merely disorient. It was itself totally irrational, a nonsense, nightmare, surreal world in which nothing was as it seemed, nothing made sense, just when it was crucial that sense should prevail. Fox pretended to be running a humane asylum. Yet everything he did was irrational, one vast defiance of society, humanity and nature. It amounted to 'insanest mismanagement', and was therefore, unsurprisingly, counter-productive. When Perceval arrived, regarding himself as a 'castaway', he was incredibly left amongst 'strangers' and not introduced to anyone. This was contrary to good manners. But it was also crazy, because it instantly produced disorientation and suspicion, panic and fear in the patient. 'I had no introduction, no explanation, no reason assigned me for my position; lunatic, imbecile, childish, deluded, I was left to divine everything.' Thereafter, the patient was habitually bossed around, never informed of decisions taken on his behalf, allowed no right of protest or power to negotiate. Here was a system designed to fix a man in permanent helplessness, rather than to help lift him out of it:

> Instead of my understanding being addressed as clear and plain as possible, in consideration of my confusion, I was committed, in really difficult and mysterious circumstances, calculated of themselves to confuse my mind, even if in a sane state, to unknown and untried hands; I was placed amongst strangers, without introduction, explanation or exhortation.

As Perceval stressed, casting a person into an asylum was tantamount to throwing him into a well, and then pelting him with stones when he tried to claw his way out. It was also foolish to treat people as utterly crazy, because the nature of lunacy involves a complex interweaving of the imbecile and perverse with the rational and the willing. The residues of reason were never given the support they needed.

Perceval believed that Fox's Quaker quackery sustained a system wholly unmitigated in its evil. It denied the patient the privacy to which he was entitled as a gentleman. For example, the doctor required a servant to sleep in the same room as the patient. It also robbed him of his rights. Thus, patients could not send out letters without their being read, censored or stopped. It erected a permanent 'inquisition' over the patient. It thought madness was 'impenetrable' because it never attempted to penetrate it. It had no spirit of humanity. Asylums like Fox's prided themselves on their humanity. But such humanity as lay within did not come from the psychiatric regime at all: 'The humanity of the asylum consisted in the conduct of the patients, not in that of the system and of its agents.'

And, not least, the asylum enshrined a series of Kafkaesque Catch-22 situations. The regime itself was intrinsically so mad and maddening that any patient with normal, healthy impulses would indeed be driven mad by it. Yet the system also demanded the aquiescence and compliance of the mad themselves. The inmate who protested against the order of the asylum was thought to be mad, indeed suspect, suffering from 'suspicion' which constituted part of his 'delusions'. Yet of course those who really were rampantly suspicious – those who opened correspondence and spied on patients – were the 'sane' authorities. The treatment moreover was 'cruel mockery', but 'if he resists the treatment, he is then a madman!' Put another way, 'the world, in their treatment of lunatics, are as insane as the lunatic himself'. It was

185

a system for creating rather than curing madness, by systematically making confusion worse confounded.

Reflecting upon a 'whole system' of 'confinement and contradiction' that 'contradicted the principles of . . . tangible science', Perceval was unsure how to judge Fox's motives. 'The treatment I have described can only be that of madmen or villains.' But which? Was Fox mad or bad? In some respects Perceval was inclined to see him simply as cruel. His system was 'intended to insult'. His psychiatry was foolish, and, worse than that, mere 'charlatanism', ignorance culpably masquerading as science. Having got 'a stranger into their nets', the Fox family were out to profit from him as much as possible. Sometimes Perceval regarded the psychiatric regime as the instrument of Satan, 'agents of that destroying spirit'.

At other moments, Perceval thought of Fox essentially as the 'dupe of his own system', 'living in a lie'. In other words, the doctor himself was the victim of a stupendous delusional system, focused upon the hallucination that he was curing the mad. This was a dangerous, rather than a harmless, lie, for it was one of the delusions which all society had come to espouse. Either way, Perceval was convinced that lunatics knew more about the nature and cure of insanity than did the 'lunatic doctors'. Society must cease to entrust lunatics to the care of 'men of little education, and of low *origins*'. For they were 'like swine or sloths set to judge over the manners of greyhounds and fleet coursers'. Perceval never denied the reality of lunacy, and he admitted the need for care and treatment. But, for him, truly salutary treatment meant individual care in private surroundings.

Perceval, as we know, recovered. How did he explain this? It owed nothing to the asylum regime, which at best prolonged the episode of insanity. It owed everything to his own experience, and not least to his capacity to resist, fight and beat the system. Fighting psychiatry, as he saw it, had made him strong and sane. 'Every struggle I had with those controlling me, served to strengthen my mind and to dissipate my errors'. In other words, 'I have proved that the power of the patient is equal to that of the oppressor': the echoes of the spiritual autobiographies of Bunyan, Baxter and others are loud and clear.

Perceval explained how, slowly but surely, his delusional voices came to lose their hold upon him. He began to see that to doubt in psychiatry, in religion, was not in itself sinful. He began to be able to challenge the spirits, resist them and mock the mockers. After all, as he discovered, God was a God not just of 'the sincere, the grave, the sober, and the chaste only', but also 'of fun, of humour, of frolic'; the human constitution 'is double' – one almost wants to supply Perceval with the terms 'Apollonian' and 'Dionysian'. 'This nation is morose and religiously mad,' he adds.

It is not very clear what in Perceval's view had permitted his powers of resistance to grow. But the process occurred in tandem with another important change. For he began to reinterpret his 'delusions'. What once for him had been absolutely literal, now assumed a metaphorical or a figurative meaning. What formerly had literally been palpable, aethereal spirits, now turned into symbolic spirits. Benevolence became the 'spirit of benevolence', understood not as a tangible entity or person, but as an attribute. Whereas he had once unquestioningly accepted the commands to suffocate himself on his pillow, now he knew a higher meaning in the commands; what he must do is to 'suffocate' his grief on the 'pillow' of his conscience, or in other words, not to abandon himself to his feelings, but to control them. 'Thus lunacy is also the mistaking of a command that is spiritual for that which is literal.'

What exactly precipitated this absolutely fundamental shift in cognition from the literal to the figurative? It is unclear. But it may be helpful to think of it against the background of parallel general debates at the time. Scriptural theology of course was racked with discussions about the relations between the world and figurative symbols, not least in the interpretation of Scripture. And contemporary theories of cultural progress saw the history of the evolution of human thought as involving a similar shift, from the very literal-minded mythologies and cosmologies of primitive peoples, with their pantheistic gods for every tree, up to the 'personification' in the 'poetry' of the moderns.

Perceval also found a physiological explanation. He discovered that his *voices* were, indeed, real *sounds*. But they were not independent utterances from outside. Rather they were largely of his own making: the 'breathing of my own nostrils', his heartbeats, the chomping sounds he made while eating; or they were natural and external, the rattling of chains, the hiss of the gas jet. Upon these real but actually meaningless sounds, which produced a 'juggle upon the senses', he had imposed verbal meanings. His 'delusions' had not been genuine divine voices after all. Nevertheless God had all the same designed these delusions to occur as part of his 'trial'. Let no man doubt the 'power of the Lord to confound the judgement and wisdom of man'. '*Soli Deo Gloria*': thus he closed the first volume of his *Narrative*. But amidst this reaffirmation of providence, it is interesting that Perceval recovered by finding a rational way of disabusing himself of his own delusions, in a rather literal sense by working his way through them.

'He who rules the imagination has the power. . . .' Lunacy is like drunkenness, wrote Perceval; it releases powerful forces within, which can ultimately work for the good, so long as a man does not abandon his own judgement. Through madness 'I loved freedom to be free.' He sounds uncannily like his almost exact contemporary, John Stuart Mill.

'Many persons confined as lunatics are only so because they are not understood,' wrote Perceval. He added: 'and continue not to understand themselves'. Perceval found himself in a maze, and all around him – his family, his doctors – merely contributed to mystifying the labyrinth still further. He was even repudiated – for being a lunatic – by the Church at Row. Perceval's madness was expressed as the bewilderment of being unable first to rationalize, and then to resolve having to live in a number of different value-worlds. He grew up a soldier and a Christian, and found the necessary violence of the one dissonant with the suffering of the other. He chose Christianity. But true religious humility contradicted the proper pride he so strongly felt as a gentleman, without however rewarding him with a firm conviction of salvation.

He had been taught to love his family (for what could be valued more highly in an early-nineteenth-century Evangelical family than filial loyalty?). Yet it was a family which (as he saw it) abandoned him to an asylum which was the negation of all that true family life ought to be; a family which degraded him by only being able to treat him as a child. Perceval's collapse marked the point in his existence when he could respond to these confusing signals and 'contradictory commands' and demands (or voices) only by guilt and abjection. As he himself so clearly perceived in his *Narrative*, he was in time able to free himself from these cages within cages, but not until his insanity enabled him to appreciate the irrationality of the prisons he had been trapped within.

10 · The American Dream

Deprived of any other outlet for his boundless manic energies during his enforced sojourn in the Connecticut State Asylum at the beginning of this century, the young Clifford Beers took to rethinking modern science. Might he become more famous than Newton? For he conceived in his mind a refutation of the physics of gravity. This was no mere abstract triumph. It would surely have its practical pay-off if it succeeded: one might be able to 'defy gravity'. 'My conquering imagination soon tickled me into believing that I could lift myself by my bootstraps.'

Speculators on the unconscious from Jung to Jong have had their say on the sexual undercarriage of flying fantasies. Here, however, the fruitful meanings are surely socio-cultural, and lodged in the upper storeys of the mind. Not only is Beers taking a flight of fancy from the asylum that was his prison. He is alluding to the American dream of individual success, taking off from log cabin to the White House. I am as good as any man. By my own efforts I will rise further. I too can be a high-flyer.

Self-help and self-perfection had long been living philosophies in the land of the free. The great heroic myths of the New World were secularized optimistic recensions of the Protestant ethic of individual salvation. The lone individual must confront the world. Through the pioneer spirit of work, energy and enterprise, he would win the success that would show his inner, spiritual qualities, his character. Self-reliance presupposed a strong self. The survival of the fittest – the Social Darwinist creed taken over by the great robber-barons, the Carnegies and the Rockefellers – would sift strong from weak egos.

Chinks in this doctrine began to appear alarmingly from perhaps the 1870s. Many Americans, it seemed, couldn't take it. Their nerves became over-stretched, they suffered lassitude and lethargy. They cracked up. Of course, amongst women this was only to be expected. The so-called 'new women' had been falsely tempted to try to emulate their menfolk, to become go-getters in intellectual pursuits, the literary scene or public life, against all the laws of psychobiology. They ended up hysterical. Once taught to resume their proper place within the home they would recover. What was particularly worrying, however, was the number of all-American men who also seemed to be caving in, unable to meet the challenges of the market which should have been the making of their manhood. For this condition, the consoling and euphemistic term 'neurasthenia' – a posh way of talking about weakness of the nerves – was coined by George Beard and spread by a leading psychiatric doctor, Weir Mitchell. Neurasthenia became widely known as the 'American disease'.

From late-nineteenth-century times onwards, the teachings of psychologists and the ministrations of psychiatrists have come to play an increasingly dominant role in moulding the American mind, to a degree surely unparalleled in any other nation. *Prima facie* this looks a paradox: shouldn't the New World be free of the 'diseases of civilization' which riddled the Old? But in reality it is not so puzzling. For one thing, the 'great democracy', to be true to itself, had to democratize psychiatry, had to put it on the free market. For another, American psychiatry itself adjusted to being a technique for adjusting achievers to their society, providing a passport to perfectibility, another string to the Dale Carnegie bow of how to win friends and influence people. Above all, over the last century psychiatry in America has been transformed from a negative to a positive force. It ceased to be simply a remedy for mental disease; it became a tonic to personal psychic health, a romantic road to self-discovery, and eventually a licence to let it all hang out in what Tom Wolfe was to call the 'Me Decade'.

The Americanization of Freud was obviously to be an important stage in the American nation's love-affair with psychiatry. Once bathed in the warm glow of Progressivism, trans-Atlantic Freudianism lost its essentially pessimistic face. Psychoanalysis became hooked up to success. Freud had portrayed the inevitable and often tragic tension between the individual – with his basic human drives – and civilization, with its demands of repression, sublimation and neurosis. The New World formulated a sort of Freud without tears: the ego could forge ahead; self-realization and social adjustment were the same.

But the way had been cleared long before this interwar consumerization of Freud. The crucial creed here was the Mental Hygiene Movement, and its evangelist was Clifford Beers. Beers wrote psychiatry into the American dream. The Benjamin Franklin of psychiatry, his talks and writings offered *Poor Richard's Almanac*-style advice on how to renounce mental malady and embrace mental muscle-power. And like all the best preachers with their personal sinner-turned-saint tales, Beers could proclaim that his gospel was true because he had been through it all himself. His credentials were better than an MD – insanity was his medical education. As he put it in a wonderfully revealing phrase, 'I believe I am one of the few who have ever successfully capitalized a mental breakdown' (he added, 'I did so not in my own interests but out of altruism, though I have received unexpected personal benefits').

In his new-style spiritual autobiography, *A Mind That Found Itself* (1908), Beers established himself right from page one as an all-American boy, born of a 'truly American' family, descended from the earliest settlers (this genealogy – Beers's myth of the hero – was probably largely fantasy). Born in New Haven in 1876 of middle-class parents, as a boy he had possessed that most winning mixture of traits, a diffident self-conscious shyness combined with enterprising-competitive get-up-and-go. His schoolday memories were of being 'business manager' of the student newspaper, and the targets he set himself at Yale were not the nobler peaks of the life of the mind: he wanted to pass, to make contacts, join the confraternities and get involved in running things. He rose to the challenge of the 'Yale spirit' and succeeded in his ambitions.

Beers went into business. First he tried selling insurance, but moved on to become a salesman for a New York architect's office which specialized in designing banks. Then calamity struck. A few years earlier, back in 1894, he had spent much time nursing his dying epileptic brother Sam. Now Beers himself became 'neurasthenic', terrified that he too was doomed to be an epilepsy victim. The fear 'possessed my mind'. Debilitated and distraught, he returned home in the summer of 1901 and made what in retrospect looks like a rather half-hearted suicide attempt. He let himself down from a fourth-floor window – it would be an exaggeration to say that he threw himself out of it – but landed on soft earth. He sustained ankle fractures which confined him in plaster for some months but suffered no permanent physical damage. Obviously, his family concluded, he needed mental treatment.

They removed him to Stamford Hall. This was a private proprietary asylum basking under the name of 'sanitarium'. Until then, Beers had simply been neurasthenic and hypochondriacal. Now he suffered serious hallucinations. He felt the victim of a giant conspiracy to persecute him (all this was due, he wrote later, to 'delusions of reference'). All those who came into contact with him were in reality policemen or their agents; those folk masquerading as his family were actually detectives in disguise. He himself was a criminal. His suicide attempt had broken state law. As soon as he recovered, he would be put on trial, tortured and executed. Racked by guilt, he played possum, and acted more ill than he was to put off this evil day.

As Beers later recalled it, his paranoia was daily vindicated by his experience. What he saw as the callous treatment meted out to him by the asylum physicians and particularly the attendants seemed like malicious torture. It would 'drive a sane man to violence'. No one bothered to get under the skin of his anguished mental state. 'My attendants were incapable of understanding the operations of my mind, and what they could not understand they would seldom tolerate.' Everyone took insanity as an excuse for incomprehension and thus brutality. But in reality, Beers insisted, there is typically reason in madness, and little insight or effort would have been needed to grasp his plight, allay his fears and speed his cure. Insanity would readily respond to rationality.

It received none. Yet Beers recovered somewhat. Moreover, his family could no longer afford the stiff fees of an asylum whose proprietor was making, Beers alleged, $95,000 a year clear profit. In March 1901, he was removed. He spent some months with a private attendant, but was then placed in 1902 in the Hartford Retreat, another private but cheaper asylum which in its better days had pioneered advanced techniques of moral therapy. Beers continued to be driven by his former delusions. He was under 'police surveillance' in an asylum full of 'detectives feigning insanity'. Nothing was as it seemed. His food was poisoned. His so-called 'friends' and 'family' were just police stooges. He lacked bearings; he was 'without a world'.

Beers's grasp of reality was restored not by the psychiatrists but by the joint labours of himself and a fellow patient. Beers had become convinced that his 'brother' was not his brother at all but a pretender. Put it to the test, his friend told him: write to your brother at his own address. Beers did. His brother arrived waving the letter. The scales instantly fell from his eyes. 'Untruth became truth,' unreason yielded to reason. He was born anew. 'My mind seemed to have found itself.' He started redating time from his 'new birth'.

Quickly Beers's depression turned to elation. He became manic, supercharged with energy, ideas, plans, schemes. He envisaged himself as a genius artist or pianist (later he bragged he would 'write a poem that will make Dante's *Divine Comedy* look like a French farce'). He started 'bossing the universe'. First he gave orders to fellow lunatics, and when that succeeded ('invariably I induced them to obey'), he started dictating commands to the attendants. He saw himself as 'sane' but 'unruly'. 'I have skipped over the border into the land of geniuses.' His blood boiled at the evils, incompetence and injustices of the asylum, and he dedicated himself to crusading for their reform. He would be a 'saviour', 'the greatest man, with one exception, who ever lived'.

Beers made his views felt. Months of battles with the doctors and staff followed. He grew demanding and, when his demands were not met, disruptive and destructive. This was (he records) not because he was genuinely out of control, but because the cruelties of the asylum provoked it. Placed under punitive discipline, he experienced the full horrors of the straitjacket. A sadistic assistant doctor (a 'Dr Jekyll and Mr Hyde') imposed forced feeding and forced medicines upon him as a punishment out of pure malice, even after he had consented to take them in the normal way. Beers began recording every injustice – on scraps of paper, sometimes scribbling on the walls – as a record of crimes against humanity and as practice for the great mission he was formulating, to become the 'saviour' of the insane. He would make it his business, he warned the doctors, to bring the evil men 'to book'.

Again family funds ran out. This time Beers was transferred to a state institution, the Connecticut Hospital for the Insane, where he was ignominiously classed as an 'indigent'. Once more he felt 'abandoned by everyone'. Yet again the staff tyrannized over him. He fought back. He tried to exert his own powers. 'I proceeded to assume entire charge of . . . the hospital.' Manic once more, he grew endlessly talkative, assertive, flamboyant. Pursuing his mission of cleansing the Augean stables, he contrived for purely investigative purposes (so he tells us) to get himself transferred to the violent ward ('the Bull Pen') so he could experience it for himself at first hand. Conditions were subhuman, the law of the jungle. Patients and attendants were locked in a circle of violence. It was 'a pocket edition of the New York Stock Exchange during a panic'.

Beers began to take effective action. He smuggled out letters to the state governor demanding investigations, campaigning for a bill of rights for the insane. He developed utopian schemes for changing the world on his release, wanting to set up, amongst other things, a new city to be called 'Beresford' after himself, entirely peopled by 'perverts, mental, physical and moral'. He wrote reams of letters to friends, family and bigwigs such as President Roosevelt, documenting the atrocious asylum conditions: a few got out; most were censored or destroyed.

Eventually, on 10 September 1903 Beers was released. He resumed his job as a travelling salesman. He read *Les Misérables* and aspired to become a latter-day Hugo, rescuing the new *misérables* of the New World. Or he would write the *Uncle Tom's Cabin* for the slaves of the asylum. In his spare time he began to compose his asylum autobiography. He dictated to a stenographer, 80,000 words in ninety hours.

Becoming overwrought once more, he was persuaded by his favourite brother George (his 'conservator') to re-enter the Hartford Retreat as a voluntary patient, on terms of freedom, so he could complete his book. By 1905 it was done. As he wrote, his strategy was shifting. Initially, he had in mind just an *exposé* of his personal sufferings at the hands of the mad-business. Increasingly, however, he wanted his book to be not just autobiographical but universal, not just critical but positive, not just a story of his own persecution but a charter for the insane. He aspired to have it launch a whole movement.

Elated and ebullient, the one-time commercial traveller astutely recognized that for his book to have maximum effect it was necessary to make friends rather than enemies. He started showing it round to men of affairs and influence, to doctors and psychiatrists. Adept at graciously deferring to authority, he won the support of such powerful figures in the American medical and academic establishment as William James, Weir Mitchell, William Welch, James Putnam and Adolf Meyer. When *A Mind That Found Itself* finally came out in 1908 it was a blueprint for the future as much as an indictment of the past and present. It told Beers's story. But it also revealed to the world his dream baby, the Mental Hygiene Movement. From then, for the next twenty years, this archetypal salesman succeeded in selling to an influential cadre of psychiatrists and policy-makers, do-gooders and philanthropists, the vision of a national crusade against mental illness, spearheaded by a new organization, the National Committee for Mental Hygiene. Its secretary, its leading spirit, its prize exhibit, was to be Beers himself.

Beers spent the rest of his life running the National Committee. He was its figure-head. His book was its bible, and one of the main sources of converts. He was its fund-raiser. He stomped around the nation – indeed, later, around the world – giving lectures, making speeches, soliciting interviews, attending in the anterooms of the rich. He loved to win friends and influence people. Selling his cause, selling himself, gave a whole new meaning to selling assurance. He endlessly retold the heroic story of his new birth, of 'Reason Triumphant' (the title he originally intended for his book), for all the world like the Ancient Mariner turned Yale businessman. He loved the plaudits of the great (subsequent editions of *A Mind That Found Itself* became ever more crammed with congratulatory letters from famous people). In 1929 he made *Who's Who in America*. The *Washington Post* with unnerving echoes of Nietzsche dubbed him a 'superman' who had climbed from the 'bogs of obscurity' to the 'tower of fame'. Finally he was snapped on the lawn of the White House.

Young-man Beers in the asylum had proved his manhood by battling against the doctors. That rite of passage over, he chose to join them. (There is an interesting parallel to Freud's shift from accusing to exonerating the father.) The mind that found itself was a mind that realized that reason really must work on the side of medicine, psychiatry and the authorities.

Of course, *A Mind That Found Itself* is a caustic indictment of the evils of the madhouse. But he intended his book as an anatomy of particular abuses – lambasting the cruelty, incompetence and stupidity which meant that 'madmen are too often man made' – not as a tract of 'anti-psychiatry' repudiating the asylum and the psychiatric profession root-and-branch. Never did Beers deny that insanity was a real, objective medical condition. Nowhere did he suggest that madness *per se* was only manufactured by psychiatry or the asylum, albeit it was often tragically magnified by their abuses. Beers was an idealistic reformer rather than a radical or a revolutionary, and he saw reform coming from within the profession.

In harmony with the meliorism of the Progressivist temper, Beers did not believe there need be any fundamental conflict between individual and state, rich and poor, doctor and patient, psychiatrist and lunatic. The interests of all should and would advance together, if only men of good will would channel their energies, talents and money into education, organization and enlightenment. The National Committee would stimulate, concentrate and popularize these efforts to create a better, healthier, saner future. Its elite of doctors and do-gooders would be the best safeguards of mental health. Almost uniquely in the history of mad people turned campaigners, Beers teamed up with the very profession which had been the 'oppressors'. And he was welcomed by them, as a man who had seen the light.

Of course, what continued to be stage-centre in Beers's crusade was the adventure story of his personal experience of asylum abuse. That was what sold thousands of copies of his book, turned him into a national figure, led movie makers to want to film his life story, made people give to the cause ($4,000,000 was donated over twenty years). But – unlike the earlier National Association for the Protection of the Insane founded in 1880, or the Alleged Lunatics' Friend Society set up earlier in England by John Perceval – Beers's Mental Hygiene Committee did not actually address itself to asylum patients and their injustices on anything more than a token scale. Of course, it received hundreds of requests for help from victimized patients. But it investigated very few of these. Indeed, Beers himself showed little interest in or sympathy for the plight of mental patients and ex-patients. To one former inmate who wrote to him about his woes and requested help in getting employment, Beers replied brusquely that 'each recovered patient must go out and get his own job just as I had to do when I left the hospital way back in 1903'. The correspondent thought this pure humbug.

Indeed, as with many others who reject their roots, who climb the ladder and kick it away, Beers's own attitude towards the insane was highly ambivalent. He never disguised the fact that he himself had once been mentally sick – never, for example, tried to make out that his 'madness' was just a label invented by a conspiracy of doctors. To have done so would have defeated his whole purpose, which was to show how mental illness was an enemy which could be conquered by will-power. But he never directly called his own disorder 'insanity'. He preferred to speak of a 'mental civil war'

195

in which 'Unreason'was eventually overcome by 'Reason'.

Furthermore, his self-dramatization was one which emphasized how his disorder was somehow 'clean' and even 'good'. It had been the understandable outcome of his very proper fraternal nursing of his brother Sam's epilepsy. Beers never testified to any shameful or shocking source of his malaise, no emotional skeletons in the family cupboard, no profound inner 'lesions of the will', no 'moral insanity'. Though the Mental Hygiene Movement had quite mixed feelings about Freud, it certainly wasn't wholly opposed to the notion of the unconscious. But there is no sign that Beers suspected any monsters from the Oedipal deep in his own case. On the contrary, he believed that, even when suffering in the depths of delusions, he had always preserved a hard core of purposive rationality and will-power. During his manic, talkative phase in the asylum (he loved to tell his audiences), he was challenged to be silent for twenty-four hours. He won his bet. Moreover, it was largely through self-help – the experiment of sending a letter to his brother George – that he had recovered. Beers had been crazy, yet there was good reason in it.

Thus Beers entertained an unspoken division between the 'deserving' and the 'undeserving' mad, and he felt most comfortable in sympathizing with those who helped themselves, once they had become rational once more. Indeed, on occasion he could display a coolness towards their plight which seems to verge on the callous. His elder brother, William, a businessman, sustained terrible financial losses in the Depression. He became deeply depressed. Clifford advised him to get admitted as a voluntary patient to Bloomingdale Asylum. He did, but soon hanged himself. Beers was quite dismissive.

Shortly afterwards, his favourite elder brother, his 'conservator' George, also became profoundly depressed. At length, on Clifford's bidding, George entered Austen Riggs Asylum (it was run by a member of his National Committee), but committed suicide on the very day of his admission. Beers's reaction was mixed. He wrote that he was gratified that George 'did not end his life without first seeking psychiatric protection against himself and his suicidal impulse' – his call for help showed he had evidently not betrayed the cause of mental hygiene. On the other hand, he saw George as essentially to blame for his own death, through not having agreed to enter the asylum earlier. There is no sign that it crossed his mind that what may have precipitated George's suicide was the very advice that he should be asylumized. George's death left Clifford feeling betrayed. What a dreadful 'irony of fate' that 'members of my own family have been unable to receive benefit from the work I started'! As he saw it, he had been made to look like the proverbial preacher unable to convert his own family.

196

Of course, sympathy is due. Beers came from a family in which his mother had been subject to depression, an elder brother had died of epilepsy, and other brothers were prone to depression; he feared that he himself was tainted. It would be no wonder if, for his own psychic well-being, he needed to put some distance between his own 'healthy insanity', hopefully conquered, and the types of malaise which destroyed others.

That need found expression in his wider visionary programme. Right from the beginning, the Mental Hygiene Movement as a whole distanced itself from the insane. William James had initially wanted the word 'insanity' blazoned in its very title, to draw attention to their plight. Agreeing with leading psychiatric practitioners such as Adolf Meyer, Beers successfully resisted. The word was too lurid. Beers (and they) wanted a movement which would be respectable, which would not scare off the Vanderbilts and the Rockefellers. Mental Hygiene became a movement not for fighting scandalous cases in the courts, but for winning over the courts – judges, lawyers and administrators – to social psychiatry. It worked through publicity, propaganda, information, pamphleteering, lobbying. It addressed its appeal both to right-thinking citizens and to society. What then did it aim to achieve?

To the individual it held out a promise of positive mental health. It told him that, through familiarity with psychology and psychiatry, he could improve his personality, think positively, gain insight into his own psyche, follow the rules of mental health, and regulate his emotions. It was a creed for psychological success. Under its umbrella, books were published with titles like *Understanding Yourself*, a self-help of the psyche advocating a sort of mental keep-fit, jogging for the mind.

To society and government it presented a different but complementary message: a battle-cry against 'poor mental health', a call to psychiatric arms. Until recently, Beers's mental hygiene literature contended, human evolution had principally been in the biological sphere, the struggle for development of higher physical powers. But now the progress of civilization required collective social psychological evolution. The future was threatened by mental maladies and misfits – by delinquents, addicts, perverts and morons. Traditional methods to deal with chronic, recidivistic criminals and trouble-making elements had become as out of date as the Inquisition and the stake. Modern scientific psychology and psychiatry alone held the keys to improvement, stressing investigation, retraining and education. Understanding the laws of mental health would simultaneously help these misfits and help society protect itself from such degenerates.

This was the mission of the Mental Hygiene Movement. It would spread education and information. It would promote prevention and treatment agencies. It campaigned for the setting up of psychiatric clinics attached to schools, jails, reformatories, workplaces, the army. Like the contemporary Social Hygiene Council in England, it advocated intelligence testing, grading, psychiatric surveys and sampling, child guidance and so forth – all these were vital for providing psychological understanding needed to manage modern society. To achieve these goals, Beers hoped to penetrate into 'all the educational and industrial spheres, courts and homes, the marriage license and advice centers'. His fantasy of reason was the goal of psychiatric man normalized by professional help within the therapeutic state.

Ironically, Beers himself never escaped from his own fantasy. In his midsixties he grew increasingly depressed. He had always been an erratic, difficult, sometimes dictatorial man – a supreme egoist in his own organization, deeply suspicious of others, often double-dealing on them behind their backs. Now his behaviour became impossible. The mind that had found itself lost itself again. Above all, he quailed before old age and the prospect of death. The sight of his own greying hair tormented him, and he started to dye it. He consulted a trusted analytically inclined therapist, Dr Ralph Banay. Banay not surprisingly tended to blame Beers's troubles on his mother, who had allegedly failed to give him maternal warmth and affection.

Admittance into an asylum was suggested. True to his principles, Beers accepted. He had his hair dye smuggled in. The old delusions flooded back. Once more he thought that he had been trapped in a conspiratorial masquerade, that nothing was real; his wife's letters to him were all 'fakes'. Increasingly nihilistic and catatonic, he died in 1943 believing that the doctors attending him were all 'impersonators'.

Crazy or sane, the irony of Beers's career sprang from his paradoxical pursuit of all-American values in an America which could no longer (if ever it could) accommodate the myths. When he entered the Connecticut Hospital, his patient record stated amongst other things that he displayed 'unrest, numerous expansive ideas, a pronounced feeling of well being, destructive habits ... irritability, egotism, mischievousness'. Might not this serve not just as a diagnosis upon the man, but as a character sketch of the civilization? Indeed, for many, would not that read not as a psychopathological diagnosis but more like an accolade, a definition of national character, or at least of its inner demon or genius? The early Beers, who read Lombroso on genius, liked to think of himself as 'abnormal'. The later Beers was glad to be called 'Superman' (or Übermensch). He was the American dream.

But he also had the 'American disease'. He recovered from it, and out of his 'expansive habits and pronounced feeling of well-being' prescribed a remedy for his society: salvation through psychiatrization, to ensure Reason Triumphant, or the progress of normality. Mental hygiene sold inner cleanliness. There was no original sin, no universal blot upon the brain to frustrate

198

the campaign. The accent was to be upon nurturing the regular guys whose thoughts and emotions squared with social harmony and integration. Those who walked in Beers's footsteps thus had the additional hazard of normality to negotiate.

Take William L. Moore for example, whose life offers an intriguing parallel half a century later. In certain superficial ways Moore's fate and Beers's took similar courses. Both grew up enmeshed in the world of selling. Both had intellectual aspirations (Beers attended Yale; Moore took economics at Johns Hopkins in the early 1950s). Both had 'expansive minds' which enabled them to criticize the tyrannies and hypocrisies of their respective asylum treatments by reference to the great liberal philosophies of Western thought. Indeed Moore now had the testament of Beers himself to draw upon. Moore was confined in 1953. He was outraged to be locked away despite never having had gross hallucinations, never having committed a crime, never having been violent, suicidal or dangerous. At some length he portrays asylum life as one evil and exacerbating system built up of a million petty oppressions. He explains how the system, by treating patients like children, cripplingly infantilizes them. He insists that he is not anti-asylums, but merely wants to make them better places. Then he stops, and simply says:

> All this has been told before far better than I could ever write it. As for example Clifford Beers wrote his *A Mind That Found Itself*, which deserves all the acclaim which has been given to the book.

But if Beers was Moore's overt hero, he is also, symptomatically at least, the evil genius at the root of all that Moore had to fight. For his own tragedy, as Moore recounts it in his *The Mind in Chains: The Autobiography of a Schizophrenic* (1955), is the story of a man whose heartfelt commitment to Beersian idealistic optimism ('the American way of life') is continually disconfirmed by the demands of his society for mental hygiene or normality. The result was a hospital diagnosis of schizophrenia. In so far as that diagnosis registered a divided self, it was a self torn between two psychiatries.

Moore was born in the late 1920s, the son of a Southern store-keeper. He grew up into a community whose gods were the Americans of Horatio Alger's stories and the myths of the movies. Trust God, work hard, play fair, be good, honour and obey, salute the flag and you'll go places, was all the message at home and school. He had been lucky to be born in 'a free country', where everyone was equal and the sky's the limit. 'I was taught that in America a man could grow up, to be anything he desired.' You should be your own man: 'in grammar school my teacher said that in America any one can grow up to be President'. Everything would turn out fine and dandy. 'In school, at home and in the movies, I was indoctrinated with the belief that people grow up and live happily ever after.' Moore's stepmother wanted all stories that did not have happy endings to be banned from the radio. Tragedy was evidently an un-American activity. Home and abroad, America stood for freedom: free thought, free speech, your right to be yourself, and, globally, justice, liberty, peace. Be a man, my son; fight for what is right.

Moore was told all this. He was told to believe it (his mother was a 'great believer in the American way of life'). He did. He must aim high. He would become President. 'I dreamed of becoming something like a combination of The Shadow and the Lone Ranger and having the powers of Superman.' His troubles started when he discovered that the adult world paid no more than casual and indeed cynical lip service to this creed. Indeed, it was deeply suspicious of anyone who took it seriously. Young Moore took it literally; others, including the parents he had been taught to love, lived it through all as a lie.

He would not stoop to lies himself. Yet that created trouble with the authority figures he had been taught to 'honour and obey'. 'You have to work hard to get on,' he is instructed. He studies; at once his protective mother stops him with some vulgarized mental hygiene: don't read too much, don't study too much, she tells him, 'you will crowd your brain'. When as a youngster he queries adult behaviour he is told, 'you're too young to understand'. When as a result he gets disheartened, distressed, lost in this maze of hypocrisy, he is wrong again. His father rebukes him: 'it isn't normal to take a little thing like this so hard! If you keep this up, I'll have to take you to see a psychiatrist.' Why can't his son just be 'ornery'?

His problem, as he saw it, was that, precisely because he was a 'model child', he *believed* all the make-believe. Thus he grew up 'not quite like other people'. Luckily he possessed a counter-balance to the cage of cosy, corny conformism: Mr Armstrong, his history teacher. Mr Armstrong was a wise old man with a mind of his own who practised what American values preached. He really believed that everyone must be his own man. Unlike the rest of supine, small-town society, this 'great hero' actually had the 'courage to think'. He 'probed the eternal mysteries of life'. He wanted to retire, buy a farm and be a Thoreau-like sage of the soil. Armstrong, however, was also an 'analyst'. By this Moore did not mean a Freudian psychiatrist. Rather, Armstrong is presented as a Lavaterian seer with his own analytical technique, who can almost read minds merely by peering hard at the cranium. Armstrong became Moore's guru but his parents' *bête noire* in a succession of adolescent struggles. Moore would go along for a weekly session of 'analysis' at his house.

Increasingly Moore found himself in an impossible world where people were 'living contradictions'. He subscribed enthusiastically to all the most cherished values of his society. But only he and his guru took them literally; for everyone else they were pious frauds best ignored in reality. He became a sort of Candide-figure or the innocent abroad in a world of candyfloss, movie-theatre illusions. For his pains he was branded as abnormal. His parents rebuked him for being a worry to them. He became isolated.

He served in the marines. There his belief in the 'true-love myth' got him into more emotional trouble. For he fell in love with a girl from Guam, who didn't understand about true romance. In 1952, he went on to college. He devised political schemes for a 'Little Utopia'. In this new Moore's Utopia, Armstrong would be Mr President. Moore himself aspired to teach Armstrongian 'analysis' – a healthy mental gymnastics – so it could help others who needed it, such as President Eisenhower, who had reneged on true idealism. For it was crucial that American values should prevail against the peril of Communism, which was the ultimate in lies and double-talk. Moore loathed Russia, a 'crazy' *Alice in Wonderland* world in which 'black is white, upside down is right side up'.

Meanwhile, however, Armstrong died. Or rather (Moore deduced) Armstrong had it given out that he had died, as part of his profoundly wise analytical strategy for making Moore truly self-reliant. Now that Armstrong was 'dead', Moore discerned extraordinary patterns behind certain chains of events. Such could not be purely coincidental; they must demonstrate the strong arm of Armstrong working behind the scenes to produce moral testing grounds for his pupil. Moore recalls that he knew at the time that all this sounded odd. Too bad. 'I cannot reconcile myself just to being normal.'

Moore tried to explain this analytic providentialism to friends, colleagues and family. Judged 'a misfit for the normal world', however, he was taken to the state hospital. They invited him to 'step inside for a couple of days and locked the door'. This turn of events merely confirmed Moore's convictions. Clearly, Armstrong had arranged it all so that he would be able to learn to 'weep with those that weep'. The asylum seemed full of stooges planted there by Armstrong. It was all a 'plot', though a very benevolent one.

The asylum doctors diagnosed him as a schizophrenic of the paranoid type subject to delusions. What constitutes delusions? he asks. True, he believes that Armstrong lives. Billions of Christians, however, believe that Christ lives. 'Yet all Christians are not put in state hospitals.' That is, he explains, because those Christians are the moral majority who have the power to define normalcy: if Christ returned now, He would be locked away for His own good. That goes to the heart of the Big Lie of his 'supposedly free country': America tells you to think big and act big, but then penalizes you big for it: 'I have dreamed wild dreams – crazy dreams if you will – in the hope of being able to make this life a better thing for us all. And that is why all windows are barred, all doors are locked, all exits are guarded.'

Indeed, the management of the asylum – reflecting the ways of the world – no longer recognized the paramountcy of truth and falsehood, right and wrong, good and bad, but only the divide between normal and abnormal. And that reduces itself at bottom to questions of who has the power to define normalcy. His doctors try to divest him of the belief that, with the aid of Armstrong's techniques, he can 'analyse people'. His parents reduce truth to authority and questions of adjustment: they tell him he must 'have faith and believe whatever the doctors tell me'. The doctors in turn tell him: 'you are a very sick man'. His problem, they explain, is that 'you have ideals which are contrary to normal society'. He replies: 'Is it not normal for a man to want world peace under law, to dream of peace on earth, good will toward men? Is it not normal to want to help others, to want to stir people to think ...? Is it not normal to believe in my ideals?' At least, he argues, his beliefs are harmless, unlike those of people who start world wars.

His visions – about Armstrong – gradually fade. But even then, once his sense of reality is restored, the asylum's roads to freedom have to do not with true and false perception, but merely with certain procedures. He will be released, he is told, only if he accepts a course of insulin treatment. Refuse, and his refusal will be taken for negativism. This is, Moore concludes, the regime of the chemical 'brainwash'. Moore is treated (he gives a long and harrowing account of coma therapy); he is released, but there is no Horatio Alger happy ending:

> Whether I go forward as Don Quixote chasing his windmill, or as the pilgrim progressing, must be left for you to decide. Indeed, in this democratic half of the world, my whole future is in your hands, at your mercy. I can only give my life. And you must make it or break it for me.

Moore's account highlights the tension in American culture between individualistic freedom on the one hand and, on the other, therapeutic conformism. If the 'normalizers' are the villains of the piece, it is noteworthy that the champion of all-American values is himself sustained by an 'analyst' who plays the part of the traditional providentialist Almighty. Moore is also a child of his time in the resolution he offers. A couple of centuries earlier a 'Lone Ranger' such as Alexander Cruden battling against the tyranny of 'the world' staunchly defended his own rationality. Moore, by contrast, tries a different tack: 'No one is sane. All the world are schizophrenics.' He himself is hooked on the rhetorical allure of the therapeutic society, on the New Deal idea that everybody needs help.

202

The life of Jim Curran rings another set of variations upon the themes sounded by Clifford Beers. William Moore felt encouraged to explore the roads to freedom and individualism but found himself trapped in a maze. Jim Curran tried to pursue those parallel goals which everyone had dinned into him since his schooldays: be a success! get rich! enjoy power! He too found they led only to the asylum. The same voices haunted him even there. 'I dream of being in a crater,' he writes from the hospital, 'and having to get to the top. . . . I know I ought to get to the top, but could not.' Like Beers, he came up with 'great schemes' of how to fly.

Curran grew up in the interwar years, the son of a manufacturer. After college, he went into the clothing business, and at one stage took a job as a travelling salesman out West. He was a dutiful son. 'I was out to make my way, and I was determined to do it.' No doubts here about the right course of life: 'I wanted business success all right.' All went well at first. His efforts were appreciated, and he rose in the firm, becoming a manager and a partner. He liked watching the happy workers stream out of the factory of an evening: 'It gave me a pleasant feeling of benign power.' But tell-tale signs appeared. He had the itch to be on the move, a 'restless desire to move on'. His concentration lapsed; he began to procrastinate: soon 'my old eager self had gone'.

The business slid: debts piled up, wrong decisions were made, the firm folded. He turned travelling salesman once more ('my training fitted me for nothing but selling'), but, Willy Loman-like, could sell nothing. His mind plagued by 'if-onlys', Curran plummeted into lethargy, a downward spiral of worry, inefficiency and more worry – above all, anxiety about being a failure in the eyes of his wife and children. 'I was weary'; 'my mind grew more tired'; he became 'mentally paralyzed'. Eventually, drowning in self-pity and self-accusation, he was no better than 'a broken spirit, a disordered mind'.

'Something was holding me back, but I did not know what it was.' Relatives thought he was just being 'lazy', that he had 'lost his grit', and they told him to 'snap out of it'. He knew that was untrue and resented the slur. Therefore he must be physically sick. His doctors thought it might be an ulcer or appendicitis ('It never occurred to me there was a mental basis for my trouble,' he adds). He had a spell in the regular hospital. It took a load off his mind and proved a great relief. For it meant 'I was ill' and 'I luxuriated in this thought,' for 'I had been relieved of the responsibility of making a living.'

He left hospital to sell life insurance, but soon underwent a complete nervous breakdown. His family despatched him to an expensive private asylum euphemistically called a sanitarium. Once again Curran felt a crushing burden of blame had been lifted from his shoulders: he was mentally sick, not lazy.

Moreover, he was not sick because he had been a failure, but rather a failure because all along he had been sick. The sanitarium doctors thus helped him in one respect: they absolved him of racking guilt, by labelling him mentally disordered. But they harmed him in another. For (Curran believed) they had a vested interest in mental illness, and they exploited it up to the hilt. The sicker their patients were, the longer they remained, the bigger the fees. The proprietor–doctor followed him around accusing him of 'negativism' and telling him 'You're crazy as a loon, and always have been,' in order (he thought) to make him worse. The whole establishment was a gross racket, offering no help, no therapy, no routine. Exorbitant fees merely bought secrecy.

Curran suffered hammer blows (not least, his wife divorced him) and he grew worse, in fact suicidal. He was removed after seven months and transferred ('admitted not committed', he stressed) to the state mental hospital, a vast institution of some 2,000 patients. It proved his salvation. St Charles's was well run by friendly and dedicated staff, cheery and caring. Once again, it disburdened Curran that things were done for him, decisions made on his behalf. 'I was cared for automatically'; it was a great relief for his 'desires to be considered'.

'I was sick, I was a failure.' But now the stigma of failure was removed. The hospital helped put him back on his feet, not least by making him work, in the carpentry shop, in the bakery, in the garden of one of the attendants. Bouts of deep depression ('a monster, a growth') still beset him, as he brooded over the wreck of his life and the loss of his family (voices told him: 'you have lost everything'). But gradually his self-respect returned. He began to look forward to the prospect of leaving, of getting work outside.

'You cannot keep a good man down.' This time there would be no mistake. 'I had to go out and make money, lots of money.' Thus he would get his revenge on his rivals. 'The man who had failed and failed, would emerge from a hospital for the insane to build up a huge fortune by his own initiative.' He would 'make a lot of money'; his 'troubles would be over'. All that was needed was a slick marketing idea, something to patent like the proverbial paper clip – a tonic, a hair-brush. At last, the big idea came. He noticed from cigarette butts that people generally smoked only half their cigarette. They clearly wanted only half a cigarette. He would patent a clipper-cum-holder which cut cigarettes in half and allowed them to be smoked conveniently. The public would see the logic, and buy it by the million. He would bring the tobacco companies to their knees. He could dictate terms to them, be able to say 'I am a power', and 'absolute dictator'.

Curran had always been prey to dreams of grandeur, in good times and in bad. The fact that he was still dreaming these air-castles, he knew, could only indicate the continuation of his sickness. Fortunately he was rescued by a wonderful psychiatrist. Dr Carlsen always cared. He was friendly and attentive but firm. He talked straight, avoiding all the silly euphemisms about 'nerves' or 'overwork', and the patronizing 'there's nothing wrong with you' which well-meaning but misguided doctors often used. He never minimized Curran's complaint, but always gave hope, and convinced him that there was light at the end of the tunnel. Gently but firmly Carlsen made Curran shed his delusions. He insisted upon realism about the future. Yes, Curran must go back into the world, because people have to learn to support them-selves: 'I must help myself along the road to recovery.' (Of course, St Charles's would always be around as a fallback.) Yes, Curran could leave, but not before time. Yes, Curran must work, but he must take appropriate work – physical not mental. Carlsen offered inspiration. Remember how General Grant had overcome his drink problem, think of Lincoln surmounting his depression, the doctors told him. But Carlsen also dispensed practical help. It was aid rather than mere advice that sufferers needed.

Eventually, Curran was discharged. He became a lift attendant (the real-world analogue to the delusion of flying). Still he was beset by doubts and depression. He spent his spare moments writing down all his troubles, penning endless letters of explanation and accusation, dripping with self-pity and vitu-peration, revolving around his 'fear of failure'. He lost his job. But this time instead of despair, he had strength. A friend got him a better one. He could now cope with office work, using his talents instead of wasting them, eaten up with fear and doubt.

Curran called his spiritual autobiography *A Mind Restored*. The affinities to Clifford Beers's title are patent. It is not clear if Curran was familiar with Beers's life, but his own recommendations in the final chapter certainly smack of Beers's own philosophy. How, he asks, can we learn from his experience and conquer this terrible curse of mental illness? Above all, society requires a better scientific knowledge of the condition, and a more understanding set of attitudes. Stigma must yield to sympathy. Early recognition and treat-ment are crucial (in his days of dreams of grandeur Curran had envisaged setting up a chain of early-treatment clinics out of his profits). Racketeering private asylums must be rooted out. The answer to insanity was indeed more mental hospitals, but they must be good and well managed. The way forward also lay in the sufferer's own hands. It was a solution which was becoming as American as apple pie. It was up to the sick person to abandon his dreams and 'learn to face reality'. To achieve this, what was necessary above all was to 'consult a psychiatrist'; it may 'save years of heartbreak'.

Curran had Carlsen in mind. It was he who had helped him to 'find my way back to normality'. Carlsen gave Curran his golden rule: 'I must learn to adjust myself to the world, and not expect the world to adjust itself to me.' Once restored to normality, 'I feel so privileged in being invited to continue my contact with him.' Curran, like so many other American sufferers from the interwar years onwards, was discovering that the key to mental health lay in the hands of the therapist. And his job, as Curran stressed, was above all to restore 'normality'. That way, failure was turned to success. Even more so than *A Mind That Found Itself*, Curran's *A Mind Restored* was – as its Introduction pronounced – 'a cheerful story' offering 'a message of encouragement' for those who despaired of 'coming back'. Horatio Alger could be right. Happy endings might be the order of the day after all.

In the three works so far considered, the dialogue between American madness and American normalcy has been conducted entirely in the good old-fashioned conscious mind. Reason and will have been assailed but have emerged triumphant. But the century of the Freudian unconscious has also seen this dialogue go underground.

'Barbara O'Brien' – it is a pseudonym – was a businesswoman working in an office in a large organization. She was efficient, well paid and ambitious. Wanting to know how to succeed in business, she became a watcher of office politics. Over a period of some years she saw that behind the bonhomie, the political economy of organization man was the law of the jungle. It was a dog-eats-dog mentality. Every executive was an 'operator', trying to get his hooks into his enemies. Machiavellian deviousness became second nature. She stayed aloof from all this and lost out in the promotion stakes.

One morning she woke up and saw three strange figures. They introduced themselves. One was an old man named Burt, another a boy called Nicky, and the third a weird drop-out figure called Hinton. They were 'Hook Operators'. It was their job in life to get their hooks into human beings (or 'Things' as they were known in Operator lingo). Once 'hooked', Things could be controlled. The Hook Operators – and there were many more besides this trio, with whom O'Brien became acquainted over the next six months – started giving her instructions. She must quit her job; she must take a long trip on a Greyhound bus (Operators had a special deal with the management of Greyhound which enabled them to control Things particularly well when they were travelling on them). O'Brien was 'on the hook', a dummy, a puppet completely at the dictation of the Operators.

Such control, however, was itself subject to a complex power struggle. For the Operators proved to be organized in many distinct and often rival groups and gangs. These outfits commonly 'just preyed on each other', though under the ultimate jurisdiction of an Operators' City Council with sovereign punitive powers. Rival Operators appeared to her, or, much more commonly, made themselves heard as voices; their instructions often countermanded each other; they fought for the 'charter' to operate her. For much of the time she was fleeing from one group, hoping for the protection of another, living dangerously. For, like mortals beset by the Greek gods, Things were the toys of Operators' games. Operators could torment and torture Things in a variety of modes sanctioned by the laws of the market place, and the most successful Operator – the one who drew the biggest emotional reaction from the Thing – won the most points. When O'Brien protested, she was reminded that these games were no different from the games people played or what humans did to dumb animals. Things were Operators' dogs.

For half a year she fled and sped from town to town, from hotel to rented room to Greyhound bus under the command of these sinister bosses. Eventually, when she was in California, one Operator told her to contact a priest who – as priests seem to do these days – sent her to a psychiatrist at a state mental hospital. He in turn apologized for not being able to admit her (the state was pursuing a policy of deinstitutionalization), but put her in touch with a Freudian psychoanalyst of European origin. He told her she was in the throes of schizophrenia, and that if the voices did not go away soon she would have to have shock treatment. On the third day they departed. She was at last on the road to recovery, though she was still numbed (her consciousness was a 'dry beach', only occasionally rolled over by refreshing waves of thought). In one moment of clarity, she noticed an advertisement for *Death of a Salesman*.

She was still far from well. She looked to her analyst for a better understanding and for practical help. He proved less than ideal. For one thing, when she failed to free-associate to his satisfaction, 'the analyst fretted and fumed'; he said 'he was going to bully it out'. (She was later to read that 'the schizophrenic, a specialist in the meaning of unreal and inappropriate behavior in his own right, will be only too quick to spot such behavior in others, especially psychiatrists'; she enjoyed the idea of turning the tables.)

For another, once he started delving into the causes of her schizophrenic disturbance, analyst and analysand became at daggers drawn. O'Brien had her own cogent theory of the meaning of her bout of delusions. She could very clearly see the parallel between what she had consciously experienced at the office and the manhandling by sinister forces manoeuvring for power which she had undergone over the previous six months. Both obeyed the laws of 'competition': 'The Operators had been businessmen.' The analyst pooh-poohed all this. No, the root of her condition lay in 'an inadequate sex life'. True love or not, a successful businesswoman needed regular outlets for the discharge of her sexual desires. A woman of her age, he told her, ought to have had at least 'one hundred and twenty five affairs'. Her best hope for a cure was to 'have a multitude of affairs' (European partners were preferable, he hinted, as American men made poor lovers): 'there's no need for becoming emotionally involved with any one'. She demurred:

> The analyst slapped his desk in irritation. 'A typical woman's point of view. And it's nonsense, do you hear, nonsense! Women don't understand themselves.'

(He had evidently just been reading Freud on Dora.)

She still resisted. He got madder. 'The only thing he could not understand ... was why, with a full six months at its disposal, my unconscious had not gotten itself into a few thousand discussions about sex.' To make up for that, he wanted to know about her dreams (O'Brien believed he was looking for confirmation of sexual repression). She went away and had one. She dreamed she was dining in a restaurant and had just discovered that her companion was a 'third-rate racketeer'. That stopped him in his tracks: 'The analyst rolled his head as if he were going to charge, and then abruptly tightened his lips and started talking about something else.' The therapy ended.

The analyst, however, provided her with one valuable insight. Unlike the somatic psychiatrist who would have seen the Bedlam cacophony in her head as meaningless, he suggested to her that her illness itself had been a healing process, that all the time her unconscious had been working surreptitiously for her benefit. O'Brien was inclined to see sense in this optimistic teleology, this wisdom of the unconscious. For in retrospect it was clear that the Operators had forced her to do many healthy things: they had made her leave her job, they had made her put a great physical distance between herself and her friends and family who would only have made things more emotionally difficult for her at a time of mental disturbance. Not least the Operators' mafia had really in some sense 'protected' her, telling her all the right things to say and do. She had, after all, travelled round America as a schizophrenic for six months without coming to any harm, without even betraying her condition. Even then, the therapeutic process was still continuing. For she had now fallen into the power of a newcomer pseudo-Operator called 'Something'. 'Something' kept on telling her to do this, do that, do the other. 'Something was evidently determined to have its own way.' All these Something-directed actions turned out right. As O'Brien later put it, common speech would call these 'hunches' or 'intuitions'. Under whatever term, the unconscious was directing her life pretty shrewdly.

O'Brien read up on schizophrenia. Interpretations of its cause and nature abounded; she found a Hobbesian war of all against all raging amongst the psychiatrists. So she introspected and developed an experiential understanding of her own case which made sense of it in the light of the American paradox. She had grown up blessed with exceptional and unusual talents – for example in English composition and mathematics. For these she had been fêted, but her very unusualness attracted the suspicion of relatives and educators alike in the rigid, restricted community in which she had spent her adolescence. Under pressure, she had chosen publicly to conform, while at the same time holding on to her private nonconformity at the cost of compartmentalizing herself. She had become a success at toeing the line, but lived in fear of turning into, or being exposed as, a 'misfit'. Her aghast reactions to seeing the Hook Operators at work had been a way of bringing her fear of life to the surface. Her schizophrenic episode made her confront her fear, and supplant it with healthy anger. In this process, the mysterious nonconformist Operator, Hinton, had obviously been with her all the way. She had learnt self-assertion, and now she knew she could compete. Schizophrenia had made her more whole, healthy and wised up. Thanks to unconscious operators *A Mind That Found Itself* had been given a new twist.

There was, however, a neat coda. Now recovered and living in California, O'Brien got another office job. What did she find?

B wanted A's job. C and D were planning to make a dash for B's job as soon as B had successfully demolished A; both helped B in his program. ... Dear God, I wondered, are all people in business like this?

This was worse than last time. Back in her home state, Hook Operators were at least apologetic about their cut-throat activities. Here in California, the hatchetmen were all so 'nonchalant'.

She saw through the false philosophy of business life. '"Face your environment, refuse to run away from it, adjust to it, face its battles realistically" is so much hooey as far as I'm concerned. ... The evidence of what I might become in time was clear. I had only to look round the office in any direction to see it.' And so she took the only sane course of action. She quit:

The day I resigned I was a little blue. Would I ever get to be a really good practising realist, I wondered. I decided, optimistically perhaps, that if I watched carefully, I never would.

11 · The Therapeutic God

Of course, orthodox Freudian analysis also took root in the New World.

Amongst the cast of monstrous phonies that populates Sylvia Plath's highly autobiographical novel, *The Bell Jar* (1963), only one person emerges as humane and caring: the psychoanalyst, Dr Nolan. The heroine, Esther Greenwood, stumbles through the book icily aloof from her contemporaries – they are appallingly shallow and stupid – yet she is eaten up with envy for them at the same time, because they are successful. Her feelings towards her long-dead father, fluctuating between love and hate, stem from an overall sense of abandonment. Towards her all-too-present mother, ever demanding and silently reproachful, she feels an inexpressible resentment which surfaces as guilt. Only Dr Nolan understands; only Dr Nolan accepts.

At last, Esther manages to give vent to her rage towards her mother. '"I hate her," I said, and waited for the blow to fall. But Dr Nolan only smiled at me as if something had pleased her very, very much.' For Esther, Dr Nolan becomes the 'good mother' replacing her biological 'bad mother', and the novel ends on an optimistic note, with the heroine recovering from a suicide attempt thanks to psychotherapy.

The Bell Jar, published only weeks before Sylvia Plath's own suicide, presents a fair picture of the author's own positive experience of 'good psychotherapy'. In 1953, after her first attempt, at the age of twenty, to take her own life, Plath had briefly been subjected to bad psychiatry, which had bombarded her with insulin, shock treatment and drugs. She had quickly, however, come under the care of Dr Ruth Beuscher. She experienced enormous benefit. 'I do love her,' she wrote to her mother in 1954.

After marrying Ted Hughes in 1956, Plath returned in 1958 to Beuscher for further therapy. As the detailed write-ups in her *Journals* show, these latter encounters proved immensely rich and stimulating experiences. Within months, Plath was producing some of her finest poetry. Therapy was perhaps its midwife.

Plath lapped it up: 'I feel I am learning so much from her.' Beuscher

210

helped her get to grips with the subterranean turmoils which had precipitated her suicidal depression, and enabled her to pour forth her true emotions in poetry. Therapy and art coalesced. Her best poems of 1959 – 'Electra on Azalea Path', 'The Beekeeper's Daughter', 'The Colossus' – capture the voice of the 'bad daughter' raging against her family. Plath's father, who had died when she was just eight, is portrayed as a rigid authoritarian tyrant. Yet the daughter's ambiguous, Electra-like longings for him are also expressed. In *The Bell Jar*, Esther is happy only while her father is alive.

If the father becomes myth, the mother becomes scapegoat. The primary target of Plath's poems at this time, as of her contemporary journals, is her mother. Like the father, she too is portrayed as powerful, overbearing and controlling. Between them they deny the daughter any breathing space of her own. But unlike the father, who had been nakedly authoritarian, the mother manipulates through selfless self-sacrifice and by stimulating guilt. She imposes herself by her effacingness. In effect, she tells Sylvia: be humble, submissive, dutiful like me, or you will be a bad daughter.

These poems specifically offer a resolution to a problem Plath had presented to Beuscher. Plath wanted to write; she couldn't. At the same time, she felt bad towards her mother, but she couldn't express it. Beuscher saw the two 'blocks' as symbiotic. As Plath recorded in her journals, the analyst explained:

> You are trying to do two incompatible things this year. 1) spite your mother. 2) write. To spite your mother, you don't write, because you feel you have to give the stories to her, or that she will appropriate them. . . . So I can't write. And I hate her because my not writing plays into her hands and argues that she is right, I was foolish not to teach, or do something secure, when what I have renounced security for is nonexistent.

Plath's writing returned again and again to these traps. It amounts to a sustained expression of her own anger towards her parents, above all her mother, and an exploration of her own confused sense of self in respect of her childhood and upbringing. How far was she her mother's daughter? Clearly she believed therapy was therapeutic. She also saw writing as 'my health'; poetry was the writing cure. Through these, she believed, she would achieve self-discovery and catharsis. She thought she was liberating herself (through madness to freedom?).

Was she? Or was what Plath considered 'working through' all an illusion, merely a case of 'acting out', of repetition? Any simple solution would of course be glib. What does seem clear is that Plath entertained a real faith in the basic undertaking of psychoanalysis. In *The Bell Jar*, after all, Esther enters therapy, is enabled through it to express her mother-hatred, and recovers. For Plath, dredging up repressed emotions from the unconscious and launching them into the world was the key to both therapy and poetry. At one point she contemplated taking a PhD in clinical psychology.

Moreover, she found its specific doctrines offered her the tools she needed. It kitted her out with ready-made concepts. When Dr Beuscher rearranges an appointment, Plath understands what that action really means: she is 'symbolically withholding herself'. Freudianism provided a language through which her father becomes an explain-all: 'If I really think I killed and castrated my father may all my dreams of deformed and tortured people be my guilty visions of him or fears of punishment?' Above all, it provided her with an armoury of vindications of her attitudes towards her mother. Mother could become the perfect scapegoat. When re-entering therapy she wrote:

> Have been happier this week than for six months. . . . It is as if R.B.
> [i.e. Ruth Beuscher] saying 'I give you permission to hate your mother'
> also said, 'I give you permission to be happy.' Why the connexion? Is
> it dangerous to be happy?

She reads Freud and he provides further illumination of how her mother is to blame for writer's block. The root of it was:

> a transferred murderous impulse from my mother onto myself: the
> 'vampire' metaphor Freud uses, 'draining the ego'; that is exactly the
> feeling I have getting in the way of my writing: Mother's clutch.

As Jeffrey Berman neatly notes, Plath had earlier as a student dedicated herself to being a perfect daughter. Now she dedicated herself to becoming the perfect analysand, dedicated to her perfect analyst, a 'permissive mother figure', to whom she wished to dedicate her first book.

Plath set to, with great zeal, on her therapeutic labours: 'I am going to work like hell, question, probe sludge and crap & allow myself to get the most out of it.' We have no way of knowing how far her solutions – her relentless indictments of her parents – were truly her own 'self-discovery' or how far they were suggested to her by Dr Beuscher; and, if the latter, were they merely quizzical hints, or were they advanced with the bludgeoning zeal with which Freud put Dora in the picture? In all this, was Dr Beuscher, herself not much older than Plath, working out her own family 'crap'? Had Plath's vision of her parents as ogres been unconsciously present all along? Or was it planted by analysis?

It is worth examining a concrete example. *The Bell Jar* concludes with two events which almost magically release the heroine: her supportive therapeutic relationship with Dr Nolan, and the suicide of her obnoxious lesbian rival, Joan Gilling (who is against babies and for careers). Plath was fascinated by alter egos and clearly intended Esther and Joan to be seen as doubles. The message seems to be that the homosexual element in Esther has to be superseded, indeed killed off, before she can properly become a mature and successful woman. If so, it is a perfect reflection of the orthodox Freudian view. Has analysis indoctrinated Plath into such a conclusion?

Here Jeffrey Berman's discussion of Plath is particularly interesting. For he argues that, through the act of rejecting her own double in the novel, Plath reveals a blind spot: she mistakenly believed that the psychoanalysed Esther at the close of the novel was healthy. She was not. She had made the mistake of splitting and rejecting where, with greater insight, she should have united and incorporated. The explanation of this error, Berman argues, lies in the fact that Esther–Sylvia suffered from 'pathological narcissism' as defined by the psychiatrist Dr Otto Kernberg.

Berman draws the character of such a narcissist: she is a person simultaneously grandiose and self-hating, hypercritical, both contemptuous and envious of others, greedy for love yet incapable of giving it, a perfectionist doomed to imperfections. Summarizing Kernberg, he explains the sources of such narcissism: above all, having a demanding mother, which produces a childhood of deprivation and aggression leading to feelings of matricide and infanticide, etc. Lo and behold: the description perfectly fits Plath and her mother. The implication is that, by stressing Oedipal rivalry and by failing to get to grips with Plath's narcissism, the understanding reached by Plath and Beuscher in their analysis was shallow; it needs to be superseded by a better one – which if, as it were, advanced at the time would have given a healthier prognosis. Berman criticizes Plath for putting Dr Nolan on a pedestal as an omnipotent magic worker.

Mutatis mutandis, however, Berman's interpolation sounds rather like Freud rewriting the appendix to Dora's case. Once again, psychoanalysis is telling women what they want, what they should think about lesbianism. Here we might see that psychoanalysis is demanding a second chance. Is there no end of futures for illusions? As Elaine Showalter has remarked, psychoanalysis may simply have been a blind alley in terms of understanding women's dilemmas, the female malady. Plath found the conflicting demands of writing, of her own sexuality, of being a mother, in a man's world, intensely pressurizing. Was becoming trapped in a patriarchalist psychiatry that trapped her in her own past what she really needed?

Many writers this century have undergone psychotherapy. A few, like Plath, have been enthusiastic. Many, like Philip Roth, have preserved an ironical distance. Some have been downright hostile. Charlotte Perkins Gilman had been exposed to Weir Mitchell's rest cure. Mitchell told her never to pick up a pen again. She became remorselessly antagonistic towards 'mind-meddlers'. As a woman and a feminist, she found Freud's conviction that sexual liberation lay at the heart of the solution offensive: it was 'the resurgence of phallic worship set before us in the solemn phraseology of psychoanalysis'.

What is indisputable, however, is that a multitude of this century's 'spiritual autobiographies' have been written from within the language and suppositions of dynamic psychiatry, above all Freudian, and many of these recount at length the history of analytic encounters. I was disturbed; I went through Freudian analysis. Here I am, better. It is a constant litany. It begins with Freud himself, the first person to be cured of a severe psychoneurosis by Freud and by the techniques of psychoanalysis.

It is not my aim here to attempt to make any contribution to the still-raging debates amongst historians and psychiatrists about the evaluation of Freud and his work. I shall not discuss whether Freudian psychoanalysis is true science, or indeed effective as therapy. I shall not explore whether the historical accounts of the origins and development of psychoanalysis offered by Freud himself and his followers are largely accurate or, as Sulloway and others have claimed, essentially 'legend'. Rather I shall examine Freud as all the other characters in this book, as one who underwent a mental disturbance, and who subsequently told his life story.

Freud published his *Autobiographical Study* in 1925, when he was sixty-eight and believed he was dying of cancer. Starting from his birth in 1856 in Freiberg, Moravia, it chronicled his family's move to Vienna when he was four, and the outstanding successes at school which led to his decision to become a medical student. Anti-Semitism amongst the doctors inured him to a 'non-acceptance' which, he says, stood him in good stead for a lifelong history of rejection. Freud recounted his studies under Brücke from 1876 to 1882, his growing recognition as a budding neurologist, and his seminal period at Charcot's feet in Paris in 1885. On his return to Vienna he married the woman whose 'fault' it was that he 'was not already famous at that youthful age' – a vacation earlier spent with her had robbed him of credit for discovering local anaesthesia by cocaine. 'I bore my fiancée no grudge.'

Freud came back from Paris enthusiastic about Charcot's investigations into male hysteria. He presented an account of it to the Vienna Society of Medicine. He received (he tells us) a wholly hostile reception. Soon he was as a result 'excluded' from Meynert's laboratory: 'I found myself forced into the Opposition.'

So he had to set up in private practice. He treated neurotics, initially by hypnotherapy. In time he came to collaborate with Josef Breuer who, recognizing the crucial importance of unconscious factors, developed the technique of treating conversion hysteria by hypnosis and 'catharsis'. Their jointly auth-

214

ored work, *Studies in Hysteria* (first published in 1893, appearing as a book in 1895), met 'lack of comprehension' and 'severe rebuff'. The faint-hearted Breuer 'felt hurt' but Freud was able to 'laugh it off'. From now on Freud had to go solo; he 'could not escape' the loss of Breuer's friendship.

On his own, and faced with 'incredulity and contradiction', Freud now erected the great theoretical pillars of his scientific temple, 'the theories of resistance, and of repression, of the unconscious, of the aetiological significance of sexual life and of the importance of infantile experiences'. These truths were discovered, Freud insists, not through speculation but scientifically, thanks to intense clinical experience. Formulating them had demanded his ability to recognize and rectify one cardinal error. He had come to see the root of the neuroses in repressed sexual conflicts. Patients told him that as children they had been subject to sexual assault by their parents. He had believed them ('Intentionally keeping my critical faculties in abeyance so as to preserve an unprejudiced and receptive attitude'). That was a mistake. He soon hit on the 'right' meaning: the patients' stories were but 'wishful phantasies'. Thereby he 'stumbled upon' the Oedipus Complex. In doing so he had, however, loaded himself with 'indignation' and 'contradiction' for his pains.

At about the same time, he perfected that technique of free association which 'guarantees' the objectivity of analysis by ensuring that 'nothing will be introduced into it by the expectations of the analyst'. A proper grasp of transference was to follow, as was the technique of dream-analysis. By the early twentieth century, psychoanalysis had thus been born. But still 'I was completely isolated. In Vienna I was shunned; abroad no notice was taken of me.' Very slowly, however, he acquired 'followers', but for many years, German science, coupling great 'arrogance' with 'contempt of logic', remained 'united in rejecting it'.

Yet even all this 'official anathema' 'could not hinder the spread' of the infant science. Nor did it suffer any real harm from the 'secessionist movements' led by Jung and Adler, who could not stomach 'the repellent findings of psychoanalysis', that is, its sexual revelations. Despite continuing resistance ('contradiction at any price and by any methods'), psychoanalysis continued to go from strength to strength. Freud himself steadily progressed from purely individual clinical studies to wider theories of psyche and society. His investigations of creativity had solved profound literary problems. '*Hamlet*, which had been admired for three hundred years without its meaning being discovered or its author's motives guessed', fell to psychoanalytic probings – though Freud added in a later footnote that he eventually came round to J. T. Looney's theory that Shakespeare was not written by Shakespeare at all. And he had gone on to decipher the riddle of the origin of religion and so forth. He

215

concludes: 'I can ... express a hope that I have opened up a pathway for an important advance in our knowledge.'

Thus Freud's spiritual autobiography. In offering this version of self as super-man, was Freud primarily speaking as an embattled polemicist? Was he being extremely ingenuous, disingenuous or superlatively self-ironical? It is hard to be sure. It scarcely needs pointing out that his self-portrait is tendentious in the extreme. He conjures up the myth of the crucified hero, battling against all the odds, repudiated and ridiculed by the world, deserted by many of his one-time friends and allies, but finally triumphant and vindi-cated. He stakes exorbitant claims for his own originality, while omitting even the merest mention of key influences and collaborators. Thus not a word about the seminal intellectual and emotional friendship he enjoyed through the 1890s with Wilhelm Fliess, the man who first developed the concept of universal bisexuality and who greatly enhanced understanding of infantile sexuality.

No psycho-historical analysis of Freud's autobiography would have any difficulty in locating elements of paranoia, megalomania and so forth – albeit perhaps no more so than is the case with most people bitten by the autobiogra-phical bug. Not least, Freud was subject to amnesia. On issue after issue, his autobiography simply isn't reliable. Thus he tells us for example that he was the first to prick the myth of childhood sexual innocence. But the clinical literature of the second half of the nineteenth century teems with accounts – not *Freudian* accounts admittedly – of childhood sexuality. Simi-larly, he tells us how his early works, e.g. on male hysteria, were ignored or met a frosty reception. But that is hardly so. As Sulloway has shown, they were widely and often quite favourably reviewed.

Such issues are, however, peripheral to present purposes. Two points nevertheless are relevant. First, it is tantalizing that Freud's autobiography is in no way a *Freudian* autobiography. It offers the barest chronicle of his outer life, being given over almost totally to his science, practice and ideas. There is no mention whatever of his mother and but the scantiest details of his infancy. His wife is referred to just once, and not by name; the sole child of his to be recorded, Anna, enters the story only as a Freudian psychoa-nalyst. Moreover, there is not the slightest introspective attempt to sift his own thoughts, feelings or motives, or to assess his own creativity. The cliché account he presents of the dedicated man of science selflessly pushing forward the frontiers of knowledge is one that no dynamic psychiatrist could even momentarily take at face value.

What is doubly noteworthy is Freud's utter silence about the fact that he himself for several crucial years had laboured under what he commonly termed a 'neurosis' and what his ardent disciple and biographer, Ernest Jones, called 'a very considerable psychoneurosis', a 'twilight condition of mind'. Freud's deep anxiety and depression during the 1890s was utterly pivotal to his career. It came in the midst of the most intellectually perilous, yet, in the end, fruitful stage in the formulation of his psychoanalytic system. It clearly marked the profound tensions unleashed by his intense speculative creativity. And, above all, the insights which its inner conflicts revealed were productive in conjuring up the very concepts of new Freud's science.

During his thirties Freud was of course subject to the usual ups and downs of being a doctor embarking upon a practice. He had a growing family (he was to have six children) but few patients; money worries beset him (he had to borrow from Breuer). Right from the time of his ill-received lecture on male hysteria in October 1886, he had felt repudiated by Vienna's academic doctors, and had isolated himself from them. In his more optimistic moments, Freud could boast of his 'splendid isolation', but that cannot mask the fact that it perturbed him that the medical community was wont to think of him as a 'monomaniac', or that Breuer eventually believed him to be suffering from 'moral insanity, or paranoia scientifica'. Treating mainly neurotics, using hypnotherapy – his practice was all in all a risky business, and it depressed Freud that his own great scientific breakthroughs in fact met with little therapeutic success (indeed, his patients were often 'running away').

But these general trials and tribulations will only partly explain the repeated references in his letters from about 1892 onwards to acute anxiety, self-doubt, insecurity, depression, misery, 'fluctuating mood changes', 'unbelievable gloom', 'hysteria' and so forth. Some of these fears were essentially psychological, such as his phobia about travelling by train. Others – e.g. his dread that he would not live beyond forty, or more generally his *Todesangst*, his 'death deliria' – were linked to manifestations of physical symptoms of disease.

Freud suffered frequent migraines, which sometimes went on for three days. His sinuses gave him trouble, both before and after minor surgery by Fliess. Above all, he had worrying heart symptoms – 'the most violent arhythmia', accompanied by feelings of constriction, spasm, dyspnoea, palpitations, shooting pains in his left arm, burning sensations, an erratic pulse and so forth. Sometimes he attributed his cardiac problems to internal disease (Max Schur, later his physician, thought a coronary thrombosis in a small artery might have been responsible). Often he blamed his own acute nicotine addiction; he regularly smoked twenty cigars a day, and attempts, under Fliess's guidance, to kick the habit never met lasting success. Moreover, it is at least plausible to argue, with E.M.Thornton, that Freud, who had pioneered the use of cocaine back in the 1880s, was still taking it. This possibility would account for various of his symptoms, not least the euphoric bouts which punctuated the gloom, and the fact that when only just turned forty Freud seemingly confessed that he had ceased to be sexually active.

But Freud's disturbance was also partly psychogenic. In the early 1890s he became profoundly wrapped up with the study of hysteria and drove himself relentlessly towards a solution to its 'superhuman' problems. But every breakthrough seemed to spell rebuff, every advance was followed by a retreat, every solution created new mysteries.

With Breuer he established that hysteria was rooted in memories, often stemming from childhood. The reliving of these memories led to the disappearance of hysterical symptoms. This finding caused Freud to grow increasingly preoccupied with the aetiology of the neuroses. From 1893 onwards, clinical encounters indicated to him that it was specifically *sexual* trauma which became translated into hysterical symptoms, and at the same time the intense cross-fertilizing give-and-take between Freud and his alter ego Fliess further convinced him of the reality of infantile sexuality.

Yet as Freud pushed on with the 'incubus' of analysis, his conceptions seemed to grow ever more wild and woolly. When Freud insisted upon the sexual origins of *all* neurotic cases, Breuer could not go along with him – leading to a split between the two which left Freud feeling permanently betrayed and embittered. Worse was to come.

Freud became certain from 1895 that he had cracked the mysteries of hysteria. Clinical experience with his female patients had pointed ever more clearly to one constant specific origin: sexual trauma. For, primed by his various techniques for dredging up memories from the unconscious, they all seemed to be telling him of childhood sexual assault (rape, seduction, molestation, etc.) by the father. Freud reassured himself that he was not suggesting this solution to them: they were presenting it spontaneously. He was immensely excited – yet also apprehensive – about his extraordinary discovery ('a source of the Nile') that hysteria thus originated in 'perverse acts by the father'. In the spring of 1896 he published his 'seduction theory', first in French and then in German, and delivered it to a meeting of the Vienna Psychiatric Society.

It met an 'icy reception from the asses': Vienna doctors saw no reason why they should transform decent patresfamilias into perverts, simply on the unsubstantiated accusations of hysterical girls. Freud put on a defiant face ('they can all go to hell'), but he was deeply distressed. Only with Fliess could he share his true feelings.

Indeed Freud had been quite enraptured with the Berlin neuro-anatomist for some years, addressing letters to him sometimes as 'Dear Magician', and meeting him occasionally for ardent 'congresses'. In all this admiration there was, he later admitted, an element of 'unruly homosexual feeling' ('how much

I owe you: solace, understanding, stimulation in my loneliness . . . even health that no one else could have given back to me', he wrote in 1896). But what primarily counted in the collaboration was Freud's profound dependence upon Fliess as an authority figure, a listener, a supporter, a fellow demon.

Yet his intellectual tripping with Fliess also forced Freud out on a limb. Fliess launched himself upon some quite eccentric flights of ideas (Freud called him 'an even greater fantasist than I'). When trying to get to the root of female sexual dysfunctions, he argued for an equivalency between the nose and the vagina, which he set out at length in his Shandeian *The Relations between the Nose and the Female Sex Organs* (1902). He also persuaded Freud of the reality of male periods (the male cycle was twenty-three days) and the male menopause. Involvement in Fliess's pet theories forced Freud into greater scientific eccentricity. It also specifically put him through a quite shattering clinical episode. Freud had a hysterical patient named Emma Eckstein. He attributed her neurosis to masturbation and, following Fliess's 'reflex nasal neurosis' theory, saw the nose as the source of her masturbatory activity. The usual treatment recommended by Fliess and Freud was a dose of cocaine to the nose, but in this case Freud agreed to let Fliess carry out anti-masturbatory nasal surgery.

The operation was carried out in February 1895. Its result was almost fatal. Thanks to a gross surgical bungle, Fliess unknowingly managed to leave half a metre of gauze stuck up her nasal cavity. When that was finally removed, Emma haemorrhaged violently, 'had no pulse, and almost died'. Unable as ever to stomach blood, Freud fled the room. Emma did not die, but she recovered very slowly. Freud's reaction was instructive. He wrote repeated letters of reassurance to Fliess, at first heaping the whole responsibility for the débâcle upon himself. 'Of course no one is blaming you,' he wrote on 8 March; it was just a 'mishap'. In any case, he should not have encouraged Fliess to perform the operation in the first place. Then, in a string of letters in April, May and June 1896, Freud modified his alibi for Fliess.

Fliess was not to blame for what had happened, Freud now argued, precisely because it was all Emma Eckstein's fault. It was her hysterical reaction, her 'longing', her attention-seeking need to provoke a crisis which had caused the haemorrhage. In April 1896 Freud assures Fliess, 'her episodes of bleeding were hysterical'. Freud's fantasy has gone a bit further by May: 'she bled out of *longing*', 'she renewed the bleeding as an unfailing means of rearousing my affection'. Freud's lively imagination continued to do Trojan service. By June he is telling Fliess, 'there is no doubt that her haemorrhages were due to wishes'.

By January 1897, his rationalization of the episode had taken final shape: 'as far as the blood is concerned, you are completely without blame', he reassured Fliess. One could consider, Freud suggested, that Emma was the precise equivalent of one of those witches of earlier centuries. They had claimed to be diabolically possessed; in reality, however, they were merely hysterical, making up stories which incriminated others. 'Why do the confessions [of witches] under torture so resemble the reports of my patients in psychical treatment?' he asked Fliess. Thus Emma, like the witches, had brought her own fate upon herself by her perverse imagination. He could understand only too well, Freud added, 'the harsh therapy of the witches' judges'.

Freud's mythologization of the near fatality of Emma Eckstein is important. For it shows how crucial fantasy was becoming in his explanatory framework, partly at least because he had had to construct a whopper to shield his comrade. For it was her own inner wishes, and not external actions performed upon her, which explained her illness. But Emma Eckstein – so Masson has plausibly argued – was one of those very patients who had told tales to Freud of childhood molestation. Time was when he had believed such stories. No longer. Perhaps all their stories were fantasies.

In the spring of 1896, Freud had believed defiantly in his 'seduction theory' (i.e. the hypothesis that fathers had assaulted their daughters, thereby producing later hysteria). But his theorizing endeavours were getting out of phase, for at the same time as he was blaming fathers in this respect, he was also coming to blame Emma Eckstein.

Something had to yield. During 1897, his confidence in the 'seduction theory' wavered. By 21 September of that year, he could frankly confess to Fliess that he had abandoned it: 'I no longer believe in my neurotica.' After a fashion, though Freud never admitted it in so many words, he had reverted to the opinion of the medical establishment (which he had dismissed so contemptuously eighteen months earlier) that the girls' stories were just hysterical fantasies. Now he was all at sea ('Tell it not in Gath,' he bantered to Fliess); indeed he did not feel publicly able to admit his appalling fiasco until 1905.

Freud never offered any very satisfactory explanation of the abandoning of his scandalous theory of paternal molestation, saying little more than that it had collapsed under its own 'improbability and contradiction'. It was, after all, 'hardly credible that perverted acts against children were so general' – or, roughly, in other words, fathers were more believable than hysterical daughters. And traditional psychoanalytically minded historians have never seen Freud's *volte face* as posing a problem at all, since it was a move from error to truth. After all, it was precisely the abandoning of the 'erroneous' theory (an act, according to Steven Marcus, of 'personal and intellectual courage') which laid the foundation stone of the true science of psychoanalysis, paving the way for the discovery of the Oedipus Complex. But some explanation is in order.

Jeffrey Masson has suggested that the Eckstein case at least created the climate for Freud's switch (which, reversing the normal Freudian hagiography, he regards as a 'failure of courage'). Freud's need to protect his only close ally symbolically meant absolving the man and indicting the woman as a hotbed of fantasy. A further factor was surely also involved. Freud's father died in October 1896. Once his own father was dead, Freud could abandon his complex negative feelings towards fathers and identify more readily with paternal authority.

Indeed, the death of his father gravely deepened Freud's disturbance. Freud had very ambiguous feelings towards his father, not least because of his ambivalence towards his own Jewish descent. Jacob's death shook him; he was 'torn up by the roots', and long 'inconsolable'. Gradually, during the course of 1897, Freud began to suffer from periodic 'intellectual paralysis'. Often he was in the 'depths'. By June he could write, 'I have been through some kind of neurotic experience.' Bereavement drove him back in upon himself, leading to a self-analysis ('the chief patient I am busy with is myself'), through which he relived his childhood and aimed to come fully to terms with the residues of his emotions towards his parents. Sulloway has argued that this process did not begin in earnest till the autumn of 1897, but the evidence is clear that it was well under way long before, involving the exploration of dreams and lengthy attempts to interpret them in his letters to Fliess.

Freud said that he was going into a 'cocoon and heaven knows what sort of a creature will emerge from it'. What finally emerged from those months when he was 'so interesting to myself', laid the conceptual foundations of psychoanalysis. For his memories, dreams and introspections totally exculpated his parents from any sexual designs upon his infant self. 'The old man plays no active part in my case,' Freud told Fliess in October 1897. Indeed, in so far as Freud had been the object of sexual attention as a child, it had been the work of a nurse, the 'primary originator' of his sexual initiation.

Indeed Freud's intense and intimate self-scrutiny had inculpated not his parents but *himself*. The core of the Oedipus Complex was first revealed to Fliess in a letter of 15 October 1897:

I have found, in my own case too, being in love with my mother and jealous of my father, and I now consider it a universal event in early childhood, even if not so early as in children who have been made hysterical.

If this is so, we can understand the gripping power of *Oedipus Rex*, in spite of all the objections reason raises against the presupposition of

fate. . . . Everyone in the audience was once a budding Oedipus in fantasy
and each recoils in horror from the dream fulfilment here transplanted
into reality, with the full quantity of repression which separates his
infantile state from his present one.

Standard histories tell us that what emerged from this psychiatric 'cocoon'
was the founder of psychoanalysis, armed with the Oedipus Complex. Seminal
works such as *The Interpretation of Dreams* soon followed. Thus the new
science was actually born out of mental trauma and a process of self-healing
by psychoanalysis. It was, suggests Ernest Jones, a creative malady:

> For that man to free himself by following a path hitherto untrodden by
> any human being, by the heroic task of exploring his own conscious mind:
> that is extraordinary in the highest degree.

Of course, as this book has suggested, there was nothing very unusual in
people emerging from spiritual crises clutching discoveries of unfathomable
value to mankind: Daniel Schreber was also rising out of such a crisis just
at that time, proclaiming his own new religion. For such people, a cardinal
credo is the notion that everybody else is systematically enmeshed in webs
of delusion from which they have been freed by mental crisis.

What seems beyond all dispute is that the more Freud's auto-analysis got
into its stride, the more intellectually confident he felt, the healthier he
became, and – gradually – his absolute emotional dependence upon Fliess
diminished. Consciously or not, Freud recapitulated the shaman's experience
of a phase of intense isolation followed by emergence armed with new powers.
Like Daniel Schreber, Clifford Beers, George Trosse and John Perceval, he
arose from his disturbance a man with a mission, bearing a gospel for the
world.

The legacy of Freud's neurosis was an extraordinary intellectual grandilo-
quence. Often he likened himself to Moses, Hannibal, Oedipus, Alexander,
Napoleon; he was a *conquistador*. His self-analysis had laid bare universal
truths. He had discovered not the Freud Complex but the Oedipus Complex.
The origins of neurosis were no longer to be blamed upon seduction by
the father but upon desires within the infant. Ever since, for all its subsequent
subtleties and refinements, psychoanalysis has shown what Freud himself
called extraordinary monotony in its preoccupation with father-figures and
infantile sexual rivalries. All Freud's published case histories are variations
upon one elemental theme, one primal scene. A glance at the very language
and dramatic construction of his case histories shows how Freud felt driven
to get their Oedipal reminiscences out of his patients (Fliess himself had
commented: 'the thought-reader [Freud] reads only his own thoughts in those
of others').

And yet, in one crucial sense, Freud saw himself not as typical but as unique. He himself noted in passing that 'true self-analysis is impossible: otherwise there would be no [neurotic] illness'. In other words, if one had the capacity to analyse oneself, one would not be neurotic in the first place. Freud uniquely performed it on himself, however, and performed it to his own satisfaction. But Freud's was the first and last Freudian self-analysis. Thereafter all analyses were to be performed by Freud, or by psychoanalysts trained and analysed by Freud, and so forth, down in unbroken apostolic succession (it is noteworthy that Freud personally psychoanalysed his own daughter, his Antigone, Anna). How then did sufferers from psychoneuroses react to analysis?

One of the utterly bizarre features of Freud's forty-odd years' practice of psychoanalysis is that he wrote up in detail only four of his own cases. It is unsurprising then that we have only the barest opportunity to view from both sides what happened in any particular instance of Freudian therapy. It is perhaps remarkable that we have any at all. But one instance stands out, the 'Wolf Man'. He underwent four years of analysis with Freud from 1910 to 1914, and Freud published his case in a report running to well over a hundred pages. The 'Wolf Man' subsequently published his own *Memoirs* under psychoanalytical imprimatur. They appeared in a volume with an introduction by Anna Freud, a review of his psychic health by his later analyst, Ruth Mack (Brunswick), who herself, like Anna, had been analysed by Freud, and some personal details by Muriel Gardiner, who had been analysed by Mack. (According to the 'Wolf Man' later, they had expurgated his own recollections.) Finally, in the 1970s, against the express prohibitions of the Freudians, he gave a series of tape-recorded interviews to an Austrian journalist, Karin Obholzer. We thus get three bites at the 'Wolf Man's' cherry.

Sergius P. was born in 1887 into a family of aristocrats from Odessa. In the best Chekhovian fashion, his mother was hypochondriacal and his father suffered deep depressions for which he was treated by Kraepelin. Sergius had a sister two years older than himself who was intellectually brilliant and precocious, and who committed suicide in her early twenties (Freud retrospectively diagnosed incipient *dementia praecox*).

At the age of eighteen, Sergius was infected with a dose of gonorrhoea. The combined effects of these two events proved traumatic. Depressed and mentally paralysed, he spent his early twenties moving from doctor to doctor and sanitarium to sanitarium until he ended up at Freud's home, Berggasse 19, in 1910. The 'Wolf Man's' main personality trouble was that he was then (in Freud's words) 'entirely incapacitated and completely dependent upon other people'. The immediate problem facing him was whether to marry

Therese, a divorced nurse some years his senior, whom he had met in one of the hospitals.

Free association on the couch, detailed in Freud's case history, brought to light some of the terrors of his infancy. He had been 'seduced' at the age of three by his sister. His peasant nanny had fiddled with his penis. When he responded to her 'seduction' by playing with it himself in her presence, she retaliated by threatening him with castration. When he saw his sister peeing, he was confronted with the reality of castration in all its enormity. Thus discovering his infant sexuality frustrated at every turn, he regressed to rages, to excessive religiosity ('obsessional neurosis') and to sexual perversions. Idolizing his father in particular, he had loved flying into tempers in his presence, so that his 'sadistic–anal' desires could be satisfied by being beaten, thus giving him 'masochistic sexual satisfaction'. What were the origins of his 'phobia and his perversities'? How were they to be understood?

The key to it all lay in a dream which the 'Wolf Man' had apparently had around the age of four:

> I dreamt that it was night and that I was lying on my bed. (My bed stood with its foot towards the window; in front of the window there was a row of old walnut trees. I know it was winter when I had the dream, and night-time.) Suddenly the window opened of its own accord, and I was terrified to see that some white wolves were sitting on the big walnut tree in front of the window. There were six or seven of them. The wolves were quite white, and looked more like foxes or sheep-dogs, for they had big tails like foxes and they had their ears pricked like dogs when they pay attention to something. In great terror, evidently of being eaten by the wolves, I screamed and woke up.

Freud's work on this dream 'dragged on over several years' (they met an hour a day, six days a week, so Sergius' neurosis took perhaps over a thousand hours to work through). To understand the 'infantile neurosis' that lay behind it and which it expressed, Freud drew on much other associative material brought to the surface by the 'Wolf Man', such as his early reading of fairy stories. Even so, in a form of words strangely mingling candour and opacity, Freud admits that his final interpretation also went well beyond material revealed (or acknowledged) by his patient, noting as he proceeded with his interpretation:

> I have now reached the point at which I must abandon the support I
> have hitherto had from the course of the analysis.

Freud construed this dream as embodying a memory of a real experience of a 'primal scene' which (Freud deduced) the 'Wolf Man' had had at the age of one and a half. Each component of the dream could in turn be decoded. That it was night and winter meant, by the common trick of reversal followed by the unconscious, that it had been light and summer at the time of the traumatic experience. The opening of the window stood for the 'Wolf Man' waking up. The six or seven bushy-tailed wolves were, Freud proved by a long and complex train of deductions, his transformed memory of seeing his two parents having sexual intercourse. Here the change of number was required by 'resistance as a means of distortion'.

Freud had inferred from other sources that the 'Wolf Man' had erotic desires for his father. Hence in the dream the wolf essentially stood for a castrating father. Moreover, a children's story the 'Wolf Man' knew involved a tail-less (i.e. castrated) wolf. Such castration was a terrifying notion, and to 'over-compensate' for this terror, the 'Wolf Man's' infant unconscious had been forced to endow all the wolves with extra bushy tails. The stillness of the wolves in the dream signified (by reversed association) the agitated motion of sex. Their whiteness was (by direct association) the whiteness of his parents' underclothes. The standing position of the wolves signified that the sex was going on *a tergo*, from behind, *more ferarum*.

In short the real meaning of the dream of the six or seven motionless white wolves was castration anxiety. The infant 'Wolf Man' – as in Freud's interpretations of the cases of Christoph Haitzmann and Daniel Schreber – had latently wished to be sodomized by his father. But his unconscious had warned him that this appetite could be gratified only at the unacceptable cost of castration. The unresolved anxiety expressed by that dream had led to his 'obsessional neurosis'. And this in turn had led to his adult neurotic sexual deviations. For the 'Wolf Man' was sexually aroused only by lower-class women with big buttocks, and he could gain sexual satisfaction from women only by taking them from behind.

The 'Wolf Man' (according to his own later account) had indeed gone along to Freud for advice about whether to marry the nurse Therese who came from a far lower social background than himself: the relationship was opposed by his family. Doubtless he had talked at length to Freud about his sexual preferences. Doubtless Freud believed that these had spontaneously shown themselves as grounded in his castration anxiety as revealed in the dream of the motionless wolves (i.e. his parents copulating). The principle of Freudian analysis would lead us to expect that the revelation to the patient of the source of his infantile neurosis would, in effect, cure it. Hence the 'Wolf Man' should have been cured of his dependency and of what Freud clearly regarded as his sexual aberration. Did this happen?

According to the psychoanalysts commenting later in the volume of the 'Wolf Man's' *Memoirs*, it did. Both Ruth Mack (Brunswick) and Muriel Gardiner claimed that Sergius had essentially been 'cured' by Freud: 'the positive results of the Wolf Man's analysis are impressive indeed', commented Gardiner. It is true that a small 'nucleus' of his neurosis had remained over, and this, according to Mack, had later resulted in a 'psychosis', which in turn had caused the 'Wolf Man' once more in 1926 to seek analysis under Freud. Too ill and too busy, Freud had diverted him to Mack, who, diagnosing him as 'paranoid', had given him intensive analysis for some months and occasional sessions for several further years. Mack confesses: 'why the patient developed paranoia instead of reverting to his original neurosis is hard to say. It may be that the first analysis robbed him of the usual neurotic modes of solution. One asks oneself if the patient was perhaps always latently paranoid.' Or one might ask other things.

In fact, the 'Wolf Man' remained intermittently in analysis right through into his eighties. He told Obholzer that the Freudians liked to treat him as a 'show-piece', a proof of the efficacy of psychoanalysis. But so far as he was concerned, precisely the reverse was true. Thanks to the transference effect, Freud had indeed become a father-figure to him after his own father's death (which Freud had called a 'lucky event'), and, far from curing him of that dependence upon others which had been his problem in 1910, analysis had addicted him to a dependence which was still going strong in the 1970s. Overall then, 'Freud didn't free me.' Freud had simply helped to turn him into the eternal patient, a nonagenarian proof of analysis interminable. Blessed with a humane despair, the 'Wolf Man' saw the funny side of it.

So far as the 'Wolf Man' was concerned, the problem of dependency was inherent in psychoanalysis itself. If transference did not operate, it was by definition useless. If it 'worked', as he thought it had between himself and Freud, then it was 'dangerous', for therapy indeed became your life.

So what did the 'Wolf Man' think of the psychoanalysts who had fantasized that they had cured him? He was jaundiced about Muriel Gardiner, who had tried to stop him even from talking to Obholzer. He remembered Mack with some contempt: 'I paid so little attention to what she said to me.' Not the least reason why he disliked her was because she had waged a vendetta against his wife Therese ('she isn't beautiful at all', 'she doesn't suit you', she had told him). During one session, she had advanced some weird ideas about his masturbating. He responded: 'She was fantasizing . . . what silliness. [She] also invented things occasionally.' When she diagnosed him as suffering from 'paranoia', he was so affronted that he got well just to spite her.

The 'Wolf Man's' feelings towards Freud himself were quite different. He had great admiration for the genuine well-meaningness of his father-substitute. But Freud was often misguided, and in any case was a blind zealot who 'overestimated his work'. The 'Wolf Man' had accepted Freud's authority in many things, and this had proved a great mistake. Apart from anything else, Freud, being interested only in the 'individual', was appallingly innocent of the ways of the world. Thus when, at the outset of the Russian Revolution, the 'Wolf Man' had wanted to return home to safeguard his assets, Freud had told him to stay on in Vienna. Thereby, he complained, he had lost his fortune. It was perhaps, Sergius suspected, out of guilt that Freud later made him financial gifts.

Looking back from near the close of his life, two things were important, however, to the 'Wolf Man'. First, there was little validity in Freud's analysis of the infantile sources of his neuroses. The root of his sexual problems, he believed, lay not in his father at all but in his sister. Freud's elaborate reconstruction of his infant wolf dream made no sense whatever so far as he was concerned. It certainly did not correspond to any of his memories. It was in any case ignorantly implausible (imagine a Russian married couple of his class having their young son sleeping in the same bedroom as they! He had always slept with his nanny). Overall, the 'Wolf Man' asked what was explained by all these dream-interpretations:

> nothing as far as I can see. Freud traces everything back to the primal scene which he derives from the dream. But that scene does not occur in the dream. . . . It's terribly far-fetched.

In any case, Freud's preoccupation with the neurotic nature of the 'Wolf Man's' proclivities (his need for *coitus a tergo*) was way off-beam. His first sexual encounter with his wife-to-be Therese was not – despite what Freud had implied – to take her from behind; rather 'she sat on top of me'. Was this, Sergius joked to Obholzer, a form of 'sitting in judgement' upon psychoanalysis? The 'Wolf Man' had certainly come to lean heavily upon Freud's authority, but Freud's reconstruction of his early life made no sense.

In any case, what was the point of all this archaeology of the mind? For, in reality, psychoanalysis had helped with none of his difficulties. You might trace problems to their roots, but why should that reduce the suffering? 'Everything is much more complicated than the psychoanalysts believe.' Sixty years earlier, he had had a compulsion for falling in love with difficult, crazy, down-market women. He still did. He had been dependent. He still was. And that was largely because Freud had insisted upon exercising his authority. When Freud explained things to him, the 'Wolf Man' remembered that he had occasionally responded to Freud:

> 'All right then, I agree, but I am going to check whether it is correct.'
> And he said, 'Don't start that. Because the moment you try to view things critically, your treatment will get nowhere.'

Clearly, neither Freud's 'Wolf Man', Mack's 'Wolf Man' nor the 'Wolf Man's' 'Wolf Man' is to be taken at face value. The aged Sergius, in all his self-delusions, did, however, have a humane sense of the irony of life. Responding to his tale, Obholzer remarks, 'It's really very funny. I apologize for laughing,' and he replied, 'Yes, it's funny.'

The 'Wolf Man' pioneered the art of analysis as a way of living; he lived off his neuroses. The art has been greatly developed this century, particularly in America, where it has become part of the joke-world of Philip Roth, Woody Allen and others. In the case of a typical post-war successful professional American, John Balt, it became a way of dying as well.

Born in the late 1920s of New York Jewish parents, Balt graduated from Yale and became a writer. His wife Claire, also Jewish, wanted to work with children. They settled in California where Balt became a highly successful television script-writer.

Claire had a strong conviction that responsible modern people ought to give themselves a good grounding in the scriptures of psychology and psychiatry. She told her husband, 'It's a fascinating subject. A lot of people believe that you can never be free of your background unless you have some sort of psychoanalysis.' Balt himself was dubious; Claire 'did not like my point of view'. They compromised, and between them put themselves through a course of psychiatric classics:

> a book we picked up, Robert Lindner's *Fifty Minute Hour*, captured my imagination hitherto unexposed to the areas that it covered. I read some of Theodore Reik, Jones' biography of Freud, Freud's *Psychopathology of Everyday Life*, and *Interpretation of Dreams*. And one other book which, as it turned out, had special consequences, A. A. Brill's *Lectures on Psychoanalytic Psychiatry*.

California life had its strains. Balt was working very hard to keep a growing family in comfort; both pairs of in-laws lived nearby and made heavy inroads upon privacy; the children were time-consuming. Claire grew convinced that she was failing as a wife and a mother ('I haven't been myself'), and decided that she needed to see a psychiatrist. Balt initially opposed this, but when she told him she wanted it more than anything else, he agreed ('I want you to be happy'). The Freudian analyst said she needed help badly, and told her it would take two to five years, four or five times a week.

Partly to pay the analyst's fees, Balt worked still harder. But meeting rebuffs at work, he began to lose faith in his own professional abilities. The result was that in 1960 Balt himself went into psychoanalysis, initially occasionally, but by 1962 four times a week, with a Dr Edward Grossler, a strict Freudian.

Grossler explained to Balt that the reason why he felt a failure was because his wife had gone into analysis. His own problem was that he was overwhelmed by guilt. This guilt was a replay of his Oedipal urges. These needed to be worked through. At the root of his problems lay his incestuous desires for his mother. These had, of course, resulted in a castration fear which (it transpired from interpretations of the psychopathology of Balt's everyday life) was still possessing him. Thus for example when Claire served up chicken giblets at dinner parties Dr Grossler saw them symbolically as Balt's testicles, i.e. evidence to all the guests of his castration.

Dr Grossler got Balt to work deep and hard on his sense of castration. He became utterly preoccupied with his analysis, believing 'what's happening here is the most important thing in my life'. The meaning of everything revolved around the confessions of the couch:

> When Claire and I made love, it had to be discussed afterwards on the couch; and so I began to weigh much of my relationship with her even in bed against how the analyst would evaluate it.

As a result of becoming so preoccupied with analysis, his capacity to work was destroyed. He could no longer sell his writings. The family savings disappeared (they spent $20,000 on doctors in two years). And Balt came to think of himself as more and more of a failure. Grossler even told him that the therapeutic sessions were not going well: 'You've failed in the analysis too.' For once Balt answered back. 'Maybe you've failed. Maybe you've done something wrong.' Grossler replied: 'I've done nothing wrong.' Another defeat. 'Steeped in psychopathology,' Balt recalled, 'I had become convinced that I wanted to destroy myself.'

He went to pieces. He felt totally worthless, became sleepless, couldn't think, couldn't write, acted strange. He believed that the fact that Claire had a job was 'castrating him'; he wanted her around at home, to be the 'good mother'. He started grabbing his penis in her presence and yelling 'Castrated! Castrated!'

Eventually, near the end of 1962, after about a year in analysis, he physically attacked Claire, and was removed for a week to a private psychiatric clinic. At this point Dr Grossler unilaterally terminated his treatment, and Balt came under the care of Dr David Blutman, who believed not in analysis but in psychotherapeutic drug-therapy. Six different kinds of tranquillizers and sleeping pills were prescribed.

'We were broke.' Balt despaired. In his own mind he had shrunk to a eunuch–dwarf. He made desperate phone calls to Grossler, but the analyst simply replied, 'Why don't you get yourself another doctor?' and kept referring him to Blutman. Finally, quite beside himself, Balt seized a kitchen knife, accused Claire again and again of castrating him, and inflicted forty-nine stab wounds on her.

While awaiting trial for murder, Balt was endlessly tortured by voices in his head. First he heard the voice of Dr Brill, followed in close succession by Grossler and Blutman, who announced that they were going to kill him, conduct a *post mortem* and dissect his brain. He was defenceless against these torments. He hoped to plead 'not guilty' on the grounds that he had been suffering from 'psychoanalytic shock'. The court found him temporarily unfit to plead and for the time being he was sent to the county asylum. There he was treated by another psychiatrist, Dr Keszi, more behaviourist in her approach. With her help he was able to work his way through the maelstrom of despair and self-absorbed self-hatred that the psychoanalytical treatment had caused. He came to recognize how his couch-work had turned him in upon himself, divorced him from reality, infantilized him and, through suggestion, given him a vocabulary of concepts (mother-fixation, castration complex, etc.) which had completely crippled his mind and emotions. Dr Keszi would not play mother to him. Neither would she allow him to absolve himself for responsibility for his acts by saddling psychoanalysis with all the blame. She insisted that he had, and continued to have, choice. He was not the prisoner of his mother, of his infancy or of his psychiatrists. His life was in his own hands.

Balt recovered. He was put on trial, but found not guilty by reason of insanity. After agreeing to continue to undergo therapy, he was set free. He still felt bitter about Grossler, since at the trial he had refused to acknowledge any connection between his ex-patient's deteriorating condition and the effects of psychoanalysis. Some time later he ran into Dr Grossler. They made awkward conversation.

> And then, astoundingly, a gesture I never expected. He gripped my right arm just above the elbow and squeezed it. It was designed, I suppose, to convey a wish for the future and an apology, perhaps, one for which there were no words. I walked away and he stared after me, and then independently I think we both knew something we had not known before. In his relationship with me, there had been a touch of madness on his side too.

12 · Conclusion

O Major, tandem parcas, Insane, minori.
Horat. Lib. ii. Sermon. 3

This book has not pleaded a cause; neither has it had any palpable designs upon its readers. In the first instance its aim has been to focus attention on a largely forgotten body of writings, the memoirs of the mad. Through recounting and analysing a small number of them, I have aimed to show what rich archives of human experience they form. Their testimony gives a new dimension to the stories which are generally told of the development of psychiatry and of insane asylums. The history of psychiatric ideas and practices has conventionally been written as a saga of good versus bad psychiatry. It is rarely sufficiently acknowledged that the real protagonists are the doctors and patients, and the real subject the complex range of their encounters. This book has argued that there is a 'story from below' which needs telling.

The authors whose works I have surveyed have often been victims in the proper sense of the word, that is to say, innocents mastered by those possessed of more power than themselves. For these mad people, writing their own stories formed their one way of maintaining their identity or indeed fighting back, at least in their mind. The mad were victims of all sorts of beings. Their immediate oppressors mainly existed only in their heads though they were commonly the analogues of ogres out there in society, in the culture. They were their own victims as well as other people's. Above all it would be facile to portray all of them as victims pure and simple of psychiatry. Few of the mad authors discussed here were in any very direct sense persecuted by doctors: to a much greater degree their plight was due to the systems and structures erected for dealing with madness, which turned people into rigidly dichotomized patients (aliens) and psychiatrists (alienists).

Many of the writers discussed held quite peculiar notions of reality. What they write cannot be taken at face value, and it would be silly simply to 'side' with the insane. Some of them, in any case, were clearly such strong personalities that craziness made them stronger. The case of John Perceval is deeply sad. But it takes little reading between the lines of his *Narrative*

231

to see that he led Brislington Asylum a merry dance – not least in his pugnacious periods he must have inflicted a good deal of physical damage upon attendants and fellow patients alike. Likewise young Dora was more than a match for Freud, and the 'Wolf Man' knew very well how to sponge off and dine out off psychoanalysis, and in the end still make it all look pretty foolish.

In other words we witness some extraordinarily complicated, elusive relations. Psychiatry typically commands the big battalions (after all it controls the straitjackets and the ECT machines), but madness is an underground army which abides by no rules and knows how to fight dirty. And, presiding over all, a cunning of unreason is also at work. Clifford Beers, poacher turned gamekeeper, ends up back in the asylum believing in his final mad–sane state that all the psychiatric doctors are phonies.

What I have chiefly tried to convey is that the mad – or to emphasize once again, those mad people, a hopelessly unrepresentative minority, who ended up writing of the life of lunacy – can communicate stories about themselves which make their own sense, and indeed make sense with that very universe of language, metaphor, idiom and symbols which the sane themselves articulate. The mad talk about fathers and mothers, about God and kings and devils, about shock waves and inspiration just as the sane do, though the nuances are often different (or, as Perceval stressed, words acquire slightly different meanings in madness).

This puts a different complexion upon the claim so often made down the ages that madness is radically incoherent, unintelligible, meaningless. As often as not, if the speech and behaviour of the mad seem peculiar, or are difficult to interpret, it is because the mad person is deprived of the expected and approved environment for normal living, and the normal auditors, attuned to listen. As Perceval and many others emphasized, place a person in a madhouse, deprive him of normal contact, chain him up, and (above all) treat him as though he were beyond communication, and you create a madman, a monster after your own imagination. Likewise, once a neurologist examines his own psyche and sees there phantoms of love and hate towards his parents, then everyone who lies on his couch ever after fails to make sense to him until he acknowledges similar phantoms in his own head as well.

We all have phantoms in the head. Each act of conception, each account, analysis, stab at historical understanding, is an expression of our preconceptions, every bit as much as it may be (we hope) a brick of truth. It also brings out our prejudices. It would be self-deluding to pretend that these do not exist. Thus, clearly, no reader will have taken the opening statement of this Conclusion at face value. Its irony may, however, have served some purpose.

It may have suggested that no writer, after Freud, can expect to have his professions respected; he is at the mercy of forces within and without, beyond his control (as Sterne said, 'You had better tell it to your physician'). Those who write about autobiography cannot escape autobiography. It may also have provided yet another reminder that there is no definitive reading of a text, no privileged author, no privileged reader. Texts are up for grabs. I have offered one interpretation. I must leave my interpretation to the interpreters, my analysis to the analysts.

Reminders of the halls of mirrors called relativism and the problem of reflexivity may indicate that psychiatry has been less than wholly successful in making sense of madness. This is no crime. As Karl Popper has stressed, no science has instantly captured truth, and sat back and enjoyed the conquest. What may historically have been a crime is the alacrity with which certain individual psychiatrists and in some ways the profession as a whole, backed by society's mandate, have taken upon themselves the role of sorting out the mad, through the assertion that they possess the answers. Have not the true fantasists been those psychiatrists who have claimed to hold the master-key to madness? In truth, such theories and therapies have all too often proved only a philosophical warhorse useful for riding roughshod over resistance and protests. The pontifications of psychiatry have all too often excommunicated the mad from human society, even when their own cries and complaints have been human, all too human.

Reading Suggestions

Chapter 1: Introduction

This book touches on a vast range of extremely important debates concerning the standing of psychiatry; its value as a science and as therapy nowadays; and its applicability for understanding people and societies in the past. The book does not directly address many of these issues or expect to make a contribution to them, but some familiarity with them is of considerable background importance.

There has been huge discussion during the last generation about the position of psychiatry nowadays. The 'anti-psychiatry' currents have doubted the objective reality of 'mental illness', suggesting that to a greater or lesser degree mental illness is a repressive invention of society and/or psychiatry. To the historian they have suggested that the history of madness and psychiatry should be regarded not as a saga of scientific progress but as the extension of social policing. The most important statements and assessments of these positions are contained in the writings of Thomas S. Szasz. See in particular his *Law, Liberty and Psychiatry* (New York, Macmillan, 1963); *The Manufacture of Madness* (London, Paladin, 1972); *The Myth of Mental Illness* (London, Granada, 1972); *The Age of Madness: The History of Involuntary Hospitalization Presented in Selected Texts* (London, Routledge & Kegan Paul, 1975); *The Therapeutic State: Psychiatry in the Mirror of Current Events* (Buffalo, NY, Prometheus Books, 1984). Also valuable are David Ingleby (ed.), *Critical Psychiatry: The Politics of Mental Health* (Harmondsworth, Penguin, 1981); Peter Sedgwick, *Psycho Politics* (London, Pluto Press, 1982); and, most recently, Joan Busfield, *Managing Madness: Changing Ideas and Practice* (London, Hutchinson, 1986), which contains a thorough assessment of the issues and an excellent guide to the literature. Intelligent defences of the enterprise of modern psychiatry include J. K. Wing, *Reasoning About Madness* (London, Oxford University Press, 1978); Anthony Clare, *Psychiatry in Dissent: Controversial Issues in Thought and Practice* (London, Tavistock, 1976), and most recently and polemically Martin Roth and Jerome Kroll, *The Reality of Mental Illness* (Cambridge, Cambridge University Press, 1986).

One attempt to adapt the insights of modern dynamic psychiatry and psychoanalysis to historical understanding has been psycho-history. My aims in this book are quite different from those of the psycho-historians. I have primarily tried to get inside the mad person's head, and to understand on his own terms, from within, what he has said and thought. Psycho-history by contrast is first and foremost concerned with the *unconscious* dimension of individual and collective behaviour in the past, with what the actors did not know about themselves and would not have acknowledged (would have 'resisted' acknowledging). Psycho-history has zealous advocates such as Lloyd DeMause in his *The New Psychohistory* (New York, Psychohistory Press, 1975) and Peter Loewenberg in his *Decoding the Past: The Psychohistorical Approach* (New York, Alfred Knopf, 1983); and more temperate defenders, such as Peter Gay in his *Freud for Historians* (New York and Oxford, Oxford University Press, 1985). David E. Stannard, *Shrinking History: On Freud and the Failure of Psychohistory* (New York and Oxford, Oxford University Press, 1980), has by contrast argued that psycho-history is bunk. In my view, the sceptics' case has scored palpable hits to the degree that is has successfully convicted its advocates of spurious speculation in the absence of satisfactory evidence, and of neglecting particular cultural formations in favour of presupposed psychic universals (such as Oedipal conflicts). Freud's own retrospective case-studies of great people from the past (Moses, Leonardo, etc.) possess only fictional truth. Indeed one camp of pro-Freudian commentators (e.g. Steven Marcus, *Freud and the Culture of Psychoanalysis* [London, Allen and Unwin, 1983]) seems to invite us to treat Freud's accounts of his own patients on the couch essentially as superb yarns.

Undertaken, however, subject to proper controls, psycho-history can be a valuable inquiry: good examples are Christopher Hill and Michael Shepherd, 'The Case of Arise Evans: A Historico-psychiatric Study', *Psychological Medicine*, 6 (1976), 351–8, and John Demos, *Entertaining Satan: Witchcraft and the Culture of Early New England* (New York and Oxford, Oxford University Press, 1982).

This present study draws essentially upon published autobiografical accounts by (allegedly) mad people. Hundreds of these exist in the English language alone, and very few of them have ever been scrutinized by historians. Easily the fullest discussion of this genre (and of the obvious and manifold vicissitudes of interpreting such texts) is to be found in D.A. Peterson, 'The Literature of Madness: Autobiographical Writings by Mad People and Mental Patients in England and America from 1436–1975'

(Stanford University PhD, 1977) and *idem* (ed.), *A Mad People's History of Madness* (Pittsburgh, University of Pittsburgh Press, 1982), where a very full bibliography can also be found. This present study makes no pretence of examining more than a tiny and unrepresentative minority of such texts.

Chapter 2: Madness and Psychiatry Talking: A Historical Dialogue

This chapter surveys selective aspects of the development of Western attitudes towards the mad and the growth of psychiatry within that civilization. For more comprehensive surveys see E.H.Ackerknecht, *A Short History of Psychiatry*, 2nd edition, trans. Sula Wolff (New York, Hafner, 1968); Franz G.Alexander and Sheldon T.Selesnick, *The History of Psychiatry: An Evaluation of Psychiatric Thought and Practice from Prehistoric Times to the Present* (London, George Allen & Unwin, 1967); I.Galdston (ed.), *Historic Derivations of Modern Psychiatry* (New York, McGraw-Hill, 1967); J.G.Howells (ed.), *World History of Psychiatry* (New York, Brunner/Mazel, 1968); and G.Zilboorg, *A History of Medical Psychology* (New York, W.W.Norton, 1941). All of the above are the work of psychiatrists and are now rather dated. A brief but up-to-date and historiographically self-aware survey is W.F.Bynum, 'Psychiatry in Its Historical Context', in M.Shepherd and O.L.Zangwill (eds), *Handbook of Psychiatry*, I: *General Psychopathology* (Cambridge, Cambridge University Press, 1983). Valuable cross-cultural perspectives arc offered in Arthur Kleinman, *Social Origins of Distress and Disease: Depression, Neurasthenia and Pain in Modern China* (New Haven, Yale University Press, 1986) and Carney Landis and Fred Mettler, *Varieties of Psychopathological Experience* (New York, Holt, Rinehart & Winston, 1964).

More satisfactory are smaller-scale analyses. The development of the idea of mind and its maladies amongst the Greeks has been examined by Bennett Simon, *Mind and Madness in Ancient Greece* (Ithaca, Cornell University Press, 1978); E.R.Dodds, *The Greeks and the Irrational* (Berkeley and London, University of California Press, 1951); H.North, *Sophrosyne: Self-Knowledge and Self-Restraint in Greek Literature* (Ithaca, Cornell University Press, 1966); Pedro Lain Entralgo, *Mind and Body: Psychosomatic Pathology*, trans. A.M.Espinosa (London, Harvill, 1955), and his *The Therapy of the Word in Classical Antiquity*, trans. and ed. by L.J.Rather and John M.Sharp (New Haven, Yale University Press, 1970). Parallel developments in Islam are surveyed in M.Dols, 'Insanity and Its Treatment in Islamic Society', *Medical History*, 31 (1987), 1–14. Medieval views are covered in Penelope E.R.Doob, *Nebuchadnezzar's Children: Conventions of Madness in Middle English Literature* (New Haven and London, Yale University Press, 1974) and Basil Clarke, *Mental Disorder in Earlier Britain* (Cardiff, University of Wales Press, 1975); the early modern period is examined in M. Foucault, *Madness and Civilization; A History of Insanity in the Age of Reason*, trans. Richard Howard (New York, Random House, 1965) and K. Doerner, *Madmen and the Bourgeoisie*, trans. J. Neugroschel and J. Steinberg (Oxford, Basil Blackwell, 1981). Particularly valuable here is the work of Michael MacDonald. See his *Mystical Bedlam: Madness, Anxiety and Healing in Seventeenth Century England* (Cambridge, Cambridge University Press, 1981) and a number of his articles, such as 'Religion, Social Change and Psychological Healing in England 1600–1800', in W. Sheils (ed.), *The Church and Healing* (Oxford, Basil Blackwell, 1982), 101–26, and 'Popular Beliefs About Mental Disorder in Early Modern England', in W. Eckart and J. Geyer-Kordesch (eds), *Heilberufe und Kranke in 17 und 18 Jahrhundert* (Münster, Burgverlag, 1982), 148–73. For eighteenth-century England see Roy Porter, *Mind-Forg'd Manacles* (London, Athlone Press, 1987). More recent developments are examined in A. Scull, *Museums of Madness* (London, Allen Lane, 1979) and F. and R. Castel and A. Lovell, *The Psychiatric Society* (Columbia, Columbia University Press, 1981).

This chapter argues that one cultural priority which developed in the West was a rationalist individualism linked to a strong sense of the self. Illuminating here are J. Passmore, *The Perfectibility of Man* (London, Duckworth, 1968); Stephen Lukes, *Individualism* (Oxford, Basil Blackwell, 1977); and at a rather fundamental level, Max Weber, *The Protestant Ethic and the Spirit of Capitalism* (London, Allen & Unwin, 1930). Useful explanations of the development of a heightened sense of self-identity in actuality and in literature include M. Golden, *The Self Observed* (Baltimore, Johns Hopkins University Press, 1972); P. M. Spacks, *Imagining a Self* (London, George Allen & Unwin, 1976); S. D. Cox, *'The Stranger Within Thee': The Concept of the Self in Late-Eighteenth-Century Literature* (Pittsburgh, Pittsburgh University Press, 1980); and J. O. Lyons, *The Invention of the Self* (Carbondale, Southern Illinois University Press, 1978). One manifestation of this emergent individualism lay in autobiographical writing. Relevant studies include Margaret Bottrall, *Everyman a Phoenix: Studies in Seventeenth-Century Autobiography* (London, John Murray, 1958); and P. Delany, *British Autobiography in the Seventeenth Century* (London, Routledge & Kegan Paul, 1969). Important on the religious facet is Daniel B. Shea, Jr, *Spiritual Autobiography in Early America* (Princeton, Princeton University Press, 1968).

This chapter seeks to chart how one function of psychiatry has been to enhance a divide between the sane and the mad. This has become plain in stereotypes of madness, for which see Sander Gilman, *Seeing the Insane*

(New York, Brunner/Mazel, 1982) and Hans Mayer, *Outsiders: A Study in Life and Letters* (Cambridge, Mass., MIT Press, 1984). It is also visible in the clinical construction of patient–doctor relations as is shown by J.P.Fullinwider, 'Insanity and the Loss of Self: The Moral Insanity Controversy Revisited', *Bulletin of the History of Medicine*, 49 (1975), 87–101, and his *Technicians of the Finite* (Westport, Conn., Greenwood Press, 1982).

Chapter 3: Madness and Power

Freud was deeply interested in the relations between psyche and power, witness the frequency with which he compared himself to Moses, Alexander the Great and other *conquistadores*. Ever since, analysis of the neuroses of individual leaders and of collective psychopathology has been a central concern of psychiatry and psycho-historians, most notably perhaps in the account of the psychodynamics of Fascism developed by Wilhelm Reich. It is hence odd that relatively little straightforward historical analysis has examined the linguistic and cultural dimensions of the 'dreams of grandeur' entertained by the mad. The vanity and hubris of assumptions of greatness have of course been a preoccupying theme of literary scholarship. Valuable here are Robert Folkenflik (ed.), *The English Hero, 1660–1800* (Newark, University of Delaware Press, 1986) and Isabel Grundy, *Samuel Johnson and the Scale of Greatness* (Leicester, Leicester University Press, 1986). The traditions of imagining the world turned upside down are of course central. See M.Bakhtin, *Rabelais and His World*, trans. H.Iswolsky (Cambridge, Mass., MIT Press, 1968); and Christopher Hill, *The World Turned Upside Down* (Harmondsworth, Penguin, 1978) and the discussion of King Lear in L.Feder, *Madness in Literature* (Princeton, Princeton University Press, 1980). For madness and revolution see Roy Porter, 'Monsters and Madmen in Eighteenth-Century France', in D.Fletcher (ed.), *The Monstrous* (Durham, Durham French Colloquies, 1, Durham University Printing Unit, 1987).

Easily the best discussion of George III is in Ida Macalpine and Richard Hunter, *George III and the Mad Business* (London, Allen Lane, 1969), which contains a critical survey of earlier interpretations; C.P.C.Chenevix-Trench, *The Royal Malady* (London, Longman, 1964) is also worth consulting. Both provide lead-ins to assorted psychiatric readings of George of dubious merit. The fullest contemporary account in print is the diary of Robert Fulke Greville: F.M.Bladon (ed.), *The Diaries of Robert Fulke Greville* (London, John Lane at the Bodley Head, 1930). Also invaluable is Charlotte Barrett (ed.), *Diary and Letters of Madame D'Arblay (Frances Burney) 1778–1840*, 6 vols (London, Macmillan, 1905), vol. IV.

The case of James Tilley Matthews is spelt out in John Haslam, *Illustrations of Madness* (London, Rivingtons, 1810). Little has been written on Matthews; see, however, M.D.Altschule, *Origin of Concepts in Human Behavior: Social and Cultural Factors* (New York, Halstead Press, 1977), and Roy Porter, '"Under the Influence": Mesmerism in England', *History Today* (September 1985), 22–9. Haslam too deserves further study. A useful survey and introduction is contained in Denis Leigh, *The Historical Development of British Psychiatry*, vol. I (Oxford, Pergamon, 1961).

My account of Christian VII of Sweden I owe almost wholly to Dr Christine Stevenson, who is working in this area. I am very grateful to her for her generosity with this material. Helpful is W.F.Reddaway, 'King Christian VII', *English Historical Review*, 31 (1916), 59–84.

Chapter 4: Madness and Genius

Genius and madness have been associated in ambiguous and contested ways ever since antiquity. Good surveys of the shifting relationships, and introductions to bibliography, are offered in G.Tonelli, 'Genius: From the Renaissance to 1770', in *Dictionary of the History of Ideas*, edited by P.Wiener (New York, Scribners, 1973), vol. II, 293–7; N.Willard, *Le Génie et la folie* (Paris, Presses Universitaires de France, 1963); and G.Becker, *The Mad Genius Controversy* (Beverly Hills, Sage, 1978); the latter work is especially helpful as an introduction to the vast *fin de siècle* discussion of the degeneracy of genius. The equivalent for literary works, from a largely psychoanalytical point of view, is developed by L.Feder, *Madness in Literature* (Princeton, Princeton University Press, 1980); and more briefly in S.Cunningham, 'Bedlam and Parnassus: Eighteenth-Century Reflections', in B.Harris (ed.), *Eighteenth-Century Studies*, 24 (1971), 36–55. Changing conceptions of the imagination *vis-à-vis* insanity are illuminated in J.Engell, *The Creative Imagination* (Cambridge, Mass., Harvard University Press, 1981).

James Carkesse published his verse in 1679 as *Lucida Intervalla: Containing Divers Miscellaneous Poems* (London, 1679). The modern edition by M.V.DePorte (Los Angeles, University of California Press, 1979) contains a valuable introductory discussion. William Blake's own scattered expressions of his 'madness' can be found in G.Keynes, *The Complete Writings of William Blake* (London, Oxford University Press, 1966); for contextualizing biographical discussion see J.Bronowski, *William Blake and the Age of Revolution* (London, Routledge & Kegan Paul, 1972); Jack Lindsay, *William Blake* (London, Canfrolico Press, 1978); and more broadly William B.Ober, 'Madness and Poetry: A Note on Collins, Cowper and Smart', in *Boswell's Clap and Other Essays* (Carbondale, Southern Illinois

University Press, 1979). M. Byrd, *Visits to Bedlam* (Columbia, University of South Carolina Press, 1974) has a good account of Georgian madness and poetry.

The fullest biography of John Clare is J. W. Tibble and A. Tibble, *John Clare: A Life* (London, Cobden Sanderson, 1972). Clare's verse is assessed in M. Storey, *The Poetry of John Clare* (London, Macmillan, 1974); and E. Robinson (ed.), *John Clare's Autobiographical Writings* (Oxford, Oxford University Press, 1983). Best on his asylum poetry is Geoffrey Grigson (ed.), *Poems of John Clare's Madness* (London, Routledge & Kegan Paul, 1949).

Easily the best account of and entry into Schumann's mental condition is Peter Ostwald, *Schumann: Music and Madness* (London, Victor Gollancz, 1985). Ostwald surveys earlier writings on the subject. An instance of an older, psychiatric tradition of interpretation is the short piece by W. R. Bett, 'Robert Alexander Schumann (1810–1856), a Manic-Depressive Genius', in *Medical Press* (25 July 1956), 105.

A full, if rather effusive and partisan, biography of Nijinsky is Richard Buckle, *Nijinsky* (Harmondsworth, Penguin, 1975). His diary was edited by his wife: Romola Nijinsky (ed.), *The Diary of Vaslav Nijinsky* (London, Victor Gollancz, 1937). There are some interesting pages in Colin Wilson, *Beyond the Outsider* (London, Pan Books, 1965).

There is an enormous literature which attempts to analyse whether particular writers and artists were or were not 'mad' or neurotic; and an overlapping body of scholarship which attempts to diagnose such people through retrospective analysis of their poetry, novels, etc. (the 'poetry as patient' genre). Much of this is of no more than peripheral concern to this volume, but two recent works handle this problem in a particularly sensitive way in regard to that old favourite, Virginia Woolf: Roger Poole, *The Unknown Virginia Woolf* (London, Harvester Press, 1978) and Stephen Trombley, *'All That Summer She Was Mad': Virginia Woolf and Her Doctors* (London, Junction Books, 1981). Charles Lamb's essay on 'The Sanity of True Genius', in G. E. Hollingsworth (ed.), *Lamb: The Last Essays of Elia* (London, Everyman) remains well worth consulting. For a recent study of Freud's attempts to crack creativity see Harry Trosman, *Freud and the Imaginative World* (Hillsdale, New Jersey, The Analytic Press, 1985).

Chapter 5: Religious Madness

The problem of how, precisely, unusual spiritual conditions relate to abnormal psychology is old and unresolved. Classic and still fundamental as an evaluation is William James's *Varieties of Religious Experience: A Study in Human Nature* (London, Longmans, 1902). Up to the close of the seventeenth century, European thought generally accepted that insanity could quite possibly, indeed commonly, be the product of otherworldly powers, both divine and demonic. Thereafter growing objections were levelled on grounds that were overtly religious, scientific and psychiatric, and more covertly socio-political. These developments are excellently surveyed in many of the works listed under chapter 2 above, and also in Judith S. Neaman, *Suggestion of the Devil: The Origin of Madness* (New York, Anchor Books, 1975); M. Screech, 'Good Madness in Christendom', in W. F. Bynum, Roy Porter and Michael Shepherd (eds), *The Anatomy of Madness*, 2 vols (London, Tavistock, 1985), vol. I, 25–39; M. MacDonald, *Mystical Bedlam* (Cambridge, Cambridge University Press, 1981) and his other writings listed under chapter 2; D. P. Walker, *Unclean Spirits: Possession and Exorcism in France and England in the late Sixteenth and Early Seventeenth Centuries* (London, Scolar Press, 1981); K. V. Thomas, *Religion and the Decline of Magic* (Harmondsworth, Penguin, 1973); and R. D. Stock, *The Holy and the Daemonic from Sir Thomas Browne to William Blake* (Princeton, Princeton University Press, 1982). Much of chapter 2 of Roy Porter, *Mind-Forg'd Manacles* (London, Athlone Press, 1987) analyses these shifts in England. Scholarship dealing with the emergent tradition of the spiritual autobiography is briefly noted above under chapter 2.

Trosse's autobiography was published in 1714 as *The Life of the Reverend Mr. George Trosse, Late Minister of the Gospel in the City of Exon, Who Died January 11th, 1712/13. In the Eighty Second Year of His Age, Written by Himself and Publish'd According to His Order* (Exon, Richard White, 1714). A. W. Brink's modern edition (*The Life of the Reverend Mr. George Trosse: Written by Himself, and Published Posthumously According to His Order in 1714* [Montreal, McGill–Queen's University Press, 1974]) contains essays analysing this work from the psychiatric and religious points of view. Haitzmann has not been extensively written about. Freud analysed his account of his possession in 'A Neurosis of Demoniacal Possession in the Seventeenth Century', conveniently available in his *Collected Papers*, vol. IV (London, Hogarth Press, 1925), 436–73; the fullest assessment in English, strongly opposed to Freud, is Ida Macalpine and Richard Hunter (eds), *Schizophrenia, 1677: A Psychiatric Study of an Illustrated Autobiographical Record of Demoniacal Possession* (London, William Dawson, 1956).

William Cowper's *Memoir of the Early Life of William Cowper Esq.* was published in 1816. Maurice Quinlan offers a modern edition; see 'Memoir of William Cowper: An Autobiography', *Proceedings of the American Philosophical Society*, 97 (1953). See also M. Quinlan, *William Cowper* (Minneapolis, University of Minnesota Press, 1953). Evaluations of the place of madness in Cowper's life can be found in M. Golden, *In Search of Stability:*

The Poetry of William Cowper (New Haven, Yale University Press, 1969)
and C.A.Ryskamp, *William Cowper of the Inner Temple, Esq.* (Cambridge,
Cambridge University Press, 1959). Cowper's letters are essential reading.
See the admirable new edition edited by James King and Charles Ryskamp,
The Letters and Prose Writings of William Cowper, 4 vols (Oxford, Clarendon
Press, 1979–84). For Dr Cotton and Cowper's time in the asylum see
F.J.Harding, 'Dr. Nathaniel Cotton of St. Albans, Poet and Physician',
Herts. Countryside, 23 (1969), 46–8; B.Hill, '"My Little Physician at St.
Albans". Nathaniel Cotton 1705–1788', *Practitioner*, 199 (1967), 363–7; and
Richard Hunter and J.B.Wood, 'Nathaniel Cotton, M.D., Poet and
Physician', *King's College Hospital Gazette*, 36 (1957), 120.

The life of Kit Smart offers important parallels to Cowper. On him see
A.Sherbo, *Christopher Smart* (East Lansing, Michigan State University Press,
1967); and K.Williamson, *The Poetic Works of Christopher Smart* (Oxford,
Oxford University Press, 1980).

Chapter 6: Mad Women

An impressive body of scholarship has emerged of late scrutinizing the
relations between madness, women and psychiatry from various angles.
From a socio-psychiatric and critical point of view, Phyllis Chessler, *Women
and Madness* (Garden City, NY, Doubleday, 1972) is still a good starting
point. Juliet Mitchell, *Psychoanalysis and Feminism* (London, Allen Lane,
1974) represented a powerful, if forlorn, attempt to reconcile traditional
Freudian psychoanalysis with feminist aspirations and consciousness; Jane
Gallop, *The Daughter's Seduction: Feminism and Psychoanalysis* (Ithaca,
Cornell University Press, 1982) has taken up similar issues from a more
critical perspective. Accounts by female writers of the ambiguities of their
own stance as authors have been sensitively explored by P.M.Spacks, *The
Female Imagination* (London, George Allen & Unwin, 1975); B.Hill Rigney,
Madness and Sexual Politics in the Feminist Novel (Madison, University of
Wisconsin Press, 1978); S.Gilbert and S.Gubarr, *The Madwoman in the
Attic: The Woman Writer and the Nineteenth-Century Imagination* (New
Haven, Yale University Press, 1979) and, above all, by Elaine Showalter.
See her *A Literature of Their Own: British Women Novelists from Bronte to
Lessing* (Princeton, Princeton University Press, 1977); *idem*, 'Syphilis,
Sexuality, and the Fin de Siècle', in Ruth Yeazell and Neil Hertz (eds),
*Sex, Politics, and Science in the Nineteenth-Century Novel: Essays from the
English Institute* (Baltimore, Johns Hopkins University Press, 1986), 88–115,
and *The Female Malady* (New York, Pantheon, 1986).

Margery Kempe's life is available in several editions, including the

Penguin Classics version edited by B.A.Windeatt, *The Book of Margery Kempe* (Harmondsworth, Penguin, 1985), in which the text is modernized. The Catholic interpretation is offered in Katherine Cholmeley, *Margery Kempe, Genius and Mystic* (London, Longman, Green, 1947); a psychoanalytical approach is advanced in T.Drucker, 'The Malaise of Margery Kempe', *New York State Journal of Medicine*, 72 (1972), 2911–17; and historical background is surveyed in R.W.Chambers, 'Introduction', *The Book of Margery Kempe*, trans. W.Butler-Bowdon (New York, Devin-Adair, 1945). The adequacy or inadequacy of Christianity for expressing female psychic needs and aspirations is debated in Rudolph M.Bell, *Holy Anorexia* (Chicago, University of Chicago Press, 1985).

The question of links between witchcraft, hysteria and the roots of psychiatry remains deeply vexed. G.Zilboorg, *The Medical Man and the Witch in the Renaissance* (Baltimore, Johns Hopkins University Press, 1935) puts the case most forcefully for witches as psychiatrically disturbed women. That argument finds some implicit support in D.P.Walker, *Unclean Spirits: Possession and Exorcism in France and England in the Late Sixteenth Century and Early Seventeenth Century* (London, Scolar Press, 1981), but is essentially scotched in T.J.Schoeneman, 'The Role of Mental Illness in the European Witch Hunts of the Sixteenth and Seventeenth Centuries: An Assessment', *Journal of the History of the Behavioral Sciences*, 13 (1977), 337–51. The broader debate about the interpretation of hysteria is covered in Ilza Veith, *Hysteria: The History of a Disease* (Chicago, Chicago University Press, 1945). An excellent conventional historical account of a famous witch trial is Paul Boyer and Stephen Nissenbaum, *Salem Possessed: The Social Origins of Witchcraft* (Cambridge, Mass., Harvard University Press, 1976); John Demos's *Entertaining Satan: Witchcraft and the Culture of Early New England* (New York and Oxford, Oxford University Press, 1982) examines such witches both as a conventional social historian and as a psycho-historian (though one primarily interested in pre-Oedipal conflict).

Freud's analysis of Dora in *The Standard Edition of the Complete Psychological Works of Sigmund Freud*, 24 vols, trans. from German under the general editorship of James Strachey, in collaboration with Anna Freud, assisted by Alix Strachey and Alan Tyson (London, Hogarth Press and the Institute of Psychoanalysis, 1953–74), vol. VII, is the *locus classicus* for the modern interplay between women and psychiatry. It has sparked a very diverse feminist–psychiatric–literary response, much of which is conveniently anthologized or discussed in Charles Bernheimer and Claire Kahane (eds), *In Dora's Case: Freud, Hysteria, Feminism* (New York, Columbia University Press, 1985). More generally see Sarah Kofman, *The Enigma of Woman: Woman in Freud's Writings* (Ithaca, Cornell University

Press, 1985). Mary Barnes and Joseph Berke have jointly authored *Mary Barnes: Two Accounts of a Journey Through Madness* (Harmondsworth, Penguin, 1971); Barnes's case is sensitively discussed in Showalter, *The Female Malady* (above).

Chapter 7: From Fools to Outsiders

Marginal people, scapegoats and privileged outsiders have received much attention of late. A rich and deep study which examines melancholics, blacks, women, Jews and homosexuals is H. Mayer, *Outsiders: A Study in Life and Letters* (Cambridge, Mass., MIT Press, 1984). As an account of stigmatization, it should be read alongside E. Dudley and M. E. Novak (eds), *The Wild Man Within* (Pittsburgh, University of Pittsburgh Press, 1972); and Sander Gilman's two books, *Seeing the Insane* (New York, Brunner/Mazel, 1982) and *Difference and Pathology* (Ithaca and London, Cornell University Press, 1985). E. Welsford, *The Fool: His Social and Literary History* (London, Faber, 1935), and S. Billington, *The Social History of the Fool* (Brighton, Harvester Press, 1984) provide introductions to the ambiguities of playing the fool. A taste of verbal clowning is offered by J. Wardroper, *Jest Upon Jest* (London, Routledge & Kegan Paul, 1970). The literary and intellectual conventions underpinning them are explored in R. S. Kinsman, 'Folly, Melancholy and Madness: A Study in Shifting Styles of Medical Analysis and Treatment, 1450–1675', in R. S. Kinsman (ed.), *The Darker Vision of the Renaissance* (Berkeley, University of California Press, 1974); W. Kaiser, *Praisers of Folly* (London, Victor Gollancz, 1964); Rosalie Colie, *Paradoxia Epidemica* (Princeton, Princeton University Press, 1966); and M. Screech, *Ecstasy and the Praise of Folly* (London, Duckworth, 1980). A psychoanalytical approach to nonsense is spelt out in Phyllis Greenacre, *Swift and Carroll: A Psychological Study of Two Lives* (New York, International University Press, 1955).

Cruden has found one modern biographer, E. Oliver, *The Eccentric Life of Alexander Cruden* (London, Faber, 1934). It is best to return to his own entertaining writings: Alexander Cruden, *The London-Citizen Exceedingly Injured: or, a British Inquisition Display'd, in an Account of the Unparallel'd Case of a Citizen of London, Bookseller to the Late Queen, Who Was in a Most Unjust and Arbitrary Manner Sent on the 23rd of March Last, 1738, by One Robert Wightman, a Mere Stranger, to a Private Madhouse* (London, T. Cooper, 1739); idem, *Mr. Cruden Greatly Injured: An Account of a Trial between Mr. Alexander Cruden Bookseller to the Late Queen, Plaintif, and Dr. Monro, Matthew Wright, John Oswald, and John Davies, Defendants: in the Court of the Common-Pleas in Westminster Hall July 17, 1739, on an Action of Trespass, Assault and Imprisonment: the Said Mr. Cruden, Tho' in His Right Senses, Having Been Unjustly Confined and Barbarously Used in the Said Matthew Wright's Private Madhouse at Bethnal-Green for Nine Weeks and Six Days, till He Made His Wonderful Escape, May 31, 1738. To Which is Added a Surprising Account of Several Other Persons, Who Have Been Most Unjustly Confined in Private Madhouses* (London, A. Injured (*sic*), 1740). His later brushes with the madhouse are described in *The Adventures of Alexander the Corrector, Wherein is Given an Account of His Being Unjustly Sent to Chelsea, and of His Bad Usage during the Time of his Chelsea-Campaign . . . with, an Account of the Chelsea-Academies, or the Private Places for the Confinement of Such as Are Supposed to Be Deprived of the Exercise of Their Reason* (London, The Author, 1754). An early life is 'Memoirs of Alexander Cruden', to be found in *A Complete Concordance to the Holy Scriptures of the Old and New Testament; or, a Dictionary and Alphabetical Index to the Bible* (New York, Dodd, Mead, 1823).

This is not the place to explore rival interpretations of Nietzsche or to offer an introductory guide to the vast body of Nietzsche scholarship. Walter Kaufmann's authoritative *Nietzsche, Philosopher, Psychologist, Antichrist*, 5th edition (Princeton, Princeton University Press, 1974) provides just that, in the context of the wider development of modern 'irrationalist' philosophy. Ronald Hayman's *Nietzsche: A Critical Life* (London, Weidenfeld & Nicolson, 1980) is an ample biography; and *Nietzsche: Imagery and Thought*, edited by Malcolm Pasley (London, Methuen, 1978) contains several relevant essays, including Pasley's own 'Nietzsche's Use of Medical Terms', which is stimulating on Nietzsche's own heroic struggles for health.

There are two good intellectual biographies in English on Artaud: Bettina L. Knapp, *Antonin Artaud: Man of Vision* (Chicago, Swallow Press, 1969), and Ronald Hayman's *Artaud and After* (Oxford, Oxford University Press, 1971). A convenient introduction to his writings is Antonin Artaud, *Antonin Artaud Anthology* (San Francisco, City Lights Books, 1965). The succession from Nietzsche to Artaud is touched upon in Michel Foucault, *Madness and Civilization: A History of Insanity in the Age of Reason*, trans. Richard Howard (New York, Random House, 1965).

Chapter 8: Daniel Schreber: Madness, Sex and the Family

There is now a large literature in English on Schreber, mainly assessing him from a psychoanalytic rather than a historical point of view. Ida Macalpine and Richard Hunter have translated and edited his memoirs as *Daniel Paul Schreber: Memoirs of My Nervous Illness* (London, William Dawson, 1955). Their edition includes a very substantial critique of Freud's retrospective analysis, which can be found as 'Psycho-analytic Notes on an Autobiographical Account of a Case of Paranoia (Dementia Paranoides) (1911)' in *The Standard Edition of the Complete Psychological Works of Sigmund Freud* (above), vol. XII, 3–84. Amongst the more interesting discussions of Schreber's condition from within the interpretive framework set by Freud are Austin McCawley, 'Paranoia and Homosexuality: Schreber Reconsidered', *New York State Journal of Medicine*, 71 (1971), 1506–13; Philip M.Kitay, 'Symposium on "Reinterpretations of the Schreber Case: Freud's Theory of Paranoia"', *International Journal of Psycho-Analysis*, 44 (1963), 191–4; Arthur C.Clark, 'Observations on Paranoia and Their Relationship to the Schreber Case', *ibid.*, 195–200; Jule Nydes, 'Schreber, Parricide and Paranoid Masochism', *ibid.*, 209–12; Robert B.White, 'The Schreber Case Reconsidered in the Light of Psycho-Social Concepts', *ibid.*, 213–21. The summary of these opinions quoted in my text is by Philip Kitay and is located on pp. 222–3. The clinical literature on Schreber continues to proliferate, most of it endorsing, though adding refinements to, the basic Freudian position that Schreber represents a case of the essential linkage between paranoia and suppressed homosexuality. For a further recent instance see Robert H.Klein, 'A Computer Analysis of the Schreber Memoirs', *Journal of Nervous and Mental Disease*, 162 (1976), 373–84, which itself has generated a further literature.

Schreber's hospital case-records are discussed in Franz Baumeyer, 'The Schreber Case', *International Journal of Psycho-Analysis*, 37 (1956), 61–74. Important new historical material on Schreber, especially concerning his father's pedagogics, is contained in William G.Niederland, 'Further Data and Memorabilia Pertaining to the Schreber Case', *International Journal of Psycho-Analysis*, 44 (1963), 201–7; and his 'Schreber's Father', *Journal of the American Psychoanalytic Association*, 8 (1960), 492–9. Niederland offers his information about the child-torturing pedagogic practices of Dr Schreber as an interesting body of antiquarian fact which has no essential bearing on the truth of Freud's analyis, which he accepts. Morton Schatzman, on the other hand, unlike the Freudian establishment, makes the daring claim that what Schreber's father actually did to his son might have some bearing on the son's subsequent psychic state. Schatzman's fullest account is to be found in *Soul Murder: Persecution in the Family* (London, Allen Lane, 1973). Schatzman makes use of some of the ideas developed by R.D.Laing in the 1960s about the psychopathology of the family. See, amongst other writings, R.D.Laing, *The Politics of the Family and Other Essays* (New York, Vintage Books, 1972), and Aaron Esterson and R.D.Laing, *Sanity, Madness, and the Family* (Harmondsworth, Penguin Books, 1970), and for a sweeping critique of the Freudian notion of the Oedipus Complex, G.Deleuze and

E. Guattari, *Anti-Oedipus: Capitalism and Schizophrenia* (New York, Viking Press, 1977).

Chapter 9: John Perceval: Madness Confined

Central to explaining Perceval's story is the question of the rise of the lunatic asylum in England, and of concern, expressed both by patients and by the public, about its abuses. Excellent accounts of these are to be found in William Parry Jones, *The Trade in Lunacy: A Study of Private Madhouses in England in the Eighteenth and Nineteenth Centuries* (London, Routledge & Kegan Paul, 1972); Andrew Scull, *Museums of Madness* (London, Allen Lane, 1979); D. J. Mellett, *The Prerogative of Asylumdom* (New York, Garland, 1982); and the writings of Kathleen Jones: *Lunacy, Law and Conscience, 1744–1845* (London, Routledge & Kegan Paul, 1955); *Mental Health and Social Policy* (London, Routledge & Kegan Paul, 1960) and *A History of the Mental Health Services* (London, Routledge & Kegan Paul, 1972). On false imprisonment see Peter McCandless, 'Liberty and Lunacy: The Victorians and Wrongful Confinement', in Andrew Scull (ed.), *Madhouses, Mad-Doctors and Madmen* (London, Athlone Press, 1981), 339–62. Early examples of patient protest literature in England include the works of Alexander Cruden (see chapter 5 above); Samuel Bruckshaw, *One More Proof of the Iniquitous Abuse of Private Madhouses* (London, for the Author, 1774), and his *The Case, Petition and Address of Samuel Bruckshaw, who Suffered a Most Severe Imprisonment for Very Near the Whole Year . . .* (London, for the Author, 1774); and William Belcher, *Address to Humanity, Containing a Letter to Dr. Monro, a Receipt to Make a Lunatic, and Seize his Estates and a Sketch of a True Smiling Hyena* (London, for the Author, 1796). In the nineteenth century, Richard Paternoster, *The Madhouse System* (London, 1841) and Herman Charles Merivale, *My Experiences in a Lunatic Asylum, by a Sane Patient* (London, Chatto & Windus, 1879) wrote influential works in this genre.

Perceval's protest against Brislington and Ticehurst appeared as J. T. Perceval, *A Narrative of the Treatment Received by a Gentleman, During a State of Mental Derangement*, 2 vols (London, Effingham Wilson, 1838 and 1840). It has been reprinted in a condensed single-volume edition by G. Bateson as *Perceval's Narrative: A Patient's Account of His Psychosis* (New York, Morrow Paperback, 1974). Bateson's introduction treats Perceval in the light of the modern theory of the 'double bind', and construes him essentially as self-curing. Surprisingly little is known of Perceval's life or even of his activities within the Alleged Lunatics' Friend Society: for these see Richard Hunter and Ida Macalpine, 'John Thomas Perceval (1803–1876),

Patient and Reformer', *Medical History*, 6 (1961), 391–5; and N. Hervey, 'Advocacy or Folly: The Alleged Lunatics' Friend Society, 1845–63', *Medical History*, 30 (1986), 254–75. Denis Gray, *Spencer Perceval, The Evangelical Prime Minister* (Manchester, Manchester University Press, 1963) is an excellent biography of his ill-fated father.

Perceval's preoccupations need to be seen against the background of early-nineteenth-century Evangelicalism and the family. Fundamental here is Ford K. Brown, *Fathers of the Victorians* (Cambridge, Cambridge University Press, 1961); stimulating also is G. Rattray Taylor, *The Angel Makers* (London, Secker & Warburg, 1973); more generally see Lawrence Stone, *The Family, Sex and Marriage in England 1500–1800* (London, Weidenfeld & Nicolson, 1977). Perceval's story is worth comparing to the relations between James Mill and his son, John Stuart: see Bruce Mazlish, *James and John Stuart Mill: Father and Son in the Nineteenth Century* (New York, Basic Books, 1975).

Chapter 10: The American Dream

There has been vast discussion about the paradox of why, during this century, the United States of America, seemingly the most individualist and self-reliant of societies, should have become one of the most heavily in need of, and indebted to, various forms of personal psychotherapy. Obviously the paradox may be merely apparent. Such developments are described and evaluated from various angles in F. and R. Castel and A. Lovell, *The Psychiatric Society* (New York, Columbia University Press, 1981); G. Grob, *Mental Illness and American Society 1875–1941* (Princeton, Princeton University Press, 1983), and Anthony Clare, *Now Let's Talk About Me* (London, BBC Publications, 1981). Christopher Lasch has written extensively on the wider socio-cultural matrix. See his *The Culture of Narcissism: American Life in an Age of Diminishing Expectations* (London, Abacus Press, 1980). Therapy as culture is stimulatingly discussed in Philip Rieff, *The Triumph of the Therapeutic* (London, Chatto & Windus, 1966).

Clifford Beers was essentially a one-book man. *A Mind That Found Itself* (edition used: Garden City, New York, Doubleday, Page, 1923) was a runaway success. Within twenty-five years it went through twenty-two editions. The standard and excellent life is by Norman Dain, *Clifford W. Beers: Advocate for the Insane* (Pittsburgh, University of Pittsburgh Press, 1980). For background on the actual condition of asylum inmates see A. Deutsch, *The Mentally Ill in America* (New York, Columbia University Press, 1949).

Scores of accounts have been published of life in the modern American mental hospital. The most famous are fictionalized accounts of real experiences: Mary Ward, *The Snake Pit* (New York, New American Library, 1973); Ken Kesey, *One Flew Over the Cuckoo's Nest* (Harmondsworth, Penguin, 1976); and 'Hannah Green' (Joanna Greenberg), *I Never Promised You a Rose Garden* (New York, New American Library, 1964), well analysed by Jeffrey Berman, *The Talking Cure: Literary Representations of Psychoanalysis* (New York, New York University Press, 1985). No less important is the literature of legal protest, such as Kenneth Donaldson's *Insanity Inside Out* (New York, Crown, 1976). D.A.Peterson, *A Mad People's History of Madness* (Pittsburgh, University of Pittsburgh Press, 1982) offers a fine analysis of this tradition. The three works discussed in this chapter are *A Mind Restored: The Story of Jim Curran*, by Elsa Krauch (New York, Putnam's, 1937); William Moore, *The Mind in Chains: The Autobiography of a Schizophrenic* (New York, Exposition Press, 1955); and 'Barbara O'Brien', *Operators and Things: The Inner Life of a Schizophrenic* (New York, A.S.Barnes, 1958).

Chapter 11: The Therapeutic God

Scholarly writing on Freud's life, works and ideas proliferates at an unparalleled rate; it would be futile to attempt here any sort of detailed assessment. Freud's autobiography is published in *The Standard Edition of the Complete Psychological Works of Sigmund Freud* (above), vol. xx. The standard biography remains Ernest Jones, *Sigmund Freud: Life and Work* (London, Hogarth Press, 1953–7), but this is hagiographical and bowdlerized, and must be supplemented by Max Schur, *Freud: Living and Dying* (London, Hogarth Press and the Institute of Psychoanalysis, 1972); R.W.Clark, *Freud: The Man and the Cause* (London, Jonathan Cape, 1982); Frank J.Sulloway, *Freud: Biologist of the Mind* (New York, Basic Books, 1979); and J.M.Masson, *The Assault on Truth: Freud's Suppression of the Seduction Theory* (New York, Farrar, Straus & Giroux, 1983), though these last two are both tendentious in their own ways. For long the Freudian establishment permitted only grossly bowdlerized publication of Freud's correspondence with Fliess, so crucial for understanding Freud's state of mind in the 1890s. This is now at last available, edited by J.M.Masson, as *The Complete Letters of Sigmund Freud to Wilhelm Fliess 1887–1904* (Cambridge, Mass., Belknap Press, 1985). Masson and Sulloway have rightly stressed that the orthodox view advanced by Jones, that Freud 'discovered' the basic tenets of psychoanalysis as a result of the profound insights of his own self-analysis, hides as much as it reveals. An important dimension of the story consists of the wider history of the unconscious. Thorough, though rather reverential, is William J. McGrath, *Freud's Discovery of Psychoanalysis* (Ithaca, Cornell University Press, 1986). See also H. F. Ellenberger, *The Discovery of the Unconscious: The History and Evolution of Dynamic Psychiatry* (New York, Basic Books, 1971); and L. L. Whyte, *The Unconscious Before Freud* (London, Tavistock, 1962). For a tendentious account of Freud and cocaine see E. M. Thornton, *The Freudian Fallacy* (London, Paladin Grafton Books, 1986).

Freud's account of the 'Wolf Man' is to be found in the *Standard Edition* (above), vol. XVII. The 'Wolf Man's' own memoirs, sandwiched between his psychoanalysts' accounts of him, are contained in M. Gardiner (ed.), *The Wolf-Man and Sigmund Freud* (Harmondsworth, Penguin, 1973). His later conversations are printed in Karin Obholzer, *The Wolf-Man Sixty Years After* (London, Routledge & Kegan Paul, 1982).

John Balt's life story is published as *By Reason of Insanity* (London, Panther, 1972).

Sylvia Plath's views are reconstructed from: *The Bell Jar* (London, Heinemann, 1963); and *The Journals of Sylvia Plath*, edited by Ted Hughes and Frances McCullough (New York, Dial Press, 1982). I have found the interpretation contained in Jeffrey Berman, *The Talking Cure: Literary Representations of Psychoanalysis* (New York, New York University Press, 1985) highly stimulating.

Index

About the Author

Roy Porter is senior lecturer at the Wellcome Institute for the History of Medicine in London. Among his many previous works are *The Anatomy of Madness*, which he co-edited, *Mind-Forg'd Manacles*, and *English Society in the Eighteenth Century*.